THE
DREAM
FACTORY

*A Proven Formula
to Turn Your Dreams Into Reality!*

PETER H. THOMAS

ISBN: 978-1-962402-93-4 (hardcover)
978-1-962402-92-7 (paperback)

Edited by Robert Joseph Ahola

Published by

Fideli Publishing, Inc.
119 W. Morgan St.
Martinsville, IN 46151
www.FideliPublishing.com

Dedication…
For longtime "brother from another mother"
Michael O'Brien and to his memory.
Until we meet again old friend,
"May God hold you in the palm of His hands."

MISSION STATEMENT:

The Dream Factory is designed
to inspire those hungry young minds among us,
longing to find that undiscovered Entrepreneur
in themselves…and, once they do,
to empower them to reach for the stars
and beyond.

TABLE OF CONTENTS

THE FIRST PILLAR

THE BLUEPRINT

Believe. Visualize. Realize.

Accept the fact that you are Limitless. Examine the power of self-belief and its role in unlocking your true potential. Learn practical strategies and exercises to help cultivate self-confidence, overcome self-doubt, and tap into your inner Genius. Along the way, find your "GQ." (Your Genius Quotient.) Learn that it's tied directly to your passion.

Learn the **Power of Visualization:** Explore the art of dreaming "Impossible Dreams" (even as you discover that all dreams are possible) and the significance of power-constructing your most daring life scenarios for yourself. Learn how to tap into your imagination, clarify your vision, and create a vivid mental image of your desired future.

In these crazy times we are going through, where it seems like planning and maintaining our lives is something others do, I suggest you spend well-directed time focusing on setting up a **Decision Making Framework.** No solid blueprint for success should be without one. **Here's mine: Clarity. Focus. Execution.** It not only inspires the rest of this journey, but also establishes solid criteria against which all other benchmarks inside the Dream Factory are measured.

THE SECOND PILLAR
THE FOUNDATION
Solid. Sure. Impeccable. Unbreakable.

THE THIRD PILLAR
YOUR STRUCTURE
If You Build It, They Will Come...

The most important key to setting your structure is learning to Take Action. Study the importance of taking consistent, progressive steps toward achieving each of your goals. Learn practical tips for overcoming procrastination, managing time effectively, and developing habits that support progress and momentum.

Time is your ultimate currency in life: Don't squander it. Mastering the art of time management to optimize productivity is a trait most successful people have learned. Here you'll discover techniques for prioritizing tasks, setting boundaries, and leveraging time effectively to make the most of each and every day.

Here you get to learn the importance of discipline in staying committed to your design...as well as strategies for creating "happy habits," developing regimens that work and overcoming distractions along the way.

Truly, "knowledge is power." Your commitment to your personal and professional growth is crucial to being successful in achieving your long-term goals. It's also essential to always seek new knowledge, discover new horizons, embrace feedback, and adapt to change to fuel progress toward your dreams.

The cliché holds true: "It isn't what you know. It's who you know." Here you learn how to explore the power of networking and collaboration as effective means of expanding your opportunities. We also offer a practical guide for how to build a strong network, nurture relationships and leverage the collective wisdom of a truly strong "support team."

Life involves risk, if you are going accomplish anything at all. It creates whole new worlds...if you learn how to manage it intelligently and with purpose. If you're going to do that, this chapter will teach you how to identify and analyze your risks—even as you develop strategies and redefine your success.

THE FOURTH PILLAR

THE DREAM...IT'S YOURS!

Now that you've got it. Here's what to do with it!

THE DREAM FACTORY

A Proven Formula
to Turn Your Dreams Into Reality!

INTRODUCTION

About this Peter Thomas guy…It's hard to describe a book like *The Dream Factory* without first getting to know the man who inspired it, conceived of it, wrote it and ultimately pulled it all together. In all the ways that really matter, they're are inseparable. Because Peter Thomas has done more than just create this book called *The Dream Factory*—he has lived it fully and to the ultimate extent of its potential.

It is also nearly impossible to refer to this multi-hyphenate, world-class entrepreneur without resorting to both superlatives and clichés. And yet, when you really get down to it, we must.

In every sense a true Renaissance man, Peter Thomas has managed live to out every one of his dreams. His goal now is to empower others to accomplish the very same thing. What's more, he has a plan to do it, and a manifesto: *The Dream Factory*.

British born, Peter Thomas is a canny investor, four-time author, public speaker, major media influencer and dedicated philanthropist. Founding partner and Chairman of Century 21 Canada, Ltd. (a company which, by the time he sold it, had attained $9 billion in annual sales), Peter later became CEO of Samoth Capital Corporation (aka Sterling Centrecorp, Inc.). After that, he became Founder and Chairman of Thomas Pride International, and its spinoffs and affiliates, including Thomas Franchise Solutions, and LifePilot.

In 2011, Thomas founded and is still Chairman of Thomas Franchise Solutions (TFS), a private equity firm that specializes by investing in, and developing businesses in North America that have franchising as their core expansion strategy. TFS made its first portfolio investment into Dogtopia, a dog daycare, boarding and grooming franchise in the fall of 2012. In the ten short years since his acquisition, Dogtopia grew from 20 franchises to 250 open locations with an additional 161 in the pipeline. Along the way, and for a very long time, he has been a former Member of the Board of Directors of YPO (Young Presidents Organization) and one of the initial master minds who created YEO (Young Entrepreneurs Organization) that has now morphed into a later incarnation in the EO (Entrepreneurs Organization) —both groups dedicated to empowering entrepreneurs all over the world...as well as anyone with a true desire to rise to the level of their dreams.

That's his resume in brief. But what about the man behind the credentials?

The Ancient Greeks were known to pose a simple question at the end of a man's life: "Did he have passion?" If he did, they knew he had satisfied the gods.

Very simply, Peter Thomas is a man who lives with passion...every day of his life—with abundant joy and a contagious sense of fulfillment. And in that Passion, Peter is *Limitless*...because he believes there is no limit to what he can do. (He also believes everyone else can be just as *unlimited* if they will but tap into the Genius within—and if anyone can show you how to achieve both, it is Peter. This has become his Ultimate Dream and what remains on his life's path.)

Above all else, anyone who knows the man, knows Peter walks the walk and talks the talk. That's because he can visualize his dreams and create the means to achieve them—each and every one.

The owner of his own jet, and his own yacht (fueling his 37-year passion for the open seas), a former car-collector and auto racer who owned his own fleet of (42) collector cars, he is also a man who learned how to ski "the blacks" just by watching a Jean Claude Killy video and envisioning himself doing the rest.[1] A skydiver, a snow-catter, and a retired long-distance runner, Peter is a non-stop mentor and motivator of an entire generation of young achievers—as well as someone who has devoted his life to fulfilling his dreams and empowering others to achieve that same level of success.

Hence this Book.

---

1 A three-time World Champion skier, Jean Claude Killy is a Triple Gold Medalist in the 1968 Winter Olympic. A feat only matched twice in the last 55 years.

"I know the exceptional potency of envisioning and that everyone possesses that power if they will but unlock the genius within," Peter Thomas insists. "I especially want to reach out to young entrepreneurs: Gen X, Millennials, and Gen Z—because I see the fire in their eyes, and the hunger to learn and improve. And that's what has inspired me to take this on."

The author of four other books—*Be Great, Never Fight With a Pig, Life Manual,* and *Business Ground Rules*—Peter's "Vision" is to make *The Dream Factory* the consummate summation of his success philosophy, as well as a melding of the *best of the best* of his other works to date. With that in mind, he has not only introduced us to his original formula for "making your dreams come true," but he has also invited a number of his highly successful friends, associates, mentees and co-conspirators to provide their Success Stories to fortify the message he brings to these pages. In that regard, this book becomes something of a Success Anthology, if you will, of people who have not only "done it," but are also willing to share their experiences with you. This is Peter's way of announcing to the world that he's not the only one with a lot of great ideas. Still, for Peter the mantra holds and the basics remain the same:

"See it! Believe it. Embrace it. Become it! And then work as hard as you can along the way to bring it all together"

That pretty well epitomizes Peter Thomas's vision for creating *The Dream Factory.* It also defines our role in this as we help him to do just that.

~ The Editors

AUTHOR'S NOTE

(Read this first...)

The idea for my latest book, *The Dream Factory*, comes from my direct interaction and sponsorship of the students who apply to compete in the Global Student Entrepreneurs Awards (GSEA) Program, an outreach program developed by the Entrepreneurs Organization. Watching these enthusiastic young people confirms my belief in people and observing the long-lasting effect it can have on them when they start to believe in their own Genius. I use the term Genius with a capital "G," because I truly believe that everyone—and I mean everyone—has the seeds of true Prodigy inside them. Most of us living a normal life are born with a certain "Genius," just as we've been blessed with two ears, two eyes, two hands, two legs, two feet... one very beautiful sponge of a Brain and one very huge Heart, if we will but open them up and let what Abraham Lincoln referred to as "the better angels of our nature" fly in.

This often-untapped brilliance comes in many incarnations, but one thing is certain: **Yours is Unique to You!** The challenge you and I have comes in two forms: *The First* is defining, understanding, embracing and cultivating our own Creative Power. *The Second* comes with helping others to discover theirs. It is born in Belief; not just Faith, but Belief! Once people believe in their own Genius, the rest will follow—as it is this very *belief* that will make them successful in their endeavors. Belief is oxygen to the spirit. Without it, the individual will eventually wither and die...or else descend into a life of low achievement and loss of even the ability to dream at all.

I have a lifelong friend, relationships counselor Pat Pearson, who wrote a wonderful book about an individual's "Deserve Levels," and how mastering them can remove barriers and help empower us all. In her groundbreaking research, Pat discovered that people almost always attained exactly what they felt they deserved in life—no more, no less.

Many times, we are programed to feel that we *do not* deserve to be successful. We are stifled by so many things, such as other people's off-handed opinions or parental conditioning not to pursue our greatest passions...or the dictums of some teacher or coach who fails to recognize our potential. Some of these negative mental implants take place day-in, day-out, until it becomes habitual. And *Habits turn into Realities* that convince us nothing can change. So much so that, over the years, we get all jammed up with loads of limiting thoughts that weigh us down and lead to lives of "Quiet Desperation."

Week after week, month after month, year after year—we are force-fed such self-confining thoughts as, "I don't have a college education, so I can't get into any high paying profession," or "My father was a carpenter; therefore, I can never be a mathematician. I can never be anything but a carpenter,"[2] or..."We are poor. We've always been poor. That is our lot in life." At the core of us, we know that this is not true, and yet it becomes a gnawing reality to those unfortunate people who are taught to worship the "false gods of inhibition."

It is through that numbing loss of faith—faith in themselves and others—that they are stuck with their lot in life as it was handed down to them. These precepts are shackles to the soul and concrete to weigh us down. Don't doubt it for a minute—just as you should never doubt that there are ways out of the wilderness of low expectations and into the light of infinite possibility.

The Dream Factory, "A Proven Formula to Turn Your Dreams into Reality," will teach you and those you care about that you are not STUCK with your lot in life. You and you alone can determine your destiny: You only have to

---

2   BTW, there's nothing wrong with being a carpenter if that's your "jam." (Jesus was one. So was Stradivarius.) If that is truly your calling, this book will not only help you confirm that, but also teach you how to become an even better woodcutter. You may end up designing and manufacturing a Hepplewhite roll-top desk, or carving out the perfect violin. Or developing your own local chapter of Habitat for Humanity.

learn the formula that teaches you how to believe in yourself, and let your true *Genius* emerge.

You don't need to rely on the opinions of others who are seldom, if ever, as informed of the issues facing you as you are. People usually don't realize they can almost always be whatever they want to be or have whatever they want to have. They truly can chase their dreams and catch them—every single one!

Once they discover who they really are, they can rise to levels far above and beyond their expectations—so much so, that their new *Undiscovered Self* will be a beacon to the world. One that will take you from the soft-bias of low expectations from family, friends and all the other armchair counselors who readily give you all the reasons that you can't make it in life. Bless them. They probably mean well for you, but "well" is not "great." And Greatness is the seed that your true Genius contains. All you need to do is see it, believe it is possible, and take the first step...

The good news is that you've already started. You started by picking up a copy of *The Dream Factory!* And it comes with Four Pillars that form the stairway to completion: *Blueprint. Foundation. Structure. Living the Dream.*

By applying these Four Pillars, you will learn this (proven) Success Formula dating back to the Greek philosophers Socrates, Plato and Aristotle and the Roman philosopher/emperor Marcus Aurelius—timeless insights that powerful people throughout the ages have used and shared to attain their highest aspirations.

In the early chapters of this book, we set the stage for the transformative journey that lies ahead. We emphasize the power of dreams, the importance of taking action, and introduce the concept of *The Dream Factory* as a system that will guide readers toward their desired reality—making their most dearly held fantasies come true.

At this point, it bears repeating that this formula and its Four Pillars are time-tested. It's something I've personally worked on with some of the finest minds in the world. And we are all united in wanting to share them with you: here and now! Along the way it's been an intricate process, but we can make it simple for you. Just follow the plan as it's laid out, and know that your mentors are there for you: on these pages and in so many other places you've never thought of before.

I'm also releasing this book just in time for this wonderful Christmas Season. So consider this a special Holiday gift for you—to help you jump-start your New Year with *Resolution, Purpose and your Dream Machine* custom-built just for you. It's easy to assemble. And all the parts are motile: ready to kick into gear as soon as you are.

Wishing you the Best of Everything.
And all your Dreams Fulfilled!

~ Peter Thomas
Christmas, 2023

THE FIRST PILLAR

THE BLUEPRINT

Believe. Visualize. Realize.

CHAPTER 1

Unlocking Your Inner Genius Through Self-Belief

I n the vast tapestry of human potential, there exists a realm of limitless creativity, innovation, and brilliance waiting to be awakened. This realm is within each and every one of us, residing deep within our hearts, minds and souls. It is the realm of Genius—a boundless source of ideas, talents and abilities that can transform our lives and shape the world around us. But here's the secret: the key to unlocking this inner genius lies in one's unwavering belief in oneself.

THE POWER OF BELIEF: Belief acts as a catalyst, igniting the dormant embers of our potential. It is the Blueprint by which all great accomplishments are built. When we believe in ourselves, we tap into a reservoir of confidence and courage that propels us forward, despite obstacles or doubts. This belief is the driving force that pushes us to explore uncharted territories, take risks, and pursue our dreams with unwavering determination. Most of the great inventors, artists, scientists and major moguls in the world shared in common an unshakable confidence in their own genius, because it was almost always accompanied by a kind of single-minded obsession with their craft compounded by a passionate pursuit of the Truth that drove it.

Sometimes it borders on arrogance. (And occasionally it has to, if it propels us to excel.) World famous surrealist and fabulist artist Salvador Dali once candidly observed, "There are only two geniuses in the world today: Myself and my son."

A bit over-the-top perhaps, but point made: you have to bring both confidence and self-belief into the game—any game—if you want to succeed. They are what give you the courage to just break ground and dig deeply into your own self-awareness.

EMBRACE YOUR POTENTIAL: Believing in ourselves allows us to embrace the vast possibilities that lie before us. It opens our minds to new perspectives and ideas, empowering us to think beyond limitations and convention. When we recognize our own Genius, we begin to see opportunities where others see roadblocks. We become willing to challenge the status quo, break free from societal norms, and venture into unexplored territories.

OVERCOME SELF-DOUBT: Self-doubt is a common adversary on the path to self-belief. It can instill uncertainty and fear and extinguish the flame of our genius. However, by embracing self-belief, we learn to silence these doubts and replace them with affirmations of our own capabilities. We realize that failure is not a verdict on our potential but a stepping stone on the path to growth and mastery. With each challenge overcome, our belief in ourselves grows stronger, fueling our genius even further.

EMBRACE THE JOURNEY OF SELF-DISCOVERY: When we truly believe in ourselves, we embark on a profound journey of self-discovery. We begin to unravel the layers of our being, uncovering hidden talents, passions, and strengths that have been lying dormant within us. That Discovery of your Genius is what will encourage you to delve deeper into your interests, to learn voraciously, and to embrace continuous personal growth. It enables you to recognize the unique contributions you have to offer the world and emboldens you to share those gifts with others.

A classic case of this would be the story of Thomas A. "Tub" Tominsky.[3] Something of a standout high school football player in Oklahoma in the 1960s, TA was nicknamed "Tub" by his B-team coach because he was a 5'9" and 230-pound tackle who seemingly lumbered clumsily about ...and as such was something of a Ferdinand the Bull. Easy going and a bit lethargic, until

3   The name is fictionalized, to be sure.

he turned into a beast on the football field, "T.A." still managed to make a difference in every game.

Mistakenly perceived as none too bright, "Tub" was what might have been considered *dull normal* and didn't rank very highly on his IQ test. He struggled in school, staggering through with B's and mostly C's for 3 years...*except in math* where he constantly excelled with all A's for the entirety of his high school years. Sharing a class with him, his football teammate Carl S. noticed that he was uniquely skilled when it came to "problem solving" in mathematical topics like trigonometry and calculus and could even extend the answers beyond the parameters of the solutions set by the teachers. Commenting on it more than once, Carl constantly encouraged Thomas to overcome his self-doubt and not to listen to those who demeaned his mental capacities.

"Get yourself to college," Carl encouraged him. "Major in math and science. You have a gift. Never doubt that for a moment." Carl spoke. T.A. listened. And, after slipping into Tulsa University on a football scholarship, T.A. "Tub" Tominsky turned out to be something of an arithmetical savant.

Because he heeded Carl's encouragement (as well as his calculus teacher) "Tub" went on to obtain an MS degree in mathematics and later a PhD in Critical Math theory from Oklahoma State University. He finally retired in 2009. A tenured University of Kansas professor and a consultant emeritus to the State of Oklahoma Department of Energy.

FIND YOUR "GQ." YOUR GENIUS QUOTIENT: Genius is a word that scares a lot of people to death. It shouldn't! When people speak of genius in the world, it immediately conjures images of Leonardo da Vinci, Nikola Tesla, Carl Sagan, Helen Keller and Thomas Edison. And yet it was Edison himself who insisted more than once that, "Genius is 10% inspiration and 90% perspiration."

It's tied to Self-Belief to be sure. But it's also umbilically connected to your Passion. So many people can't find their own genius with a searchlight and a pack of *greatness-sniffing* bloodhounds, mainly because somewhere along the way they've been talked out of doing what they love and into "doing what it takes to survive."

So it is here that we'd like to give you a quick *GQ Test* to help you discover just where your Genius may lie.

1. **If money was not an object, and you could work at any career you wanted in life, what would it be?** Don't be shy when you answer this. And don't feel as if any aspiration is either too wild or far-fetched for you to achieve. If you have passion, passion will find a way.

2. **Are you doing it now?** And if you're not, what is holding you back? Don't feel as if you're alone in this. When polled, across America in 2023, 45% of workers said they were either satisfied or extremely satisfied with their jobs, while only 20% felt very passionate about their jobs, 33% believed they had reached a dead end in their career, and 21% were eager to change careers. In this study, the most surprising statistic of all was that, of this 55% who were at some level of dissatisfaction, 80% were under 35 years of age.

3. **Are you willing to break out of the "I can't afford the education" trap?** Everyone knows that it costs money to get a college degree—to become a doctor, lawyer or engineer. And yet there are numbers beyond counting of young men and women who've put themselves through school to achieve their degrees and pursue their personal path to discovering their own genius. Frankly, higher education (or a lack thereof) can too often be an excuse for not accomplishing something when there is a list a yard long of some of the most successful people in history who never finished school. Albert Einstein was a high-school dropout. So was Apple's Steve Jobs. So was Microsoft's Bill Gates. Helen Keller was born deaf and blind (and mute because of it) and yet became one the most brilliant and articulate speakers and authors in defense of the Handicapped in the history of the world. And let's face it: Your only handicap is believing that you have any at all.

4. **Do you have a hobby or avocation that you prefer over your job?** That is often where your career lies, hidden behind the enthusiasm. Never doubt that your true love and favorite hobby may hold the key to your inner genius. There is the story of a somewhat characteristic Millennial woman named Angela S. A fairly successful sales rep for an online marketing firm, Angela felt OK about her job but looked forward to those weekends when she could spend virtually 90% of her time playing video games. (One of the 22% of video game aficionados who [at the time] were women.)

Yes! The cliché holds true: Video Games are very often looked upon as the ultimate in escapism, the Millennial's ultimate retreat from the grim realities of today, and yet a very male-dominated pursuit where violence was almost always "the name of the game." But Angela saw it differently, and applied as an apprentice producer at a leading video game company. Determined to see to it that Video games became less violent and had more appeal to women, she started designing her own "less violent themes," and at the ripe old age of 34 soon became one of the leading Video Game producers with one of the largest companies in that $222 Billion a year industry.

The object lesson is twofold: First, sometimes what appears to be a vice or a bad habit is actually the heart's desire crying out for completion.[4] One merely needs the power of self-belief to bring it to light, and to clarify the purpose behind it. Second, No dream—no matter how far-fetched or lightly regarded—should be left to die.

5. **Make a List of the 3 to 5 things that you're best at.** *And whatever you do don't Succumb to the "Michael Jordan" Syndrome!* OK. We get it. You love basketball but you can't score 60 points and a triple double in every game…and slam dunk from the top of the arc. However, Bill Russell notwithstanding, neither MJ nor any great player in any sport has ever made an outstanding coach. (Perhaps because they expect too much of themselves and others.) And it's absolutely a fact: The greatest coaches in the world in any sport—football, basketball, baseball, ice-hockey, soccer—have almost always been those "Journeyman Players!" Coaches like the LA Lakers Phil Jackson (aka "The Zen Master") or Dallas Cowboys Superbowl Champions and Miami Hurricane national champions Jimmy Johnson, or Notre Dame's legendary Knute Rockne (the inventor of the "forward pass" and the savior of American gridiron football). Why? Because they possessed the passion combined with an innate intelligence and applied it diligently to the game, sport or profession that they loved; which made them great leaders and terrific strategists with their own imprint on the game.

---

4   Some common sense applies here. Addictions such as smoking dope or getting drunk or eating 20 pounds of pizza don't qualify you for any kind of genius on the path to your life's pursuit.

This is the point: if you truly love what you do you will find a place where your Genius can express itself to the fullness of its arc. So maybe you'll make a wonderful coach, teacher or mentor. Julia Child was a terrible cook when she started out, but kept at it because her cooking pleased her husband. And *Voila!* 50 years, 13 TV programs, *The French Cook,* and 16 Cookbooks later, Julia was the most highly regarded food expert in the world, and a superb chef, as well as a name synonymous with making the culinary art accessible, approachable and fun. That is a brilliance in itself.

6. **Genius invariably comes with its own equation: P + S x R=A. Passion plus Skill times Repetition equals Achievement.** And, more often than not, High Achievement. Your Genius is waiting. By now you should at least know how to tap into it. Especially if you have a quality called Resilience. So…

BELIEVE IN YOURSELF: When you Believe in yourself, it serves as a safe-haven against the storms of adversity that life inevitably presents. It infuses us with a kind of steely persistence—a steadfast determination to persevere and bounce back from setbacks. When we face challenges with unwavering self-belief, we tap into our genius for creative problem-solving, finding innovative solutions where others see only dead ends. Along the way, we become dauntless. Our rock-solid steadfast nature becomes a beacon of inspiration, not only for ourselves but also for those around us.

WHATEVER YOU DO, "DON'T LET ANYONE KNOCK YOUR COW": When, at age seven, I first came over from England to Canada with my Mom I immediately was enrolled in grade two (Second Grade for you Yanks). We had an art teacher named Miss Belmont. I was in her art class, and as part of her instruction, she had the class all draw a picture of a cow. For some unknown reason, she came to my desk and took my picture of the cow and held it up for all the class to see. They all laughed, while I in turn was mortified by their response. (And I might add, Miss Belmont did nothing either to defend me or articulate my effort.)

Crestfallen by the ridicule, I never drew again. Much later in life, in my early forties, I went to an art gallery in London and saw a picture of a cow painted by none other than Pablo Picasso. (Yes! *That* Picasso.) And wouldn't you know it? I discovered on the spot that *my cow, at 7, was much better than Picasso's at 77!* So ultimately who's to say…art is subjective. So is Self-Belief. But since I let the other students' laughter discourage me from ever drawing again, I never got to find out. The moral of this story is something that's hard to sell to a 7-year-old. We are all so uncertain in those first 7 years of our lives. And peer groups can be cruel.

And yet…and yet, there is an admonition to all the parents among us. Self-belief starts at an early age. Encourage those you love when discouragement is the poison that society often peddles. Offer empowerment and reinforcement as well. And behold what kind of product you help to create. As the song goes from the musical, *Into the Woods: "Careful of what you say. Children will listen. Careful of what you do, Children will see…and learn…"* So be there for those you love. And also learn to love yourself. Your destiny is to not let people intimidate you or blunt your dreams. Be strong and fight for what you believe in. Do not let others tell you how good or how not good you are.

INSPIRE OTHERS: Our belief in ourselves and the cultivation of our genius does not exist in a vacuum. It has a ripple effect, inspiring others to believe in their own capabilities. And when you get right down to it, **your GQ** isn't nearly as significant if you don't bring in a little **EQ (Emotional Quotient)** with it. *So bring your EQ to their GQ.* Never hesitate to be Kind. Be Expansive! Share what you have with others…especially those who come to you with success-focused questions of their own. When we embrace our inner genius and fearlessly pursue our passions, we become beacons of possibility for those who witness our journey. And we're able to encourage others to explore their own potential, to break free from self-imposed limitations, and to embark on their own paths of self-discovery and growth.

BRINGING IT ALL TOGETHER: *Belief in oneself is the key that unlocks the door to our inner Genius.* It is the difference between mere potential and transformative success. I've always felt that the world is full of ordinary people who are capable of extraordinary things: *if they will but believe in themselves.* When we believe in ourselves, we tap into an infinite reservoir of creativity, innovation, and brilliance. Our self-belief fuels our passion, propels us through challenges, and inspires us to continuously grow and evolve. So, dare to believe in your genius, for within you lies the power to shape your destiny and create a future beyond your wildest dreams.

CHAPTER 2

Dream Big!
Define Your Vision

Live in the Present. Invent the Future.

~ Karl Lagerfeld

Welcome to the world of visualization, where dreams are transformed into reality. In this chapter, we will explore the remarkable ability of the human mind to create vivid mental imagery and how harnessing this power can unlock your full potential. No matter who you are or what your dreams are at this point, visualization can be a game-changer, allowing you to tap into your imagination and bring your aspirations to life.

THE MAGIC OF MENTAL IMAGERY: Close your eyes for a moment and imagine yourself standing on a pristine beach, feeling the warm sand between your toes and hearing the gentle lapping of the waves. As you inhale, you can almost smell the salty sea air, and as you exhale, you feel a sense of tranquility wash over you. What you just experienced was the power of visualization—creating a vivid mental picture that evokes emotions and sensations as if the scene were real.

Visualization is a natural ability of the mind, allowing us to generate images, sounds, and feelings internally. It's a tool that great artists, athletes and innovators have harnessed throughout history to achieve remarkable feats and accomplish great things. By harnessing the power of visualization, you can align your thoughts, beliefs, and actions to create a harmonious pathway towards your goals.

THE SCIENCE BEHIND VISUALIZATION: Numerous scientific studies have explored the effectiveness of visualization in any number of domains familiar to all of us—such as sports, communication, broadcast, education and personal development. One such study conducted with basketball players revealed that those who regularly visualized successful free throws showed significant improvement in their actual performance compared to those who didn't engage in visualization exercises.

Historically, the classic case of this would be Golden State Warriors and Houston Rockets star forward Rick Barry. Barry (who played from 1965 through 1980) would often spend hours at a time just standing at the free-throw line and envisioning the ball going into the basket before he even attempted his world-famous underhand toss. A standout at forward, he was also the ABA and NBA free-throw record holder at .900, until Stephen "Steph" Curry broke his record 32 years later starting in 2012 at .909.

When we visualize, our brains activate the same neural pathways that are triggered when we physically perform an action. The intricate connection between our minds and bodies allows us to simulate experiences mentally, strengthening the neural networks associated with those experiences. By repeatedly visualizing success, we can prime our minds and bodies to perform at their best when the time comes to take action.

THE ART OF DREAMING WITH INTENT: Visualization is not just about creating mental images; it's also about dreaming with intent. Fashion icon and master designer Karl Lagerfeld had a perfect masterplan for that and was notable not only for creating new brand names (such as his own eponymous Lagerfeld house) but also for resurrecting "dead" fashion brands like Chanel and Fendi—turning them again into household names synonymous with high-end, cutting edge styles and breakthrough designs. Crossing over from fashion into everything from film-making to video games, Lagerfeld once admitted privately: "I spend a lot of time dreaming. Then I act upon those dreams. It might even be said, I live in a dreamworld. Not a bad place to be."

Famous for being ruthlessly practical when it really counted, Lagerfeld often applied the three principles of *Clarity, Focus* and *Execution*. (A "Design Directive," that we will cover in the following chapter.) "I always live in the present," he said. "But my canvas is the future. I visualize. Then I create. And I never cease co-creating until the work is done."

TO START VISUALIZING EFFECTIVELY, FOLLOW THESE STEPS:

1. *Define your Goal:* Clearly articulate what you want to achieve. Be specific and write it down. Then check-in from time to time to make sure you stay focused on it. Goals can often be fragile things unless you understand their value. They are your GPS to the future, and will hold you fast to your magnetic North.

2. *Create a mental image:* Close your eyes and imagine yourself already having achieved your goal. Visualize the details—the sights, sounds, smells and feelings associated with it. Make it as vivid and real as possible. As Ralph Waldo Emerson once noted: "When you stay focused on what you desire, the Universe conspires to support you."

3. *Engage your emotions:* Feel the joy, satisfaction, and excitement of having accomplished your goal. Emotions fuel the power of visualization, enhancing its impact. They're also contagious (for better or worse). When you're positive, it spills over into everything you do. You become a magnet to good events and better outcomes.

4. *Repeat and reinforce:* Practice visualization regularly, preferably in a quiet and focused state. The more you visualize, the stronger your neural connections become, making your dream more tangible and attainable. "Muscle memory," also applies to the brain as well as the rest of your body. It is both the strongest and the most fragile organ you possess. So feed it. Stay focused. And don't clutter it up with contradictory thoughts or splayed objectives.

OVERCOMING CHALLENGES THROUGH VISUALIZATION: Life is full of challenges, and visualization can be a potent tool to overcome them. When faced with obstacles, take a moment to visualize yourself successfully navigating through them. See yourself finding creative solutions, staying calm under pressure, and emerging stronger on the other side. By consistently reinforcing positive mental imagery, you can train your mind to view challenges as opportunities for growth and success.

MAKING IT HAPPEN: *Visualization* is a gateway to turning dreams into reality. By tapping into the power of your imagination and aligning your thoughts and actions with your desired outcomes, you can create a powerful force of manifestation.

Try a Vision Board. It works! There are many proponents of this. And I happen to be one. Sometimes when you objectify, your imagination needs a little help. So, help it. Find those images—photos, pictures, designs or illustrations—that best depict what you desire. Cut them out and put them up on a cork or magnetic blackboard. It's OK to constantly have them on-screen on your laptop, iPad, or iPhone. But having the physical image there, right in front of you can often make all the difference, because it even feels more real. When it's there in your office or your den, someplace you can see it several times a day, that image takes on a life of its own—whether it's car, a boat, a plane, or a trip to some exotic part of the world, or even your ideal significant other or the kind of business you want—there it is. And when it is…it's tangible and clear. I can certainly vouch for this: I'm living proof that it works.

YOUR OWN LEARJET. SEE IT. BELIEVE IT. OWN IT: Let me underscore that by offering a little story of my own. When I started selling mutual funds many years ago (at the age of 28) I was reading a business magazine, and in it I saw a picture of a Learjet. To say it was "love at first sight" would, at the very least, be accurate. For me, it was the most beautiful thing I had ever seen in my life. Right then and there I knew in my heart that I wanted one of those. I cut the picture of the very plane I wanted out of the magazine and put it up on the wall directly across from my desk…where I could see it and virtually experience it every day I sat there. Call it the power of concentration (call it what you will). But six-years later I actually owned that jet.

The purpose of this story is self-revealing and posted here to let you know: that, with the *Power of Visualization*, all things are possible. It is simply one of the most powerful motivating tools you will ever have—and you have it at your disposal every day of your life. There are many reasons why it works that are much more eloquently explained by psychologists. But what I know from experience is that visualization does the job and then some…and I have used it many times to attain goals that I would have thought unattainable.

SUMMARY

THE ONE THING YOU NEED TO DO: *Leave no room for doubt!* Embrace the art of visualization, and watch as your dreams come to life within the infinite realm of "It Can Be." Remember, The Dream Factory is waiting for you to design and build the life of your dreams through the transformative Power of Visualization.

CHAPTER 3

Design a
Decision-Making Framework

Nothing can prove a more valuable ally than the *Power to be Decisive*. That requires seeing things clearly…and acting upon your insights. In these crazy times, we as a society are constantly going through different layers with mixed messages—where it seems as if we have control over nothing and where normalcy in planning and maintaining our lives is something that others do. Put on the brakes when you see that happening, because it should be just the opposite. And for that I offer an antidote: I suggest you spend adequate time (and then some) focusing on "Your Today."

No solid blueprint for success should be without a hard and fast Matrix for Decision-Making. So, here's mine: *Clarity. Focus. Execution.* Let those three words inspire the rest of this journey, and you'll be able to establish a solid a criteria against which all other benchmarks inside *the Dream Factory* are measured.

In every sense of the word, it starts *Right Now:* Plan to make today the best day of your life. Every morning when you awaken spend a few minutes thinking and planning the entire day ahead of you. Put in time for a random walk with a family member or friend. Ask yourself who can you call, or write a short email…just to cheer them up and make their day better? Who in your world needs a little pep talk? Who would it be fun to call? Pick up your phone right now and call them.

"CLARITY. FOCUS. EXECUTION." 'Three little words that create such a huge impact. That's because, intelligently applied, they form a decision-making framework that helps you make better choices every single hour of every single day of your life. As such they are the stair steps that propel you up to the entrance of your Dream Factory:

By following this formula, individuals can make well-informed choices that are aligned with their goals, minimize the risk of errors, and increase the likelihood of successful outcomes. It helps streamline the decision-making process by breaking it down into manageable steps that encourage thoughtful consideration and action. I live by this formula. I recommend printing a copy and having it close by for reference. That way, you can refer back to it until it becomes an ingrained habit.

1. **CLARITY:**

    *   Gain a clear understanding of the situation or problem at hand. And cut to the chase when you do. Too often people become distracted by the little stuff that spins out of a challenge rather than the challenge itself. So, take a hard look at things when you do this. And understand that the issue bringing you the most pain or dissonance is the one you really need to address…first!

    *   Define the goals, objectives, and desired outcomes. There can be more than one to be sure. Just make sure they're achievable. Whatever you do, don't spread yourself too thin. True Goals have a "clarity" about them. That is how you recognize them.

    *   Identify relevant information and gather data to inform your decision. If what you're learning is something you can put immediately to use, this will be the path that's clearest for you. So start your gathering there. Rule of thumb: Does it empower you? If it does that's the ticket.

    *   Consider the potential implications and consequences of different choices. Yes, Mary Jane, it's true: Actions have consequences. As such, they require a sense of responsibility. That entails some personal maturity in the deciding. And in every sense of the word, "Let your conscience be your guide."

    *   Avoid making decisions based on assumptions or incomplete information. The Second of the Four Agreements applies here: "Never Make

Assumptions." Do your Due Diligence and make sure you've covered all the bases. People will respect you when you've taken the time to do it. (Nothing can be more painful than trying to explain away your mistakes.)

2. FOCUS:

- *Narrow down your options to the most viable and relevant ones.* This can be a tough one, and yet it is essential. Very often because sometimes you have to cut away some superfluous things that seem attractive but may be nothing more than "cotton candy" in your life. Sometimes it's good to apply a three-step rule: a) Is it absolutely essential; b) is it a good thing to do; c) does it create a "win-win" scenario?

- *Prioritize the factors that are most important and relevant to your decision.* Once you've narrowed down your options, it's also important to rank them. Which ones are most important? Which could you do without if you have to?

- *Consider the alignment of your decision with your long-term goals and values.* Short term and long-term goals should align with one another. But there are those occasions when they do not. When it comes to cutting them out, always try to align your short-term and long-term goals so they both help you accomplish your end-game objective.

- *Eliminate distractions and external pressures that might cloud your judgment.* Some genuine discipline applies here (and we'll get to that in a moment). For now, keep in mind that distractions have their place… but seldom in the beginning. If they don't contribute to Item No. 1, *Clarity,* then cut them loose. The sooner the better.

- *Focus on what truly matters and avoid getting overwhelmed by minor details.* Absolutely pay attention to details. Because, as you know by now, so many effective Decision-Making Frameworks can get tripped-up for lack of them. The challenge comes with recognizing which details contribute to your objectives…and which ones are false directives that get you tangled up in unnecessary clutter.

3. **EXECUTION:**

- *Develop a clear plan of action for implementing your chosen decision.* We'll have an entire chapter on "Taking Action" in a moment; it's *that* important. So we set the touchstone here. The important thing to remember is that action "requires a plan." This, more than anything, needs its own Blueprint. So keep that in mind when you apply this effective 3-Step mandate.

- *Allocate necessary resources, time, and effort to execute the decision effectively.* As you know by now, nothing takes place in a void. You need alliances. You need support groups. And you need resources: time resources, money resources, natural resources, and resourceful people. Best suggestion: Make a list. They'll solidify once you do. (Remember the first rule is "Clarity." It's No. 1 for a reason.)

- *Anticipate potential challenges and create contingency plans to address them. Challenges!* They're ruffles and ridges in the blueprint. They're also *Opportunities,* once you see them for what they are: *a chance to rethink your focus.* If you plan for them in the beginning, they'll be easier to deal with once they present themselves. So when "trouble" comes (as if often does) you will be ready.

- *Monitor progress and adjust your approach if needed to ensure successful implementation.* Whatever you do in setting up your Decision-Making Machine, always take a pause to reassess and re-evaluate. It will be worth the time spent. And it's part of the Critical Matrix for every successful endeavor.

- *Take responsibility for the decision and its outcomes, and learn from any mistakes.* It's as simple as this: Taking responsibility for your actions announces to everyone that you are the grown-up in the room. There is something ennobling about it. And once you recognize the value of it, it serves you in a couple ways: First, it helps you realize (as the poem "Invictus" implies) that, "You are the Master of your fate. You are the Captain of your soul." Second, it becomes an invaluable tool in helping you evaluate others. Take a look. And if you see other people running around pointing fingers, making excuses and shouting "It's not my fault," it's probably a good idea to learn from them but avoid them, and drop them from your horizon ASAP.

SUMMARY

So there you have it. Three Steps—*Clarity, Focus, Execution*—that seem complicated at first. And yet once you've mastered them, you've refined your Blueprint for *The Dream Factory* to come. And you've made it so much easier for all the steps that follow to fall neatly into place. BTW, I feel that it's important enough to offer a pocket version of this. So, cut it out. Paste it up. And put it in your pocket. (Or snap a photo of this on your smart phone.)

DECISION MAKING FRAMEWORK

1. **CLARITY:**
   - Gain a clear understanding of the situation or problem at hand.
   - Define the goals, objectives, and desired outcomes.
   - Identify relevant information and gather data to inform your decision.
   - Consider the potential implications and consequences of different choices.
   - Avoid making decisions based on assumptions or incomplete information.

2. **FOCUS:**
   - Narrow down your options to the most viable and relevant ones.
   - Prioritize the factors that are most important and relevant to your decision.
   - Consider the alignment of your decision with your long-term goals and values.
   - Eliminate distractions and external pressures that might cloud your judgment.
   - Focus on what truly matters and avoid getting overwhelmed by minor details.

3. **EXECUTION:**
   - Develop a clear plan of action for implementing the chosen decision.
   - Allocate necessary resources, time, and effort to execute the decision effectively.
   - Anticipate potential challenges and create contingency plans to address them.
   - Monitor progress and adjust your approach if needed to ensure successful implementation.
   - Take responsibility for the decision and its outcomes, and learn from any mistakes.

THE SECOND PILLAR
THE FOUNDATION
Solid. Sure. Impeccable. Unbreakable.

CHAPTER 4

Establish Your Core Values

Core Values. So many people don't even know what they are or how to identify them. And yet they are essential if you are ever going to set all the pieces of your Dream Factory into place. This chapter will help you identify and define your core values...because they are the *Concrete for the Foundation* upon which you build your dreams. On the next few pages, we will delve into the establishment of your values as a crucial aspect of personal and professional development.

Your values serve as the guiding principles that shape your decisions, actions, and overall outlook on life. Discovering these principles—once you understand their importance—will help give you solid footing toward achieving purpose-driven life. Let's explore why these values are so essential and how they can positively impact your journey towards success.

CHARACTER COUNTS...FOR A LOT! The Greek Philosopher Heraclitus once observed that, "Character is Destiny." So we begin this chapter with the conundrum that your ambitions only rise to the level of your awareness of right and wrong...and your willingness to apply that awareness at all the important junctures in your life. Success is not necessarily money, power and all the riches those things can buy. There are many rich and powerful people who are not successful, because they have no Core Values to redeem them, and often spend both time and money trying to compensate for that hollow place inside.

So when you consider your core values, I offer this *Rule Of Thumb:* Ask yourself if they meet four criteria: 1) Is it good? 2) Is it necessary? 3) Is it kind? 4) Is it a benefit to you and the world around you?

Once you meet these standards, everything else will fall nicely into place.

DEFINING VALUES

Values are the deeply held beliefs and principles that reflect what truly matters to you. They form the moral compass that guides your behavior, your choices…and ultimately the outcome of who you become as a human being. They are also an offshoot of that "integrity GPS" because… *Values are subjective and unique to each individual,* influenced by personal experiences, upbringing, culture and education. Identifying your values requires introspection and self-reflection, as you need to uncover what resonates with your authentic self.

A classic case of defining one's values came to me in 1974 when I attended my first Young Presidents Organization University. It was held in Hawaii and I was very excited about attending classes, meeting new people and expanding my horizons. There was a menu of fascinating lecturers to attend. And a fellow named Red Scott got my vote. Prior to our getting acquainted, someone told me that Red had 17 companies that all qualified to meet YPO standards. I knew how difficult it was for me to be accepted into YPO. So it occurred to me that, with 17 companies already filling the bill, this was a man who could teach me a lot about business and how to grow one. After all, I was there to learn how to become a bigger and better businessman. We went into the classroom, and there were about 14 other students. Red came in with a big smile, looked around at the crowd and stated, "It is far too nice outside. Let's go down to the beach." And out the door he went. Dictum set by our leader, we all followed along like puppies.

Once at the beach, we sat around campfire style, and Red proceeded to talk about what our values were and whether or not our lives were being lived according to those values.

To demonstrate what he meant he gave us all an 8 x 11 notepad and asked us to write down everything that we felt were our values on that pad. The entire group worked feverishly for about 10 minutes when Red shifted gears and asked us to write down on another page all the priorities that were most important in our lives. That took me longer, but after about 20 minutes I had a full page.

Then Red asked us to check the priorities against the values and see whether or not each priority reflected one of our values. Well, big surprise:

I recall that probably half the things that were taking up my day were not related to a value. And I realized immediately that some major changes needed to be made in my life. I had what I now call *an epiphany*. As a result, within 90 days I had moved from where I lived out to the West Coast and literally started my life over—intent on ensuring that everything coming into my life from that point on was first measured against my values. What's more, I have lived my life for the last fifty years according to the lessons I learned back on that beach in Hawaii in 1974.

The point of this story is to help you understand (as I did) that goals and values are linked together in a chain of destiny. And if one aligns with the other, your chances for success will multiply 10-fold. The other point come with an emphasis on "Mentors" in our lives. They often come when they are least expected and to our greatest benefit. I am forever grateful for Red Scott.

WHY ESTABLISHING YOUR VALUES MATTERS...

1. *Clarity and Purpose:* Values provide clarity about what is important to you, helping you understand your purpose and meaning in life. When you align your actions with your values, you experience a sense of fulfillment and purpose, knowing that you are living in accordance with your deeply held beliefs.

2. *Decision-Making:* Values act as a decision-making framework, helping you make choices that are in alignment with what you hold dear. When faced with difficult decisions, your values can serve as a guide, allowing you to make choices that are consistent with your principles. Oftentimes this requires listening to your GUT feel. (Your Great Universal Truth.) Because it is innate to every human being that we know at our "core" what is right and what isn't. Once when asked about his religious beliefs, Abraham Lincoln famously answered: "When I do good things, I feel good. When I do bad things, I feel bad. *That* is my religion."

3. *Personal Authenticity:* Living in alignment with your values allows you to be true to yourself. It enables you to express your authentic self and fosters a sense of integrity. When your values are clear, you can

confidently navigate various aspects of life, remaining authentic and genuine in your interactions with others.

4. *Goal Setting and Achievement:* Values provide a solid foundation for setting meaningful goals. By aligning your goals with your values, you create a sense of purpose and motivation. Goals that are rooted in your values are more likely to inspire and drive you toward success, as they resonate deeply with who you are and what you believe in.

5. *Resilience and Well-Being:* Establishing your values strengthens your resilience and enhances your overall well-being. When faced with challenges or setbacks, your values provide a sense of inner strength and determination. They act as a source of both motivation and strength, enabling you to persevere through difficulties, while helping you maintain a positive outlook on life.

DISCOVERING YOUR VALUES

1. *Reflect on Core Beliefs:* Take time to master introspection and (through that mastery) identify your core beliefs. Consider what is truly important to you and what principles you hold dear. Think about the qualities and characteristics you admire in others and the values you aspire to develop in yourself.

2. *Prioritize and Evaluate:* Once you have identified a list of potential values, prioritize them according to their significance in your life. Evaluate how well these values align with your current actions and behavior.

3. *Test Your Values:* Put your values to the test by examining your decisions and actions. Are they consistent with the standards you have identified? If there are any inconsistencies, reassess and make adjustments.

4. *Refine and Fine-Tune:* Refine your values over time as you gain more self-awareness and life experiences. Remember that values can evolve and change as you grow as an individual.

LIVING YOUR VALUES

1. *Integrate Your Values Into Daily Life.* It is statistically acknowledged that it takes 15 days to establish a habit. (So create "happy habits.") Incorporate your values into your daily routines, habits, and interactions. Strive to make choices that align with your values, both personally and professionally.

2. *Communicate Your Values.* Clearly communicate your values to others, ensuring that they understand what you stand for. This helps build trust, authenticity, and meaningful connections with like-minded individuals. It also announces to the world exactly who you are: what you stand for, and what principles dictate the course of your life.

3. *Evaluate Opportunities and Relationships.* Assess opportunities, relationships, and experiences based on how well they align with your values. Surround yourself with people and engage in activities that support and uplift your values. Say "No!" to *Doctor No* and "Yes!" to *The Good News Fairy.* Get rid of Energy Vampires and surround yourself with "Yes men and women"…people with a can-do attitude who will always say, "Yes, we can do that!"

4. *Practice Self-Reflection.* As Socrates once observed: "An unexamined life is not worth living." Regularly reflect on how well you are living in accordance with your values. Assess your actions and decisions, making adjustments when necessary. Introspection is a vital tool for helping align your values—as long as you're honest with yourself when you do it.

VALUE ADDED

THE WHOLE IS ALWAYS GREATER THAN THE SUM OF ITS PARTS! *It's all a matter of Synergy.* And once you've established your core values, you've taken that fundamental step towards personal growth, fulfillment, and success. Your Core Values serve as a compass, keeping you focused on *True North*, guiding you toward a life that is authentic, purpose-driven and meaningful. They provide clarity, inform decision-making, and shape your goals. By understanding the importance of values and actively integrating them into your life, you can create a solid foundation for a truly fulfilling journey of personal and professional development. Remember, your values are unique to you, and living in alignment with them will allow you to unlock your true potential and build the life of your dreams.

CHAPTER 5

Meet Your Mentors: Virtual and Real

On this journey of personal growth and success, the role of mentors cannot be overstated. Mentors are individuals who possess the wisdom, experience, and guidance to help us navigate the complexities of life and achieve our goals. In this chapter, we will explore the importance of having mentors, provide tips on how to find them, and address the question of how many mentors one should have.

RECOGNIZE THE POWER OF MENTORS: Mentors act as beacons of knowledge, offering valuable insights gained through their own experiences. They serve as trusted advisors, providing guidance, support and encouragement. Mentors can help us gain clarity when it comes to our aspirations, identify our strengths and weaknesses, and develop strategies for success. They offer a different perspective, challenging our assumptions and helping us grow beyond our comfort zones.

LEARN FROM OTHERS: One of the greatest advantages of having mentors is the opportunity to learn from their mistakes and successes. They can impart invaluable lessons that might take years to learn on our own. By sharing their wisdom, mentors help us avoid common pitfalls and navigate the complexities of our chosen path more effectively. Their guidance can save us time, energy, and resources, propelling us toward our goals. They often help us get rid of those confusing "gray areas" in our lives. And they may come by ways and means that none of us expects.

GETTING RID OF THE GRAY: *A Classic Example* once came to me when I was in my late 20s and was something I never expected. Early in my management career I found myself in a selling contest between all the regions of the mutual fund company I worked for. I was the youngest and probably the most aggressive new branch manager. I very much wanted to win. I had the best salesmen and we were virtually unbeatable…or so I thought. Then it happened: In the last week of the contest I found that two other branches were running neck and neck with ours.

WHAT SHOULD WE DO? I had to confront the challenge of possibly being "second best," which was not something I looked forward to. We had a meeting on Sunday and schemed out a strategy. My group would divide into teams and work as teams for that week and all head out to any territory where they felt they could get sales. As this was Canada, we were licensed to sell anywhere in the province but not out of that province. My guys left for their missions early Monday morning and some of the more eager ones late Sunday so they were all in place for their bouts of Monday morning selling. When they came back on Friday they all had sales, but two of them had written an unbelievable amount of business way up in the corner of the province where it bordered another one. As I went through the sales figures, I soon found out that most of their sales were actually written in the next province.

My dilemma this early in my career was that these extra sales would have put us over the top and we would have won the contest hands down—what to do? My teams had all worked hard and they had delivered, even if they had to bend a few rules to do it. There were several things I could have done, all of which were quickly suggested when I brought the culprits in to explain to me why they did what they did.

Their answers were that these out of province sales would in fact qualify because their PO Boxes were in the province we were licensed in; they lived just on the other side of the line. They went to the town in our province for all their groceries and supplies and in all ways except their actual residences they qualified to buy the mutual funds we were selling. The salesmen had thought about actually registering the home addresses on the mutual fund applications as in our province office, but they discarded that idea for some unknown reason. Again, what to do? It was a little gray. And the salesmen had a good point. As their manager, I had to decide whether to accept the sales or not? Well, whenever "gray" areas come up, if I can't quite figure it out I have always had mentors or people I could go to for advice.

This time I felt the situation was so specific that the only person who could help me was the President of the company. He listened to what I had to say and answered me this way.

"Peter, he asked, "Where did the people live that your salesmen sold the mutual funds to?" I answered that they actually lived in the adjoining province but…?

He then asked, "What province are these salesmen licensed to sell in?" I answered which province it was. After which, he asked "Then what is your question?"

By that time, the answer was so obvious that I was ashamed to have sought his counsel. So, I thanked him for his time and turned to leave.

This is when he gave me one of the best lessons of my life and one that I always think of when there are "gray" decisions to make. He told me that usually most of the questions have very simple answers, *if you think of things in black and white.* They only get complicated when you think of them in multiple shades of gray.

He further told me something I never forgot: "You should think of all issues in black and white. Then draw an imaginary line. Behind this line draw another imaginary line. The space between the two lines is the gray area— don't go there, stay with the black and white decisions. You will find that 99% of the time all your decisions will be black or white. If they ever feel gray to you then hopefully you have surrounded yourself with mentors who you can go to, like you have come to me today and have them help you define what is black and white and what is gray. It may be easier for them as they will not be emotionally attached to the answer." (Such great advice!)

Oh, by the way – we won the contest without their out-of-province sales.

I tell you this story here and now to illustrate one thing: *to show you how simple it can be to make what appear to be difficult decisions into something simpler:* Is there a realm of Black and White? There can be, and will be, occasions when there is. Very often this is simply a metaphor for what's right or wrong. You always want to make the "right" decision. And always let your *Conscience* (the ultimate mentor) be your guide.

FINDING THE RIGHT MENTORS: To find mentors, it is crucial to be pro-active and intentional. Start by identifying individuals who have achieved what you aspire to accomplish or possess the expertise you desire to acquire. Consider mentors from various areas of your life, such as personal development, career, relationships, or specific skills. Look for mentors who align with your values and can provide honest and constructive feedback. When you get down to it—whether you read them, watch them on a podcast, or are fortunate enough to have them in your life 24/7—truly great mentors have one thing in common: They will always ultimately help you find that hidden power within yourself. They will invariably bring-in *The Light*. They will shed it and they will share it.

On Apple+TV, there is a limited (3 Season) series that is an object lesson in Mentoring. It's called *Ted Lasso*. Starring Jason Sudeikis, it's a Master Class in Humanity, Humor, Personal Transition, and Character Development in all the right ways. A winner of countless Emmys, Golden Globes and SAG Awards, *Ted Lasso* deals with the adventures of an American High School Football Coach who is brought across the pond to the UK to "head up" a Premier League Soccer Team that is rife with dissention and losing so badly it is about to be dropped down to a lower division (financial death to a big league "football club"). Hired by the club's (female) owner who hopes he will fail miserably, Ted Lasso knows zero about soccer but *Everything about human nature…and how to motivate others.* Never once letting a negative thought enter his mind or a demeaning word cross his lips, Ted and his zany assistants uplift and inspire the complicated, egotistical players, unify the team and bring the Richmond Football Club back to its days of glory. And when on an outrageous 18-game winning streak in Season Three, he is asked by reporters for the secrets of his success, Ted Lasso simply replies: "It's never about the wins and losses that take place out there on some patch of grass. It's about making all these young men into the best version of themselves."

That is true Mentorship. And *that is what you should look for* in the mentors and coaches that you seek: someone who wants to make you the best version of yourself.

APPROACHING POTENTIAL MENTORS: When approaching potential mentors, remember that it is a mutually beneficial relationship. While you seek guidance, mentors often derive satisfaction from helping others succeed. Start by building rapport and expressing genuine admiration for their achievements or knowledge. Be clear about what you hope to gain from the mentorship and demonstrate your commitment to learning and growth. Respect their time and availability, and be open to the possibility of rejection while remaining persistent.

RECOGNIZE THAT MENTORS CAN COME FROM MANY SOURCES: It is a common misperception people tend to believe—that their mentors have to be in their lives on a daily or weekly basis; and please let me be the first to disabuse you of that. If you've been trying to improve your life at all, you've probably already had a dozen or so mentors in your life and didn't even know it.

To be sure, we've all had coaches, teachers, professors, parents, bosses and major peer-group influencers in our daily interactions that have made a major impact on our lives. If we're lucky, they have proven to be role-models and those who are able to "lead by example." Doubtless they have been invaluable. And yet they come in so many other forms. If you've read the New Testament, Jesus is bound to be the ultimate mentor. Or maybe you've read the works of Ralph Waldo Emerson, Marcus Aurelius or (more recently) Napoleon Hill, Wallace Wattles or Dale Carnegie. You've taken a course from Tony Robbins or read *Chicken Soup for the Soul*, co-authored by Jack Canfield and (our good friend) Mark Victor Hansen. You've watched Oprah and subscribed to *"O"* *Magazine*. Or followed the career and teachings of Marianne Williamson.

Each of these individuals and so many others have made a significant impact on our lives. And they can neither be ignored nor denied. They also need to be put into context. Because, who you choose as your mentors also reflects on you and what you want in life.

They also arrive at times and in places that none of us expects.

THE QUANTITY OF MENTORS: To all of this there is a caution: "Don't overbook the room." The number of mentors one should have can vary based on individual preferences and circumstances. Some find great value in having multiple mentors, each specializing in different areas of expertise. This allows for a diverse range of perspectives and insights. However, having too many mentors can lead to conflicting advice and confusion. It is essential to strike a balance and focus on quality over quantity. Start with one or two mentors who can guide you effectively and then expand your network gradually, as needed.

NEVER UNDERESTIMATE THE POWER OF VIRTUAL MENTORS: When I started my first company my lawyer told me that I needed to appoint some directors who could give the company wisdom, direction, strategy etc. I was 31 years old and had not met enough people at that time that I felt could give me the advice that I would need. I kept thinking about this situation and tried to think of people who could help me in this growth stage of my life. At home we had a coffee-table book of black and white personality portraits by the inimitable Yousuf Karsh.

In the book were extraordinary photos of such historical icons as John F. Kennedy, Martin Luther King, Mahatma Gandhi and Ernest Hemingway. I thought to myself *These people can become my directors; they have a lot of wisdom and could advise me on what I need to do.* So I cut their pictures out of the book and actually took the time to "frame" each of them, putting them up in my den, and reading everything about them that I could get my hands on.

In that form, in a very good way, they were kind of "in your face" during my every waking hour. As challenges came into my life I would ask each one of them what they would do about the particular issue. I found that JFK was the business advisor. MLK was the person who could provide moral balance and help me to better discern right from wrong. He was a wonderful decision maker, and contributed greatly to making me one as well. *Gandhi* was my spiritual guide, my metaphysical "clarifier." And Ernest H. was the "pull-no-punches," bare-knuckles and straight-talk, writer/rogue advisor. If I needed an excuse to have a little fun I would be sure to check-in with Hemingway…one man to another.

Mind you, I had never met any of these people face to face (though, heaven only knows, I would have loved to). Still the act of having them there, and putting their images in front of me, gave them all a life of their own…and their thoughts and wisdom with it.

The purpose of this *Virtual Mentorship* is to open your mind to the idea that you do not need living mentors (though you certainly should have them) but you can have access to the wisdom of the ages if you open your mind to the idea of having virtual mentors to inspire you as well. The advantage is that they're available to you 24/7 every day of your life. All you have to do is pick up a book or go to them online. Once you select who your virtual mentors are going to be, I suggest that you immediately go down to your favorite book store or point and click on Amazon.com or BarnesandNoble.com and buy an autobiography on your first mentor. Then take it home and read it cover to cover. Once you've finished, buy a book on your next virtual mentor and repeat the process. The more books you buy and read about your virtual mentors, the more wisdom they will be able to impart to you. Again, the impact is quite organic; so don't ask me how this works. Just give it a try and recognize that it does.

IN A FINAL MOMENT OF MENTORING...RECOGNIZE THIS FACT: Mentors play an integral role in our personal and professional development. They offer us the wisdom, guidance, and support we need to overcome challenges and reach our full potential. By leveraging their experience and insights, we can accelerate our growth, avoid unnecessary setbacks and achieve our goals more efficiently. Remember to be proactive in seeking mentors. Be open to learning and cultivate meaningful relationships. Embrace the power of mentorship and unlock your true potential on the path to success.

As you embark on your construction of your Dream Factory, let your mentors be the guiding stars that illuminate the course of your life, helping you turn your dreams into reality.

CHAPTER 6

Set SMART Goals: Make Your Dreams Attainable

Not all goals are created equal. It's only logical and yet too often goes ignored that occasionally "the road less traveled" leads to a dead end. Super highways are set to connect us for a reason. And sometimes those shortcuts to our dreams end up taking us on a rocky path indeed, one that might very well run us off a cliff. So be imaginative to be sure. But also apply a little logic in the pursuit of your dreams. As an engineer friend of ours once said: "Life is a lot easier if you start out by reading the instructions." So, let *The Dream Factory* be your instruction guide.

Setting intelligent goals acts as your personal direction-finder, guiding you toward the destination you desire. To maximize your chances of success, it is crucial to **Get SMART: with goals that are Specific, Measurable, Achievable, Relevant, and Time-bound.** Yes! That's an acronym, and one that is carefully thought out. Because in this chapter, we will delve into the importance of setting SMART goals and provide a practical framework for turning your dreams *into actionable targets.*

The Significance of SMART Goals: Setting SMART goals is a powerful tool for transforming dreams into reality. They provide clarity, focus, and direction, ensuring that our efforts are purposeful and aligned with our aspirations. SMART goals help us break down our dreams into manageable steps, making them more attainable and measurable. They motivate us, drive our actions, and enable us to track progress effectively. By setting SMART goals, we lay a solid foundation for success.

SPECIFICITY: Define Clear Objectives. Specificity is the cornerstone of setting SMART goals. And the adage holds true: "Freedom is greatest when the boundaries are clearly defined." Clear definition is what you want to achieve by answering the **Five Ws:** *What do you want to accomplish? Why is it important? Who is involved? Where will it take place? When do you want to achieve it?* By honing in on the specifics, you create a clear vision that helps you crystalize the patterns and pathways you've set for yourself.

MEASURABILITY: *Quantify Your Progress.* To make your goals measurable, establish criteria that allow you to track your progress objectively. Set quantifiable targets or milestones that indicate you are moving closer to your dream. Break down your goal into smaller, measurable components, enabling you to celebrate achievements along the way. Measuring your progress not only provides a sense of accomplishment but also enables you to make adjustments and stay motivated.

ACHIEVABILITY: *Balance Ambition and Realism:* While dreams often require stretching beyond our comfort zones, it is essential to set goals that are achievable. Assess your skills, resources, and circumstances to ensure your goals are within reach. *(Question: How do you eat a hippopotamus? Answer: One bite at a time.)* Consider the challenges and potential roadblocks, and develop strategies to overcome them. By striking a balance between ambition and realism, you set yourself up for success, building confidence as you make steady progress towards your dream.

RELEVANCE: *Aligning Goals with Your Dreams:* To stay motivated and engaged, your goals must be relevant to the objectives you'd like to achieve. Evaluate the significance of each goal in relation to your vision, values, and passions. Coordinate your goals with your long-term aspirations, ensuring they contribute meaningfully to the fulfillment of your dream. When your goals are relevant, they become a natural extension of your purpose, propelling you forward with unwavering determination.

TIME-BOUND: *Establish Deadlines and a Sense of Urgency.* At the same time, remember that time is your best currency. So use it intelligently. And be realistic. But also remember Parkinson's Law. (A highly important maxim we shall cover shortly.) Setting deadlines creates a sense of urgency and helps you prioritize your actions. Establish specific timeframes for achieving each goal, allowing you to track your progress effectively and maintain momentum. Break down your goals into short, medium, and long-term targets, providing structure and a sense of progression. Remember, deadlines are not meant to create pressure but to provide a sense of direction and ensure that you make consistent strides towards your dream.

SUMMARY

GETTING THERE: Setting SMART goals is a transformative step on the journey to attaining your dreams. By making your goals Specific, Measurable, Achievable, Relevant, and Time-bound, you enhance your focus, motivation, and progress tracking. With clarity and direction, you can break down your dreams into actionable steps and celebrate each milestone along the way. Embrace the power of SMART goals, and let them serve as the foundation for turning your dreams into tangible achievements.

As you navigate your path to the Dream Factory, remember that setting SMART goals is the bridge that connects your goals to your reality. It empowers you to take intentional actions, overcome obstacles, and ultimately bring your dreams to life.

CHAPTER 7

The Power of Belief:
Cultivate a Success Mindset

Automaker Henry Ford once said it best: "If you think you can do a thing, or think you can't do a thing, you're right!" So when others in his profession told him that the automobile could never be mass-produced, that it would always just be a "rich man's toy," he invented the Assembly Line in 1908, and out of that created the Model-T—the car that everyone in America could afford. In so doing, he altered the course of the auto industry forever.

In the quest to transform our dreams into reality, one of the most influential factors is our *State-of-Mind.* Our beliefs shape our thoughts, actions, and ultimately, our outcomes.

Bruce Lee, the man who transformed martial arts for Western Civilization said it with ultimate purity: *"Man's mind and behavior are one. Inner thought and outer expression cannot contradict each other."* It's something everyone nods their heads to, but there are very few who actually put this into practice. Cultivating a success mindset is essential for navigating challenges, embracing opportunities, and achieving our dreams. In this chapter, we will explore the power of belief and provide insights on how to cultivate a success mindset in the journey towards the Dream Factory.

THE ROLE OF BELIEF: Belief acts as the foundation upon which our dreams are built. It is the unwavering faith in ourselves, our abilities and the possibility of achieving our dreams. When we believe in our potential, we tap into a reservoir of strength and resilience. Belief fuels our motivation, helps us overcome setbacks, and propels us forward even in the face of adversity. It is the driving force that transforms dreams into reality.

SHIFTING LIMITING BELIEFS: Often, we hold onto limiting beliefs that hinder our progress. These beliefs create self-imposed mental shackles that shut down our sense of initiative and prevent us from fully embracing our dreams. To cultivate a success mindset, it is crucial to identify and challenge these *monsters of limitation.* Examine the narratives you tell yourself (and others tell you) and challenge their validity. Replace negative self-talk with empowering affirmations that reinforce your capabilities and potential. By shifting your limiting beliefs, you create space for growth, possibility and greater achievements.

EMBRACE A GROWTH DYNAMIC: *A Growth Dynamic* is the belief that our abilities and intelligence can be developed through dedication, effort, and a willingness to learn. Embrace the idea that setbacks are opportunities for improvement, and as such are merely the illusion of rejection. Cultivate a curiosity for new knowledge, seek out challenges, and view obstacles as stepping stones to success.

VISUALIZE SUCCESS: Visualization is a powerful tool for cultivating a success mindset. Create a vivid mental image of yourself achieving your dreams. Envision the emotions, the sights, the sounds, and the sensations associated with your success. Immerse yourself in this visualization regularly, allowing it to reinforce your belief in what is possible. Visualizing success not only strengthens your belief but also helps align your actions and choices with your desired outcomes.

SURROUND YOURSELF WITH POSITIVITY: The company we keep has a profound impact on our mindset. Surround yourself with positive, supportive individuals who believe in your dreams and uplift your spirits. Recognize the fact that, once you apply yourself, you are *Limitless,* and that's just where it begins. And along the way remember to **"Fire the Handicapper General!"** (That's the person who tries to make you feel inadequate, unworthy and generally bad about yourself, accompanied by the dogs of conformity and a lack of imagination.)

Brilliant satirist and American Author Kurt Vonnegut once wrote a seminal work of dystopian fiction in short story form called "Harrison Bergeron." In it, the America of the future has degenerated from being a "Meritocracy" into becoming a "Mediocrity" where no one is permitted to be better than anyone else. And instead of a President, the United States is now governed by a Handicapper General who has placed all the high-achievers in [electronic] mental and physical shackles...and who hunts down those who dare to excel and blows them in half with a 12-gauge shotgun.

Whether you recognize them or not, there may already be Handicapper Generals in your life. You can find them everywhere, and once you've learned how to identify them they become easy to spot...because they're the ones who try to tell you that you "Can't" accomplish what you really want in life. So, "Can the Can'ts" and kick to the curb those who use that kind of language. Fire those Handicapper Generals in your life.

Instead, fill your life with all the good things, good people, and smart mentors—both virtual and real. Engage in communities, attend seminars, and read books that inspire and motivate you. Seek out mentors and role models who have achieved what you aspire to accomplish. By surrounding yourself with positivity, you create an environment that nurtures and reinforces your success mindset.

ALONG THE WAY, LET YOUR AMCs KICK-IN: I have always been interested in what makes some people successful while others just can't quite seem to get it together. So a few years ago we asked many successful people what they felt were the reasons they were successful and received a lot of different answers—from hard work to just being lucky. We asked them to give us 10 reasons and the 3 Characteristics all successful people had in common. Although the 10 Reasons vary somewhat, the 3 Commonalities were almost always the same.

First, they had good **Attitudes**. Second, they were easily **Motivated**. They were almost always "self-starters" and, more often than not, knew how to motivate others. Finally, they were the type of people who made **Commitments** and kept them. These three character traits resonated with me because they were consistent, indelible and easily explained. I've come to call them my AMCs and have used them for years in recruiting people and in my advising and mentoring activities.

Certainly, the *Laws Of Attraction* apply here as well. Because your AMCs are contagious. And if you have all three in place, you will be drawn to others who have theirs together as well. You'll recognize them instantly. Because they'll announce themselves to you—with *"can do" attitudes* and *enthusiasm...* and a passion and *motivation* for all things. And as surely as the rainbow follows the rain, their *commitment* will be there for you as well.

CELEBRATE YOUR PROGRESS: To develop a success mindset, it is essential to celebrate every step forward, no matter how small. Acknowledge and appreciate your progress along the journey. Celebrate achievements, milestones, and even the lessons learned from disappointments. This practice reinforces your belief in your abilities and fuels your motivation to keep pushing forward. Remember, success is not solely measured by the destination but by the growth and progress you've made along the way.

SUMMING IT ALL UP: Over 120 years ago a man named James Allen wrote a life changing book. It was only 110 pages, but the title summarized it all: *As A Man Thinketh.* And it opened with the immortal first seven words: "As a man thinketh, so he becomes." Cultivating a success mindset is a fundamental aspect of turning dreams into reality. By harnessing the power of belief, challenging limiting thoughts or confining precepts, embracing a growth mindset, visualizing success, surrounding yourself with positivity, and celebrating progress, you lay the groundwork for remarkable achievements. Your *PMA (Positive Mental Attitude)* becomes the driving force that propels you forward, enables you to overcome obstacles, and ultimately guides you to the total realization of your dreams. As you embark on the careful construction of your personal Dream Factory, nurture your success mindset. Believe in yourself. Find new ways to grow. Align your thoughts with your actions. Once you do, extraordinary things become a way of life.

CHAPTER 8

Turn Obstacles into Opportunities

O bstacles are inevitable when pursuing our dreams. They try our patience, challenge our determination, and sometimes make us question our path. For those of us who recognize them for the strengtheners that they are, *Obstacles* also become our best friends along the way to testing our *Resolve*. Challenges are often friends in disguise. Because it is when we are tested in the fire of adversity that our true inner-power is revealed. In this chapter, we will explore the art of overcoming obstacles and turning challenges into opportunities on the path to the Dream Factory.

THE NATURE OF OBSTACLES: Obstacles come in various forms: they can be external or internal, tangible or intangible. They may manifest as setbacks, failures, social shackles, extrinsic occurrences (out of the blue) or even a bout self-doubt. Along the way, we also have to decide whether or not they are *Imagined…or Real!*

In a perfect track and field metaphor, 3 Time Olympic Gold Medalist and 10-time World Champion in the 400 meter hurdles, Edwin Moses, was once asked the secret of his success. "I never see the hurdles," Moses answered, without a moment's pause. "I see the finish line." While obstacles may seem daunting, it is crucial to recognize that they are an inherent part of the journey. By shifting our perspective and embracing seeming blockages as opportunities for growth, we can harness their transformative power. And sometimes, it's easier said than done. (Or is it?)

"CUT YOUR LOSSES," THE SOONER THE BETTER: If you've lived any time at all on Planet Earth, you've experienced some kind of loss in life. Whether it's a personal tragedy such as an illness or even death of a family member, or a professional calamity such as a sudden crash in your chosen field of endeavor—having the bottom drop out of a market or a potential Chapter 11 Bankruptcy. When these events take place in our lives we're all at choice to take either one path or the other: to succumb to these demons of denial or to rise above them and move on.

Sometimes it's exceedingly difficult, because both kinds of loss can, for a time at least, seem insurmountable. Since we all know that "time is relative" and can last a moment or a decade, the question is set before us: What steps do we take next?

Our good friend Pat Pearson (who I mentioned in my "Author's Note") offers an excellent course about how to handle these little crises in our lives. It provides the perfect antidote. And her insights are pretty uncanny when you see them laid out before you. It is virtually axiomatic that *loss* often becomes *grief.* Grief turns quickly into *Fear,* and fear can quickly tumble off into that chasm called *Obsession.* And once you become obsessed over something (anything) it can subsume your consciousness and dominate your life. Once you've gone down that "Rabbit Hole" it's very hard to climb out because now you've fallen *Through the Looking Glass* into a realm where everything's upside down.

So what is the answer? ***"Letting Go."*** Forgive the source of the loss and grief and overcome the fear. Remember, if you've learned anything by this time, that *you are Limitless.* If you're Limitless you are also *Fearless.* And soon enough you recognize that fear is the ultimate illusion and little more than a fog. So whenever this suddenly pops up in your life, eliminate this vicious cycle. And do it without pause. Remember every challenge in your life comes with its own solution. And along the way your innate ability as a "Problem Solver" will kick-in.

CULTIVATE A PROBLEM-SOLVING MINDSET: The next step in overcoming obstacles is to adopt a problem-solving mindset. Rather than succumbing to frustration or defeat, approach challenges with a proactive attitude. Break down the obstacle into smaller, manageable components. Analyze the situation, explore alternative strategies, and seek creative solutions. By focusing on finding solutions instead of dwelling on the problem, you empower yourself to overcome even the most perplexing logjams set in your path.

LEARN FROM SETBACKS AND FAILURES: Believe it or not, more often than not "Failure can be your friend." Setbacks and speed bumps are valuable teachers on the road to your success. Embrace them as opportunities for growth and learning. Reflect on the lessons they offer and extract wisdom from each experience. Genius inventor and owner of 2,332 patents, Thomas Edison once observed: "I've never failed. I've just found 1,000 ways that haven't worked." Edison also acknowledged the power of taking that 1001st step that leads to success…and in using all those "failures" as teaching tools to finally get to that *Eureka Moment!* That breakthrough that invariably takes you to achieving your objective.

Understand that setbacks are not indicative of your worth or potential. Instead, they provide insights into what needs improvement, even as they offer you the chance to refine your approach. Use failures as stepping stones towards success, resiliently bouncing back stronger and more determined. World famous scientists, explorers, inventors, tech nerds in IT and futuristic architects—all have one thing in common. They have learned to consciously acknowledge the "F" word (FAILURE) along the pathway to their discoveries. In fact, in the parlance of Silicon Valley *Failure* is embraced! It's part of the *quantum soup* of making things happen. It also serves as a "welcome sign" that you are getting that much closer to achieving *Your Desired Result.*

No one exemplifies this better than Apple Co-founder and inspirator, Steve Jobs. Fired from the company he founded, not once but twice, Jobs bounced back stronger than ever both times because he knew that, "You have to be willing to fail…you've got to be willing to crash and burn." He repeated that mantra often and loudly because Steve Jobs, like many other innovators, had multiple failures on the way to accomplishment but never gave up because he believed in Overcoming Obstacles. Through failure, we learn from our mistakes and we get better and better at what we are trying to achieve. With enough hard work and effort, we can push forward to achieve what we set out to do originally and so much more. When an Apple product failed to gain traction or when he was forced out of his own company, Steve Jobs like many other successful men and women did not give up but went on to form other breakthrough companies such as animation giant PIXAR and NeXT computers. They learned from their mistakes and became even better at what they did…and, as a result, ended up being even more in demand.

"If you're afraid of failing, you won't get very far." Jobs added when asked later in his career. "To put it bluntly, failure happens to everybody. Nobody in the world succeeds 100% of the time at everything they do." Along the way, his many failures and those of his brilliant staff ultimately evolved into such phenomenal triumphs as Macintosh Computers, the iMac, the iBook, MacBook Air, the iPhone, the iPad, iTunes, spinoffs like Apple+TV and now finally Apple Vision Pro® (breakthrough VR with the *entire universe of technology at your fingertips*)...leading to the first $1 Trillion Dollar Company in the history of global commerce.

BUILD RESILIENCE. "FLIP THE SCRIPT:" Resilience is the key to overcoming obstacles. Cultivate inner strength and fortitude by developing a resilient mindset. Embrace challenges as opportunities to build character and enhance your abilities. Practice self-care and prioritize your well-being to stay mentally and emotionally strong. Surround yourself with a supportive network of friends, family, and mentors who can offer guidance and encouragement during difficult times. With resilience, you can navigate through obstacles and emerge stronger on the other side. And along the way remember, you can "Flip the Script," at will, virtually turning lemons into lemonade every single time. Once you do you'll not only perceive yourself differently, you'll also start to command respect from others who recognize your "Bounce-Back Factor" and rally to your side.

GET UP AND GET BACK ON THE HORSE...LITERALLY. Well, the old cowboy trope holds true (as any experienced horseman is sure to tell you): "Never a horse that's never been rode. Never a cowboy that's never been thrown." A bit colloquial, I admit. But it carries its own life lesson that is tough, durable, and innately contains a truism that cannot be denied.

When I was in my early teens—thirteen in fact—I was quite an avid horseman, skilled I thought, and always inclined to bring my rides to full gallop pretty quickly after I climbed into the saddle. So there I was on a familiar trek, and urging my steed to top speed when, for some reason, he veered with a jerk from the path we always took at a full gallop. Understandably, the laws of inertia came into effect. And when the horse cut away, I kept on going straight ahead. And, flying off the saddle head-first, I tumbled to ground and got knocked out in the bargain. But I was thirteen, and the thought of giving up never entered my mind. So when I came to, I quickly dusted myself off and went off to catch my horse, climbing back into the saddle and riding away with my pals.

EVEN IF IT'S A POMMEL HORSE: An even better example of this comes with a story about our granddaughter Shae. An accomplished gymnast at an early age (as they invariably have to be) Shae was first up to perform for her school team and started with her strongest event—the Balance Beam. Unfortunately, at the very beginning of her routine, she fell off the beam and lay on the floor devastated…but only for a moment. Acting as if it had never happened, she got back on the beam, continued her discipline to perfection and ended up winning five medals in the combined. Ultimately, other than losing one point for falling off the beam at the beginning, she continued on to have a perfect score. So—no matter what your event in life—if you fall, dust yourself off and get back onto the beam, the horse or whatever else challenges you. Because that's what winners do.

WHEN YOU THINK ABOUT IT, BOTH STORIES OFFER A COUPLE OF MORALS: The First is that Life is like that. Sometimes for no reason it "veers" on us and there is no use in trying to figure it out. "*Why me?*" Should never be the final question asked. Instead tell yourself that, *This is my opportunity to really make it happen.* The Second is even more important: WE ARE NATURALLY RESILIENT. Resilience is as innate to human nature as breathing in and out. At 13, I was too young to even consider failure as an option. So…just like the song says, I followed that melodic advice; "Pick yourself up. Dust yourself off. And start all over again!" At about the same age, Shae even topped me, took her setback and molded it into *Gold,* setting an example—and a model for winning—for others along the way.

SEEK SUPPORT AND COLLABORATION: You don't have to face obstacles alone. Reach out for support when needed. Seek guidance from mentors, advisors or experts in relevant fields. Collaborate with like-minded individuals who can provide you with different perspectives and share their relevant experiences. Remember that seeking help is not a sign of weakness but an acknowledgment of the power of collective wisdom. By joining forces with others, you can overcome obstacles more effectively and accelerate your progress.

MAINTAIN FOCUS AND ADAPTABILITY: Obstacles can be distracting, causing us to lose sight of our goals. And there is one antidote to all that virtually never fails: *Stay focused. (Remember: FOCUS is Item #2 in our Design Directive.)* So, it is essential to maintain focus on the bigger picture while addressing the immediate challenges that you face. Remind yourself of your original vision and the reasons behind your pursuit of the dream. Be adaptable and open to adjusting your strategies as circumstances evolve. Embrace change as an opportunity for growth and innovation. With a resilient mindset and adaptable approach, you can navigate obstacles with grace and determination.

OVERCOMING IS BECOMING: Overcoming obstacles is an integral part of the journey towards *The Dream Factory*. By embracing a problem-solving mindset, learning from setbacks, building resilience, seeking support, and maintaining focus and adaptability, you can transform challenges into opportunities for growth and success. Obstacles cease to be roadblocks and convert into stepping stones that propel you closer to your dreams.

Keep ever mindful that it is not the absence of barriers that defines your journey but rather your ability to recognize, navigate and conquer them. With unwavering determination and a resilient spirit you possess the power to overcome any obstacle that comes your way. Welcome the challenges, learn from them, and let them fuel your journey to the Dream Factory, where dreams turn into reality.

THE THIRD PILLAR
YOUR STRUCTURE
If You Build It They Will Come...

CHAPTER 9

Take Action!
It's the Key to Success

Taking action is the fundamental ingredient that transforms our dreams into reality. If you do so, it is virtually assured that your Dream Factory will reach completion. Without it, you'll probably fall asleep, only to awaken too late and watch someone else's dreams come true. In this chapter, you'll not only learn the importance of taking action, but also discover some remarkable techniques that will show you how to do it…and explore strategies to unlock its potential on the journey to the Dream Factory.

There is the paradox about dreams. You have to have them (literally during your REM sleep) if you're to survive at all. In fact, if people cannot have dreams, they literally start to go mad. And yet, unless you act upon them, you become nothing more than a drifter…because daydreams are lovely only as long as they motivate you to do something.

Personally, I've never quite understood the point of having dreams—or having aspirations and desires—and not acting upon them. As you will recall, when I wanted to own a Learjet I visualized it, and then followed that up by taking action. I did what was necessary to own it and I still own one to this day. When I wanted to own a Ferrari and race it, I took the necessary steps to do that. Ditto when it came to purchasing and traveling the high seas on my own yacht, *Happiness II*. I've also believed that it is not only important to follow every dream with an action-plan to achieve it, but also to teach and empower others to do the same (hence this book).

Once you start visualizing, once you make it a part of your daily discourse, it will take place as surely as day follows night that you will start applying the means to make it happen. You will take action. There is a saying in the United States Marine Corps: "Attitude is everything!" A *can do* attitude is the key you insert to turn on the engine of your action.

THE POWER OF ACTION: Action is the force that propels us forward, bridging the gap between where we are and where we want to be. It is through action that we bring our dreams to life, turning them into tangible outcomes. Action innately has the power to create momentum, build confidence and unleash our fullest potential. Without action, dreams remain stagnant fantasies, unfulfilled and unrealized.

SET CLEAR AND MEANINGFUL GOALS: Before embarking on any journey, it is essential to set clear and meaningful goals. Define what you want to achieve and why it matters to you. As a point of review, remember to establish *(SMART)* goals that align with your dreams. ***Specific, Measurable, Achievable, Relevant,*** and ***Time-Bound...***and it bears repeating here. Because goals act as guiding stars, providing a sense of both direction and higher purpose. They give you something tangible to work towards and serve as a roadmap to keep you right on course...and not be fooled by all those imitations of success.

BREAK DOWN GOALS INTO ACTIONABLE STEPS: Large goals can be overwhelming, but by breaking them down into smaller, actionable steps, they become more manageable. Divide your goals into smaller milestones and tasks that you can tackle one by one. This approach allows you to make consistent progress, build momentum and celebrate achievements along the way. Breaking down your goals into actionable steps transforms the seemingly insurmountable into concrete benchmarks that help you successfully chart your path.

DEVELOP A PASSION FOR TAKING ACTION: To turn dreams into reality, it is crucial to cultivate passion for taking action. Avoid falling into the trap of waiting for the perfect moment or seeking absolute certainty...because if you do, that moment will never come. As legendary Green Bay Packer football coach Vince Lombardi once said: "Perfection is impossible. But on the way to seeking it, we may achieve Excellence!" Know in your heart of hearts that excellence is yours already.

When you take the initiative and embrace a mindset of taking action you are already on the way to achieving excellence in the way that you pursue it: with intention, focus and resolve. Recognize that mistakes and failures are inevitable. Also acknowledge that they provide valuable lessons and opportunities for growth. Embrace the idea of "learning by doing" and trust in your ability to adapt and recalibrate from every action taken.

OVERCOME PROCRASTINATION AND RESISTANCE: Procrastination and resistance are common obstacles that can hinder progress. To overcome them, it is vital to understand their underlying causes. Identify any fears, self-doubt, or limiting beliefs that may be holding you back. Once you discover what they are, *lean into them!* Make the very things that you're putting off a priority in your life. Turn aversions into habits...and habits into wins.

Develop self-awareness and devise strategies to overcome procrastination. Set deadlines, create a supportive environment, break tasks into smaller, manageable parts, and hold yourself accountable. By taking proactive steps to combat procrastination, you empower yourself to take consistent action towards your dreams.

SHIFTING GEARS AT 51: It's also never too late to shift gears and pick up something new. I have been a long-distance runner all my life, running at least 30 miles a week, and any number of 10K races and marathons virtually every year. It was always a great means of staying in shape and also a terrific way to wind down and get into a rhythm with nature when I needed to. So, it was both inspiration and sanctuary for me, up until it started taking a toll on my body. Because of that long-term wear and tear, my back started aching so badly that I could no longer run.

All you runners know what kind of a sentence this is after a lifetime of running. I slacked off, and you would be amazed at how quickly I got past not running each day. Then, as I started to gain weight, I realized that I had to do something. So, I turned to the exercise bike with a certain sense of disappointment.

All my life, I wondered how anyone could go through the monotonous ritual of riding those bikes while it was so great outside: warm sun, wicked winds and all those adventurous courses that Mother Nature had to provide.

By contrast, there was no way that I wanted to ride that boring exercise bike. But I decided, instead of setting my goal to ride the bike for 30 minutes at a time, that I would only ride it for 5 minutes a day. And you would be amazed how quickly I was able to introduce this new program into my life. In a very short time, I could not imagine not riding my bike for 30 minutes a day. And it all began by taking action with small steps like starting with five minutes. That way, I was not setting myself up for failure but for winning.

And even though now, several years later, I've downshifted from 30 minutes of cycling to treadmills and power walks, I still apply those same principles with any project that I find difficult to get myself excited about. Just as the Nike ad says – *Just Do It!* When you get down to it, that's the only language that Life understands.

The reason I'm retelling this story is to give you the confidence to START NOW no matter how daunting the task may seem. The longest journey begins with the first step. In Japan, the Samurai have a wonderful word for it: *Kaizan!* (It means "little baby steps." And when you think about it, just the sound of the word propels you into action.) So whenever you're faced with a trial or two, Shout *kaizan* to yourself! Break up your task into small pieces and take those baby steps. You will be amazed at the results when you do...and how quickly you'll be enthusiastically setting new goals and enjoying your "happy habit."

LEARN FROM ACTIONS, THEY ARE YOUR TEACHERS: The actions you take are not merely means to an end, they are also sources of invaluable feedback and learning. Once you adopt a mindset of continuous improvement, they become like bricks and mortar for your Dream Factory. You build upon them day by day and piece by piece until you have the entire plan—brilliantly put together to your exact specifications just as you visualized it.

After that, you evaluate the outcomes of your actions, both successes and failures, and extract lessons from each experience. Use this knowledge to refine your strategies and approach. Embrace the concept of "failing forward"... seeing setbacks as stepping stones towards growth and refinement. With each action taken and each lesson learned, you become more adept and aligned with your goals.

I pause here to advise you as well that this can be a trap. Because you need to make adjustments or else your failures become a "habit" (and not the good kind). I use for this, a classic example of my *experience with "The Fly."*

One afternoon, I came by and saw a fly buzzing frantically against the window pane in my house. It was one of those windows not easily opened—and only from a certain angle. The fly, of course, didn't know that and—able to use its 3,000 sets of eyes to see the great outdoors on the other side—just kept buzzing away. When I looked again in ten minutes, the fly was still buzzing away...and then buzzing away another ten minutes later. About three hours later, I walked by the same window and the fly was no longer there. When I glanced down, there was the dead fly along with several others on the window sill, casualties of their own persistence, devoid of intelligent thought. The irony in all of this was that—just across from where the flies were buzzing, trying to get out the window—was a door to the outside, left wide open and unscreened. Those flies had thousands of sets of eyes to see the other side, yet not one fly had two brain cells to rub together to seek an alternate route, or simply to fly to the source of the breeze blowing-in from across the room.

THE PURPOSE OF THE FLY STORY: I could not help but think that this was a lot like the way some people lead their lives. Too many of us spend too much of our lives pursuing dreams and objectives—"buzzing" against the window, without trying to make adjustments. (Because all they could see was the other side, and NOT the ways to get there.)

All too often it happens on the human level as well. We can see the goal in front of us and feel if we just "buzz" harder and longer we will be rewarded, when in fact we should stop our "frenzied flying," back away, reassess and look around for that other open door.

SUMMARY

START TODAY. ACT ON YOUR DREAMS. Taking action is the catalyst that propels us towards the Dream Factory. By setting clear goals, breaking them down into actionable steps, embracing a bias for action, overcoming procrastination and resistance, and learning from each action taken, we unlock the potential within us to make our dreams a reality.

Remember, *Action* is the transformative force that turns dreams into tangible outcomes. Approach it with determination, perseverance, and a willingness to learn. Each step forward, no matter how small, brings you closer to the fulfillment of your dreams. Embrace the power of action, and let it propel you towards a future filled with achievement, fulfillment, and the manifestation of your deepest aspirations on the path to the Dream Factory.

CHAPTER 10

Master Time Management: Maximize Productivity

Work expands or contracts
in direct proportion to the time allotted to it.

~ Parkinson's Law

As the cliché goes: "Time is on our side": It is too… as long as you learn how to *Master* it, and not let it master you. Time is your *Ultimate Currency* in life. Time is the bank for your energy, and your inventory for the effort you expend—every day and every week of your life! From the moment you get up in the morning until you drop off to sleep at night, the clock is ticking. And you are already rich beyond your wildest imaginings…provided you recognize it for the gift it is, and once you learn to use it efficiently.

Mastering the *Art of Time Management* to optimize productivity is a trait most successful people have learned and virtually all those who have failed have not.

Here we show you all those techniques for prioritizing tasks, setting boundaries, and leveraging time effectively to ensure progress toward your goals. Remember: *Time is not your enemy; but it is your Scorekeeper.* And anyone who has ever participated in a game or a sport knows the importance that the clock can play when it finally comes down to winning.

On the way to building our dreams, Time is a precious resource that must be managed effectively. Taking charge of time management is crucial for maximizing productivity and staying on track towards the Dream Factory. In this chapter, we will explore strategies and techniques to optimize time management and unlock your full potential on the path to success.

UNDERSTAND THE VALUE OF TIME: Time is a finite resource, and each moment holds the potential for progress or stagnation. Recognize the value of time and the impact it has on your ability to accomplish your goals. Understand that every minute spent wisely brings you closer to your dreams, while wasted time drains your productivity. Adopt the jarring reality that time is a precious asset, and by managing it effectively, you gain a competitive edge in everything you do.

While you're doing this, there's something to keep in mind that I referenced at the beginning of this chapter. It's called *Parkinson's Law:* Parkinson's Law actually contains several rules of thumb. But *The First Law* is most important, and it is this: "Work expands or contracts in direct proportion to the time allotted to it." And there's no question that philosophy can be taken to extremes.

In the mid-1980s there was a book that came out called *The ONE Minute Manager* that stressed, if not overstressed, the importance of maximizing one's time. In it, the reader is constantly challenged with ways to "cut to the chase" and optimize their time while minimizing the pitfalls and perils of getting through the arc of a busy schedule, project or business objective. Its premise was that you could do just about everything in one minute and less than 250 words and reach your desired goals. Based on Sun Tzu's belief (in *The Art of War)* that all battles are won or lost before they are even fought, it adopted the premise that most tasks and meetings are already decided before they ever take place. On the downside, it tended to eliminate the human factor, because it turned Time into the Beast that constantly had to be fed. And it ended up creating a kind of "panicked" management technique. On the upside, it offered one excellent concept called *The Monkey.*

In effect, "Monkeys" were what are now known as OPPs *(Other People's Problems).* And the last thing you ever wanted to get burdened with was having to pick up a lot of monkeys. So learning how not to take on other people's problems became a key issue of effective management in all aspects of business.

As we like to cherry-pick the best of good ideas, the one element you can extract from this concept is "Time can and should be used effectively." And absolutely avoid the monkeys. *That means learning how to say "no" when the occasion demands.* Just learn that your success and your dreams are directly reliant upon your focus: how to get there effectively and fast, and yet with optimum emphasis on quality of content for what you want to achieve.

SET CLEAR PRIORITIES: Effective time management begins with setting clear priorities. Identify your most important goals and determine the tasks and actions that will have the greatest impact on their achievement. Prioritize your activities based on urgency, importance, and alignment with your long-term vision. By focusing on high-priority tasks, you ensure that your time and energy are directed towards activities that bring you closer to your dreams.

CREATE A SCHEDULE AND ROUTINE: Developing a well-structured schedule is essential for maximizing productivity, thereby ensuring a balance between work, rest, and personal life. *Dedicate specified blocks of time for important goals,* minimizing distractions and virtually eliminating interruptions during these periods. By adhering to an intelligent routine, you establish discipline and create a culture of consistency that optimizes your productivity when it counts the most.

ELIMINATE TIME WASTERS: Identify and eliminate time-wasting activities that hinder your progress. Be mindful of distractions such as excessive social media use, aimless web browsing, or indulging in unproductive habits. Recent research has shown that excessive social media use can lead to a range of negative outcomes, including increased feelings of loneliness, anxiety and depression.

Social media use has also been linked to poor sleep quality, decreased physical activity and diminished face-to-face social interaction. It apparently also directly reflects on your ability to succeed.

In a recent 2023 *Pew Research* study, it was found that truly successful people spent less than 1 ½ hours a week on Social Media such as Facebook, Twitter (now X?), Instagram, Pinterest and TikTok. Conversely, those in lower income and poorer productivity levels (especially among Millennials) spent an average of 2 hours and 45 minutes a day on social media. (That's 17-1/4 hours a week for those of you doing the math…virtually five waking days a month out of your life.)

All the more reason to set boundaries to minimize interruptions and create a conducive environment for focused work. Especially be jealous of your own time and how you spend it; because it is the most reliable currency that you have.

That in mind, it becomes crucial to develop strategies to overcome procrastination—such as the *Pomodoro Technique* (working in focused bursts with short breaks). In essence, the Pomodoro Technique is a time-management method based on 25-minute stretches of focused work that you soften with five-minute breaks. Then longer breaks, typically 15 to 30 minutes, are taken after four consecutive work intervals. Each work interval is called a ***pomodoro***, the Italian word for tomato (plural: ***pomodori).*** Which is apparently a sweet little night-shade fruit (what we know as the Roma tomato) used as a "tiny reward" for children in schools…rather like a shiny red apple.

THE POMODORO TECHNIQUE
FEATURES THESE FIVE BASIC STEPS:

1. Identify a task that you need to complete. Make sure it meets the criteria you've set for being necessary and contributory toward your goals and objectives.

2. Set the timer on your smartphone, laptop or iPad for 25 minutes.

3. Work on a task with no distractions. Stay focused and truly become one with your project task or established goals.

4. When the alarm sounds, take a 5-minute break. And make the most of it with activity, taking a brisk walk around the room or just rewarding yourself with a refreshment.

5. Repeat the process 3 more times. Then take a longer break (say 15 to 20 minutes).

It sounds strict but in fact it is very liberating. By consciously managing and minimizing time-wasters, you reclaim valuable moments for meaningful and productive work.

DELEGATING AND OUTSOURCING: Recognize that you can't do everything on your own. Learn to delegate tasks and responsibilities that can be handled by others, freeing up your time for higher-value activities. Identify areas where you can outsource work or seek support from experts or professionals. It should come as no surprise that 48% of all companies in America now use freelancers on a regular basis. Delegation and outsourcing allow you to leverage the expertise of others and optimize your own time and energy for projects that align with your strengths and goals.

MAINTAIN A WORK-LIFE BALANCE: Yes, my dears, the trope holds true: "Don't forget to stop and smell the roses." Effective time management is not solely about productivity; it also encompasses maintaining a healthy work-life balance. Prioritize self-care, personal relationships, and leisure activities (we'll get to that later). Be sure you get enough solid, healthy nutrition, regular exercise and most of all restful sleep. Nurture your physical and mental well-being through exercise, relaxation, and pursuing hobbies. Allocate time for family, friends, and activities that bring you joy. Remember that a well-balanced life enhances overall productivity and supports long-term success.

CONTINUALLY LEARN AND ADAPT: Time management techniques are not one-size-fits-all. Continual learning and adaptation are essential to refine and optimize your approach. Stay open to new tools, technologies, and methodologies that can enhance your productivity. Seek feedback from mentors and people you trust—those who can provide insights and pathways for improvement. Continually assess and adjust your time-bound strategies based on evolving priorities and changing circumstances.

TAKE TIME TO MAKE TIME: *Summing it all up...*Mastering time management is a critical skill on your journey to building your Dream Factory. By setting clear priorities, creating a schedule and routine, eliminating time wasters, delegating and outsourcing, maintaining work-life balance, and embracing continual learning and adaptation, you optimize your productivity and make the most of each precious moment. Remember that effective time management is not about working harder, but about working smarter and aligning your actions with your dreams.

Embrace the power of time management and let it propel you forward towards your goals. By activating a disciplined and efficient use of time, you gain a competitive advantage, out-maneuver those "bumps in the road," and bring your dreams to life. Maximize productivity, seize each moment, and embark on a journey of purpose and fulfillment on the path toward completion.

CHAPTER 11

Cultivate Discipline: Commit to Consistency

Discipline is kind of a scary word when you think about it. And as such, it generally gets a bad rap. For so many of us, the term implies a punishment of sorts…like being grounded or staying after school, or being forced into something that is retributive and strict. So time dear friend to *change the game* on this one because—in its higher form of expression—it's the opposite of all that.

THE POWER OF DISCIPLINE. GET TO KNOW ITS MEANING: In its truest manifestation, *Discipline* is the mortar and concrete that forms the bedrock upon which dreams are built. It is the twin of *Consistency*. The combination of *discipline and consistency* propels us towards our goals on the path to building our Dream Factory. As such, discipline becomes your new best support system and reliable "go-to game plan." In this chapter, we will explore the importance of cultivating discipline and provide insights on how to develop and maintain this essential trait in your journey towards success. Discipline is the internal force that drives us to stay focused and committed to our dreams. It is the ability to consistently take action, even when motivation wanes or challenges arise. By cultivating discipline, we tap into a wellspring of newfound power that enables us to achieve what we set out to accomplish.

SET CLEAR INTENTIONS: To cultivate discipline, start by setting *clear intentions*. (It's that "Clarity" thing again ☺) That means you should avoid taking a scattergun approach to your objectives. So many people quit because they try to focus on too many things at once…which is the best way in the world to lose focus. Avoid that trap by clarifying your goals and the actions required to achieve them. Visualize the outcomes you desire and the impact they will have on your life. *Clear intentions* provide the foundation upon which discipline is built. And be a little bit strict about it when you do. Because when you are, you create a sense of purpose and direction that serves as a constant reminder of why you are committed to your dreams.

ESTABLISH PRODUCTIVE ROUTINES AND "HAPPY" HABITS: Discipline thrives in the realm of routines and habits. The challenge often comes when people start to look upon them as "a lot of work," or "a drudge." It is commonly known that it takes between 14 and 16 days to establish a habit. So, make that habit or routine *your new Number 1 priority.* Design daily and weekly routines that turn habits into something you actually look forward to. Once you do, it becomes easier to lock onto your goals and prioritize the actions that will take you closer to your dreams. That way you'll have a little reward already built into what you're working toward accomplishing. This will, in turn, empower you. And once you establish *happy habits,* renewed discipline and productivity will follow. Consistently engage in activities that align with your aspirations, whether it's practicing a skill, studying, or engaging in focused work. Over time, these routines become ingrained, making structured behavior a natural part of your lifestyle.

Nothing illustrates that better than performance sports like long-distance running or rugby or basketball or high-level competition swimming where you have to constantly ramp up your daily routines to get in top shape and stay there. That means developing consistency.

Along the way, through that routine of constancy, a wonderful kind of addiction takes place. Because something called *endorphins* kick-in. And they do so in a way that infuses your physical system. *Endorphins* are hormones that convert into your body's reward for keeping it in shape. They're free-radical fighters, stress removers and proven life extenders. What's more, once you've established a habit-pattern of (say) running 20 or 30 miles a week, your endorphins will start to "nag" you if you slack off. They become like a favorite dog you have to feed or take for long walks on a regular basis…or else it will (fondly) bark at you. And what a lovely bark that is! "Happy Habits" are much the same way. They're disciplined with a smile. And they will virtually transform your life once you give them a chance.

DEVELOP A PATTERN OF DELAYED GRATIFICATION: Everything we do in life involves both risk and reward. The challenge comes with most people when they decide to *devote more time to the reward than to the risk*. At this point, we should all be a bit honest about the society we live in today. It has by now been virtually set up for "instant gratification." No one is denied anything anymore. That spawns a nasty little social element called Entitlement. And Entitlement is the enemy of Discipline and the delayer of dreams.

Discipline helps you prioritize. That requires a willingness to delay gratification. It is about making choices that serve your long-term goals rather than succumbing to immediate impulses or distractions. Recognize that the path to the Dream Factory may require sacrifices and temporary discomfort. Embrace the mindset of investing in your future self and understand that the rewards of establishing a solid regimen are often far greater than momentary indulgence. By prioritizing long-term gains over instant gratification, you strengthen your discipline muscles. Then by all means, at the end of it all, reward yourself once in a while.

BUILD ACCOUNTABILITY STRUCTURES: Accountability is a powerful tool for cultivating discipline. More specifically, *self-accountability* should be the driving force behind it. Establish structures that hold you accountable to your actions and commitments. And take responsibility for them. That means you avoid blaming others and traps like "scapegoating" and making excuses. It also means setting up a system you can interweave with those inside your circle of activity. That way you have a "Feedback Support Group." Share your goals and progress with trusted friends, family or mentors who can offer perspective and hold you to your word. Consider joining mastermind groups or finding a "check-list" partner with similar aspirations. Regular check-ins and progress reports create a sense of responsibility and motivation to maintain discipline.

PRACTICING SELF-MASTERY: Discipline begins with *self-mastery*. And the first step toward achieving this is the ability to regulate your thoughts, emotions and actions. Now more than ever that entails the process of something called **Mindfulness.** You hear and see it mentioned all the time these days, because *mindfulness actually works.* It goes back hundreds of years to the Zen practice of "being present" in every single moment—your thoughts (and dreams), when you visualize what you see and when you bring it to life… because all these things are interactive and conjoined. The sooner you focus upon your dreams, the sooner they become real.

Mindfulness also entails the *art of being present with others.* How many times have you noticed when someone in your company seemed to be anywhere but where they were at the moment? They're buried in their iPhone, playing Wordle™, messaging on Facebook or in a conversation to someone far away—taking that call right in front of you, however superficial it might be—and then talking for half an hour, as if their time mattered and yours did not. It had to be unsettling; it always is.

Being present with others is just the opposite of that. When someone you meet or converse with is with you in every moment, there is a bond that forms, a connection between the two of you that solidifies and strengthens over time. They're telling you that your friendship matters; that you have significance as a human being. (And doesn't that make all the difference in the world?)

Mindfulness prompts *self-awareness* and helps you to stay centered. It solidifies intent. It firms up your resolve. Mindfulness helps make it easier to implement strategies such as meditation, journaling, or visualization to cultivate mental clarity and emotional balance. By mastering your inner world, you gain greater control over your external actions and strengthen your discipline.

OVERCOMING RESISTANCE AND OBSTACLES: Resistance and occasional obstacles are inevitable on the journey to the Dream Factory. Cultivate discipline by recognizing these challenges as opportunities for growth. Recognize the discomfort for what it is, and lean into it. That means leaving *No Room for Doubt.* Doubt is more of a stumbling block than any challenge you might face. Develop strategies to overcome resistance and help you to conquer doubt— such as breaking tasks into smaller, manageable parts or using positive affirmations to reinforce your commitment. By persisting in the face of obstacles, you build resilience and reinforce your discipline.

CELEBRATE MILESTONES AND PROGRESS: Well…let's keep it *Real* here. And it's just common sense when you think about it: you can't go through all that discipline, hard work, consistency and overcoming "stuff," and not have some tiny rewards "pop up" just when you need them.

So have a plan for that too. Set up a little "reward package" at the end of that *long and winding road* toward your success. Your celebrations can be as simple as a dinner date or a new set of AirPods™. But, no matter how large or small, be sure to reward yourself for all those special wins in your life. And honor yourself for the progress that you've made along the way. Acknowledge and reward yourself for staying disciplined and committed. Celebrations provide a sense of accomplishment and reinforce positive behavior. Use these moments as fuel to continue your journey with renewed enthusiasm and dedication.

STRONG FINISH! BRINGING IT ALL TOGETHER: Cultivating discipline is a transformative practice that paves the way to strengthening the structure of your Dream Factory. By setting clear intentions, establishing routines and habits, embracing delayed gratification, building accountability structures, practicing self-mastery, overcoming resistance, and celebrating milestones, you develop the discipline necessary to stay committed to your dreams.

Remember, *Discipline is a journey of growth and self-mastery.* It requires consistency and a willingness to adopt occasional discomfort for the sake of long-term success. With discipline as your guiding force, you possess the power to manifest your dreams, turn roadblocks into speedbumps, and create a sense of purpose on the path to *Your Dream Factory.*

CHAPTER 12

Learn and Grow:
Embrace the Power of Knowledge

"The important thing is not to stop questioning. Curiosity has its own reason for existing. One cannot help but be in awe when he contemplates the mysteries of eternity, of life, of the marvelous structure of reality. It is enough if one tries merely to comprehend a little of this mystery every day."

~ Albert Einstein

Albert Einstein, the man who reconfigured the known universe, was an anomaly in that he constantly played down his own genius. (He was, of course, a genius!) Mainly due to his own modesty, but also due to the fact that he saw his own brilliance as being attributable to what he called "constant and insatiable curiosity." And it is a given that *Curiosity* is the handmaiden to *Learning*…as *Learning* is to *Knowledge*. Einstein also acknowledged that it was an ongoing process—that learning was an active part of life, something we had to engage in every day.

You don't necessarily have to be "insatiably curious." But a good healthy thirst for knowledge never hurt anybody. And isn't it so easy to keep and store phenomenal chunks of information these days?

In fact, Einstein would have been shocked by the amount of facts, figures, data, instruction and intelligence we have available to us in today's society… virtually a keystroke away. And yet it has often been observed that, especially in America, we are, "the most media saturated and worst educated society in human history." I'm old enough to remember this. And it wasn't that long ago that if you wanted to find out anything, you had to go to a library to do the research. You had to spend an entire afternoon, or a whole day, pull a pile of books off the shelves and research and dig and wade through a mountain of tired volumes until you were lucky enough to hit upon the information you needed.

In today's point and click society, instant access to the internet has transformed all that. So that someone, anyone—college students, researchers, scientists, journalist, authors, shut-ins, seniors, hospital patients, corporate CEOs, barefoot home-schooled children in Mozambique or Kenya—can set up a scan on any subject and gather-in a host of references in a matter of minutes and in-depth comprehension in a couple of hours. You can upload 1500 books onto Kindle or Nook and have an entire library at your fingertips inside of a single day.

Those who appreciate the value of this quickly learn how to use it. They are also the same achievement-driven people who recognize that, *in the pursuit of our dreams, the journey is not merely a destination but also an integral part of the process of growth and self-improvement.* Embracing continuous learning is a vital aspect of the path to the Dream Factory. It is through expanding our knowledge and acquiring new skills that we unlock our full potential and create a life of fulfillment and success. In this chapter, we will explore the importance of embracing continuous learning and how it propels us towards our dreams.

CULTIVATE A LEARNING MINDSET: Let's be frank here. The cliché is true: *Knowledge is Power.* And the access is around us, everywhere. So, the rest is up to you. And here we have to ask the question: How powerful do you truly want to be? It has become an unsettling fact for so many, that once they leave high-school or college—once they graduate—42% of American adults never read another book again. Then there are those who recognize that Learning—the continuous, passionate pursuit of Knowledge—helps you to develop a "questing mindset," one that values both personal growth and curiosity. Acknowledge the self-evident truth that there is always something new to learn and that every experience offers an opportunity for growth, and you're halfway there already. Be open to new ideas, diverse perspectives, and feedback. Adopt a mindset of lifelong learning, where challenges are seen as learning opportunities and failures become stepping stones towards improvement.

SEEK NEW EXPERIENCES: Learning extends beyond books and classrooms. It definitely holds true that true learning can take on dozens of forms. And one sure way to do it is to become involved: in learning groups, seminars, webinars, podcasts and Zoom classes. Take a course, cultivate mentors, teachers, coaches, classes. Seek out new experiences that challenge and expand your horizons.

Be what Arnold Schwarzenegger once defined as the secret to his success: "Stay Hungry!" That takes-in a multitude of things: hunger for knowledge, hunger for self-improvement, for optimum fitness, for higher levels of achievement…for life itself. In order to accomplish that, it also requires you to step outside of your comfort zone, engage in activities that stretch your capabilities, and expose yourself to diverse cultures, ideas, and environments. Welcome the richness of life's experiences as a source of personal growth. By seeking new experiences, you gain a broader understanding of the world and discover new avenues for success.

SET UP A PERSONAL DEVELOPMENT PLAN: Create a personal development plan that outlines your learning goals and the steps required to achieve them. It is often best here to establish a "Physical Check-List." And on that Checklist, you get to identify areas where you wish to develop new skills or deepen existing ones. That way, you avoid abstractions; because without a physical presence, something you can put your arms around, abstract concepts can leave you floundering and cause you to lose that needed focus to complete your tasks. Set aside some dedicated time for learning and more— actually allocate resources towards acquiring knowledge. In today's media-saturated world, free information is a "Movable feast." Take advantage of online courses, workshops, seminars, and mentorship opportunities that align you with your goals. By creating a structured plan, you actively invest in your personal growth and development.

BUILD A NETWORK OF MENTORS AND ROLE MODELS: We've emphasized this before. In fact, we've built a whole chapter around it. So why bring it up again? Because it is *that* important. And in the case of your "higher education" in the "university of life," it is that much at your immediate disposal. The trick here is to find those mentors and teachers who share your values and will help you to better define your Structure. Surround yourself with role models who can guide, inspire you, and help you develop those final steps in the completion of your Dream. Seek out individuals who have achieved what you aspire to accomplish. Co-create a "Brain-trust" of mutual ideas. Learn from their experiences, seek their guidance, and leverage their wisdom. Cultivate relationships with mentors who can provide valuable insights, feedback, and support. I have personally found that some of the best mentors are those who lead by example. And no question, we learn best by doing. So, by building a network of mentors and role models, you tap into a wealth of knowledge and accelerate your own growth.

BEFRIEND FAILURE AS A LEARNING OPPORTUNITY: As AE (Albert Einstein) or any scientist will tell you, "Failure" is definitely part of the process of creating success. And if you think you've succeeded straight out of the gate, either play the lottery that very day…Or recognize that you might have just not done it right in the first place. Failure is a powerful teacher. It strengthens your structure and helps you navigate your path to realizing the framework of your Dream Factory.

Embrace failure as a valuable learning opportunity and extract lessons from each experience. Reflect on the reasons behind the failure, analyze your actions, and identify areas for improvement. Develop a growth mindset that views failure as a stepping stone towards growth and resilience. By learning from failure, you refine your approach, gain wisdom, and become better equipped to overcome future challenges.

PRACTICE REFLECTION AND SELF-ASSESSMENT: Allocate time for reflection and regular self-assessment. Evaluate your progress, identify areas of strength and areas that need improvement, and set new learning goals. Engage in self-reflection to gain insights into your motivations, values, and aspirations. Journaling, meditation, or seeking feedback from trusted individuals can aid in this process. By practicing reflection and self-assessment, you deepen your self-awareness and create opportunities for growth.

CONCLUSION

ONE RULE HOLDS FIRM AND FAST: You never stop learning. Once you embrace continuous learning you'll realize that it's an essential part of building up what you've started in the first place. By valuing knowledge, cultivating a learning mindset, seeking new experiences, forming a personal development plan, building a network of mentors, embracing failure as a learning opportunity, and practicing reflection and self-assessment, you embark on a course of self-empowerment that cannot be denied.

Remember, the journey towards your dreams is not solely about reaching a destination; it is about the growth and transformation that occurs along the way. Continuous learning is a Gift. Untie the ribbon on that, and let it guide you towards your fullest potential. With each new lesson learned and skill acquired, you become better equipped to navigate challenges, seize opportunities, and create a life of purpose and fulfillment on the path to the Dream Factory

CHAPTER 13

Network and Collaborate: Harness the Power of Connections

The cliché holds true here: "It isn't what you know, it's who you know." It sounds like an excuse for failure when in fact it is the ultimate trigger for synergizing your success. It is Universal Law that: "Nothing is accomplished in a void." Very much in the vein of the human dynamic, the final stages in the structure of your Dream Factory cannot and should not be undertaken alone. You need collaborators. You need co-creators and "co-conspirators." You need a solid support group: your people, your community, "Your Tribe."

Finding your tribe means networking and harnessing the power, feedback, creative synergy and genius of all those you trust, admire and acknoweldge as people of your own house. Sometimes you already know them. In other instances, you may have the opportunity to create a whole new network of your own. In every case you win when you do, because you broaden your horizons. You widen your Circle of Influence and those who influence you.

By now, if you're learning anything at all from this book, you've got to recognize that the Laws of Attraction prevail here. Mentors, mastermind groups, employees, partners and friends…all those with whom you've established relationships and more now become contributors on the pathway to success.

It is through networking and collaboration that we harness the power of connections and unlock new opportunities for growth and success. In this chapter, we will reveal some of the secrets of building those networks, and how they can propel us closer to our dreams.

NETWORK NOW...OR DISAPPEAR: I should add to that: "And learn how to do it right." I probably shouldn't insert an either/or element to this part of the lesson plan. And yet, on a practical note, *it is* that important. That's because Networking is more than just exchanging business cards or making superficial connections. It's an art form. And, properly applied, a feat of great skill that requires sensitivity, insight, persistence and a genuine sense of humanity.

It can and should also be a lot of fun. Because Networking is about building meaningful connections with like-minded individuals who can support and uplift you as you build momentum. Networking opens doors to new opportunities, insights, and resources. It's also a starting point for the synergy that comes out of relationships: *the collaboration, the discovery, the ultimate realization that two heads are better than one…and three or more heads are very often "a brain trust!"* This is especially true when you're on the same path and striving toward a common goal. It allows you to tap into the collective wisdom and experiences of others, expanding your perspectives and helping you navigate the challenges ahead.

CULTIVATE AUTHENTIC CONNECTIONS: Authenticity is the key to cultivating meaningful connections. And losers and energy wasters need not apply. By now, on the way to building your Dream Factory, you should have learned to discern. Be selective. Also, be genuine in your interactions by showing a sincere interest in the journeys and aspirations of others. If you want authenticity in your Networking, you need to be authentic yourself. This isn't always just about you and what you can get out of something. It is also what you can contribute. In fact, "the most successful networkers in the world" are able to capitalize on two things: 1) knowing their target market and 2) putting others first.

THE MARY KAY STORY: Nothing illustrates that power more emphatically than the founder of one of the world's most famous Network Marketing companies: Mary Kay Ash. In 1963, after her husband died, leaving Mary Kay a widow at the age of 45, she developed a concept to empower and enrich the most overlooked market in America: Women! (This was the early 1960s, mind you. Women were, in relative terms, still disenfranchised. Most women, by the time they reached their early 20s were either housewives, secretaries, bank tellers, waitresses or flight attendants [or if they were lucky paralegals or nurses]—and there wasn't much beyond that.) Mary Kay thought women deserved better than that and founded an MLM cosmetic company that virtually charged double for its excellent products ... and passed along the profits in the form of commissions to all her *Representatives*. "Pink" was the operative shade of choice and a symbol of its success.

In the next 20 years, Mary Kay created more female millionaires than any other business in America. Perks were things like Pink Cadillacs (or the pink car of your choice). Forget Barbie, Pink was the Mary Kay color that announced itself to the world, as a well-trained, well-taught Armada of women were given both the confidence and support to become their own powerhouse entrepreneurs.

As such, this phenomenal task force of committed, confident distaff entrepreneurs transformed the consciousness of the personal care and cosmetic field, thus creating an entity in itself: a unique and unprecedented movement in an industry previously dominated *by men*. Above all else it wasn't business. It was "personal." Because Mary Kay Ash made it a point to (her word) "mentor" each and every one of her highly motivated "account executives" with as much information, moral support and superb product as possible. In so doing, Mary Kay referred to her sales people (most of whom she knew by name) as her "Daughters." Mary Kay Cosmetics was a "family." And by the 1980s it was a billion-dollar company. Most of all, it is inspiring to note that all of it started as a Dream—with $5,000 of borrowed (family) money and a middle-aged widow with a Vision!

Mary Kay Ash was an object lesson for what true networking is and on the importance of understanding the needs of others—their hopes and fears, their challenges and their dreams. Understanding that and using it, or something like it, as your role model will empower you to approach networking as an opportunity to give rather than just receive. Share your knowledge, skills, and resources with others, and offer support and encouragement. By fostering authentic connections, you create a network of individuals who genuinely care about your success.

EXPAND YOUR NETWORK: To expand your network, seek out opportunities for connection both online and offline. Attend industry events, conferences, and seminars where you can meet like-minded individuals and experts in your field. Engage in online communities, forums, and social media groups related to your interests and goals. Be proactive in reaching out and initiating conversations. Remember, every interaction has the potential to lead to new possibilities and collaborations.

BE ECLECTIC. MAKE IT DIVERSE: A Diverse Network is a valuable asset on the journey to the Dream Factory. Seek connections with individuals from different backgrounds, industries, and areas of expertise. Embrace diversity in all its forms, including age, gender, race, and culture. A network based in diversity offers unique perspectives, fresh ideas and a broader range of opportunities. It challenges your assumptions and expands your horizons, making you more adaptable and resilient. By the same token, be selective. Make intelligent choices. And to learn the secret of that, I offer this advice…

FROM THE DEAL BOOK OF PETER THOMAS: This is my "perfect world." When I am out there doing deals, the most important thing for me is to first understand the people I am dealing with…so I can make it a "win-win" for everyone. Since I've always emphasized the *Value of Relationships,* the personal connection for me is even more important than the deal. Generally, I have pretty good instincts. So I would not do a deal with someone that I could not relate to.

I am speaking about when you have an ongoing relationship within a transaction. Knowing this rule going-in when I meet people, I spend a little extra time to get to know them and like them. Then I share with them by saying, "I want to tell you about my perfect world." From that point I paint a picture of "the ideal." I tell them how their deal will fit for me in my world. I will tell them that I cannot pay crazy money, but I can pay fair money. I really outline the outcome I expect. I find this is good as I try and cover the hard questions right up front. I deal with questions like. "I will not give up control." As a counterpoint, I just keep talking about my perfect world. When I come across deals I want to go after, I really let the sellers know up front what my expectations are, or in other words… "my perfect world"

I always say yes and work my way to "no." Initially I imagine this new deal is already my deal. I say "Yes," and I imagine I now own the building or the company and I can feel like an owner. I then see the deferred maintenance and realize that this project has not been taken care of and my budget for getting the building in perfect shape will simply cost too much and I need to change my yes to a "no" or a "maybe." You understand the idea. Saying "Yes" opens your mind, allowing you to visualize what happens after you say "yes."

There are really two kingdoms at play here, each fronted by a door. So it's crucial to understand which door to walk through and why? If you immediately choose the door marked "No," nothing lies behind it. It's an empty wasteland and all possibility dies there on the spot. However, if you choose the door marked "Yes!" you've entered *the realm of pure potential.* New universes reveal themselves, and all the wonders therein. (If something goes sideways later on, at least you gave it your best…and probably learned a boatload of things that enhanced your total awareness—teaching you a little more about what works and what does not.)

COLLABORATE FOR MUTUAL GROWTH: The best kind of Networking is a two-way street because, more often than not, it entails Collaboration. When you collaborate, you synergize. You accomplish something that is mutually beneficial. And that in itself is a powerful tool for achieving shared success.

Look for opportunities to collaborate with individuals who share similar goals or skills that complement your own. Identify areas where you can combine efforts, leverage each other's strengths, and create synergistic outcomes. Collaborative projects foster innovation, enhance problem-solving capabilities, and expand your network even further. By embracing collaboration, you unlock the potential for exponential growth and impact.

NURTURE AND MAINTAIN RELATIONSHIPS: Good relationships are very much like Gardens. They need sunlight. They need positive energy, lots of emotional nutrition, proper watering and looking after. (They definitely require positive energy, and "classical" music helps [especially with plants].)

It is also important to recognize that Networking is not a one-time activity. It's an ongoing process of interaction, "staying in touch," and seeing to the needs of others. Always try to be there for your connections and cultivate credibility by offering support, by just "being you," by celebrating their achievements, and providing value whenever and wherever you can. *Engage* in regular communication. And it can come in many forms—whether through emails, calls, FaceTime, Zoom conferences or meetings. Show gratitude and express appreciation for the contributions of others. By simply embracing tthe human factor in one another, you create a superstructure that is solid, and that can help to fortify those final steps in your Structure.

GIVE AND RECEIVE SUPPORT: Networking is a two-way street, and it is important to both give and receive support. Offer your expertise, advice, or resources to others when needed. Actively listen to the challenges and needs of your connections and find ways to assist them. Similarly, be open to receiving support and guidance from your network. Be willing to listen to their suggestions. Wisdom comes from all sources. And be mindful of giving back in equal measure when you can. Reciprocity is more than a custom. It is a new kind of culture: the kind that reminds you that the good things we put out are returned to you a thousand-fold.

SUMMARY

LEARN TO BECOME THE CONSUMMATE NETWORKER: *When you think about it, it's the ultimate case of balancing, "PUSH and PULL." And I have a little story for that:*

A businessman was going to give a speech, and his driver was driving him to the conference where he was to be the keynote speaker. When they arrived, the businessman said to his driver: "I have a terrible headache. You have taken me to a thousand of these things. So, if you would, please go in and give this speech for me."

The driver said: "Oh no I never could do that. I have nothing to talk about."

To which the businessman replied: "Don't worry about that, just be positive. And it will all work out."

The driver thought about it for a moment and, finally figuring he had nothing to lose, said, "OK, boss!" And inside he went.

As he walked up to the glass doors at the front of the building, one said "Push," and the other door said "Pull." The driver took a second look at this and thought, *That is what I will talk about: having "Push" and "Pull".*

So, he strode up to the microphone and started to talk to this packed house of prominent people, thanking them for having him there to speak to this notable crowd.

He said: "When it comes down to it, there is one quality you must have if you want to be successful. You must practice it every day. You must visualize yourself doing this all the time. And ladies and gentlemen that 'thing' you must do every day is written on every door you go in and out of in every building in the world."

He pointed to the door and said: "There!"… the word PUSH was written on it. He went on to say, "Ladies and Gentlemen, the door says PUSH, and that's what you must do to open it. When it comes down to it, having a little PULL makes it so much easier. Then again, where does having PULL come from? Having lots of PUSH."

The driver got a standing ovation.

Both networking and collaboration are powerful tools for fortifying our *Dream Factory*. In an ultimate rule of thumb: Your connections will only be as authentic as you are. And if they are, they'll expand your network, help you diversify, engage in projects and concepts that benefit everyone. Still, there is a moral caveat to all this: *Everyone wins only if you all play by the rules*. And observe the best aspects of respectability, nurturing relationships, and mutual support. Opportunities will always spring out of the best managed connections—ones that grow into friendship, regard and mutual respect.

Remember, your network is far more than just a collection of contacts. It is a community of individuals who can inspire, guide, and uplift you on your journey. Embrace the power of collaboration, and let it fuel your progress toward your Dream Factory. With each connection made, you broaden your horizons and increase the potential for achieving your dreams.

CHAPTER 14

Manage Your Risks: Calculate Your Potential for Success

R isk: Reward. It's the name of the game if you understand the subtext. And it comes at so many levels that it carries with it a virtual rainbow of potential. In the pursuit of our dreams, taking risks is an inevitable part of the journey. However, managing them effectively—and using the right kind of direction-finders to do so—is what separates those who succeed from those who stumble and fall.

It is here that the twice-told tale holds true: 90% of people who win the Lottery or the Powerball end up broke inside of five years. And that semi-tragic undoing of their wealth occurs for several reasons:

In the first place, one can rest assured that they never had a plan, an investment strategy, or a team of experienced financial advisors who could teach them how to manage their money, temper their newfound wealth with both patience and resolve—and shield them from the predators that come clawing at the gate. To be sure, the last thing you want to do once you've reached certain levels of financial security is squander it on high-risk investments or succumb to the army of "needful things" that will draw-down on your reserves.

"Every investment involves some risk." You see the disclaimer every day on ads for Wall Street brokerage houses. They're required. And it's true. But that's life. Life involves risk, if you are going to succeed at all. Some people are risk averse—that is their choice to be security motivated. But you're not those people. Or you would not be reading this. So be bold. Make bold moves. As long as they're intelligent ones backed by information—education and considerable research.

The Secret is that risk can be phenomenal. It creates Whole New Worlds IF you understand the nature of it. And if you learn how to manage it intelligently and with purpose. This Chapter will help you find some wondrous ways to manage risks effectively…and, once you have, how to apply them on *your journey to success.*

You'll learn some very simple but effective strategies for assessing risks—high, low and medium—make informed decisions, and embrace some proven effective moves that minimize setbacks and maximize opportunities.

Once you've achieved your dreams and goals both personally and financially, you have to look beyond the basic material things. Once you've bought that house and car and perhaps an executive toy or two—once you've built up your 401 K, so that it's now "rock solid," and once you've set up, as everyone should, intelligent multiple-streams of income—you have to have a plan for what comes next. And this is where it can become something of a scramble.

People who only know me from the press or three degrees of separation feel that I am a big risk taker. That was how, by reputation, I became successful, when the real story is far more carefully woven than that.

In truth, I have never considered myself to be a risk taker. I am a risk assessor. I feel that I go to the ends of the earth in what we call due diligence when I am looking at making a major investment. If I decide to invest, I do not feel it is as risky as it looks. I have been very fortunate several times in my business career in spotting new business trends before they reached *Consciousness 3.* Investments that we made in the start-up of both Century 21 Real Estate and Dogtopia proved to be very lucrative—at least partly to do with the fact that I did my homework. My investigations of these concepts before they hit mainstream America proved enough to me that they both provided untapped areas of potential, as long as we understood how they would play out.

Risk is an inherent part of any endeavor. It involves stepping out of your comfort zone, facing uncertainty, and potentially encountering any number of false fronts along the way. With risk comes the potential for reward and growth. Understanding the balance between risk and reward is key to managing your ventures effectively.

In that regard, the first thing you do is assess the potential benefits; then weigh them against the projected downsides. Do that to set the stage before making decisions or taking actions. Ask yourself how far you are willing to go, and if the end result is worth both the time and money you will spend.

Today they have *Algorithms* that can help you through the process: computer programs based in mathematical constructs that assess markets and evaluate potentials for every individual and corporation in the world. You can use them to bake a cake or design your next LLC. You can use them to project market trends or calculate ratios of success and failure. But like any IT product, an algorithm is only there to serve—and still relies upon the human factor to have any life at all. It offers options. But the final decisions will always be up to you. And taking responsibility can often be the scariest thing of all.

MAKE INTELLIGENT RISK ASSESSMENTS...AT THE BEGINNING AND AT THE END: All risk entails a paradox. Because you have to confront it at least twice: when you start out and as you near completion. And you have to establish your own *rules of the road*. About half a dozen steps to guide you on the path to financial freedom: 1) Before embarking on any significant endeavor, conduct a thorough risk assessment; 2) Fingerprint your ventures and evaluate their likelihood for success; 3) Consider both internal and external factors that could affect your journey; 4) Develop contingency plans and mitigation strategies to minimize the impact of potential sidesteps; 5) Once you intelligently assess your risks, you gain a clearer understanding of the challenges you may face and can plan accordingly; 6) It's important, at this point, not to delude yourself. Constantly take a reality check. And above all else, know yourself: your commitment to your dreams...and whether or not you are willing to go all the way to achieve them.

Then, when your Dream Factory is close to being fully formed, take the time to reassess and develop a strategy that will carry you the rest of the way. This means you have to know your market and your personal value. And make sure that what you've become matches what you've dreamt of.

MAKE CALCULATED MOVES: Successful risk management involves making calculated moves rather than reckless gambles. Gather relevant information and conduct thorough research before making decisions. Consider both qualitative and quantitative factors, weighing the potential benefits against the risks involved. Seek advice from mentors, authorities, or individuals with experience in similar situations. Definitely, if you can, get in touch with those experts in your chosen field of endeavor. Go to school on the steps they took to succeed and the pitfalls they avoided to reach their objectives. Let their learning curve become yours as well. So you never have to take those unnecessary detours on the journey. By making calculated moves and studying every aspect, you minimize unexpected setbacks and increase the likelihood of a favorable outcome.

ONE RULE OF THUMB THAT IS PRETTY ROCK-SOLID: *It's always better to seek out financial advisors who are far richer than you are.* They've been there. They've done it. And they don't need your commissions to make a living. They're there as monetary partners. Fiduciaries are often the most solid because they're not trying to churn and burn you into trades. Check track-records. Vet reputations. Consult those who have long-term relationships with the advisors that you seek. No risk is infallible. But at least you've done your homework. And you've established relationships with people who are good at doing theirs.

EMBRACE A GROWTH MINDSET: Managing risks requires adopting a growth mindset. Recognize the often ignored fact that those losses you experience often offer opportunities to become wiser and smarter. See setbacks as temporary obstacles rather than permanent defeats. Cultivate resilience and the ability to adapt in the face of unexpected challenges. By embracing *a growth mindset,* you develop the mental fortitude to navigate risks with confidence and bounce back from any setbacks.

BUILD A SUPPORT SYSTEM: Above all else remember that you got this far by believing in yourself. And so now is the time to make that "self-belief" contagious. "Conviction is catching," it is often said. And when you truly believe, you can approach others and create that splendid synergy that almost always works. Strong support systems are invaluable when it comes to managing risks.

Surround yourself with individuals who not only believe in your dreams but are also willing to provide guidance and support. Seek out mentors or advisors who can offer valuable insights and help you make informed decisions—like-minded individuals who share similar goals and can provide additional perspectives. By building a support system, you gain access to diverse perspectives and collective wisdom to help navigate risks more effectively.

CONTINUOUSLY MONITOR AND EVALUATE: Managing risks is an ongoing process that requires continuous monitoring and evaluation. Regularly chart the progress of your endeavors and monitor for shifting sands in the marketplace or changes in circumstances. Stay updated on industry trends, and other relevant factors that may impact your growth; then adapt accordingly. By continuously monitoring and evaluating, you remain proactive and maximize your chances for success.

LEARN FROM BOTH SETBACKS AND SUCCESSES: We've covered this before, and yet bring it up again, because it is *that important.* And we do so here, because it's one of the hardest things for some people to admit. Mainly because we've been trained to loathe the word…and because most people confuse *failure* with *quitting altogether,* when in truth the two have little or nothing in common. Quitting, the dreaded "Q" word, is a dagger to the heart. It is announcing to the world that you've resigned all effort—that you have given up on things; and that's a truth that hurts.

Also in truth—and this Truth is indelible— ***Failure can be a powerful teacher.*** British author, political reformer and originator of "Self-Help" Samuel Smiles said it best in 1883 when he observed: "We learn wisdom from failure much more than from success. We often discover what we will do, by finding out what we will not do; and probably he who never made a mistake never made a discovery."

Each success and every failure, both hold valuable lessons. Reflect on both your successes and failures to extract insights and identify patterns. Understand the factors that contributed to your "wins" and learn to replicate them. Analyze the reasons behind your "losses" and identify your areas for improvement. Learning from past experiences helps refine your risk management strategies and informs future decision-making.

WHATEVER YOU DO…AVOID KING ARTHUR'S DISEASE: By now we all know the tale of *Camelot* (or should): the Legend of King Arthur who—armed with the magical sword Excalibur and the ongoing mentorship of Merlin the Magician—formed the ideal kingdom that included a Roundtable of noble knights, invincible to the man, (ostensibly) free of moral flaw and on a quest to only do good in the world. Of course, this tale became a metaphor for arrogance in all its forms—the fact that perfection at any level is virtually impossible—and soon enough Camelot started breaking down under the weight of its own expectations.

I offer this comparison because, in a way, I also once caught the "Camelot Syndrome" or what I often refer to as "King Arthur's Disease." So let me pass my story along as *a cautionary tale*—to help you on your trajectory to success.

After a few years in business I began to have several what some might call "phenomenal successes." And so I began to get quite a high degree of confidence and notoriety that some felt was legendary in scope. I began to be sought out to give advice to other business people and soon was asked to speak to various organizations on how I had managed to become such a "Win Magnet" in such a relatively short period of time. During this period, I did give credence to the fact that the country was going through an unprecedented period of growth, and that I was lucky to be in a business niche that could take advantage of that.

Many of my business contacts at the time just smiled and reminded me that, while it was true that lots of people were not making it, I was truly rare and impervious to failure, and as such was "infallibly" wise and special. It was very difficult not to agree with them as they fed directly into my ego, and deep-down inside I think I tended to feel the same way—if not wholeheartedly, pretty substantially.

As I continued on my upward path, I had more and more deals offered to me and I less frequently sought the advice from others I always used to seek. (After all, who else was really making all these brilliant decisions?) Some of these deals turned out to be remarkably successful. And, even for the bad ones, I had usually structured exit strategies without getting too burned. It was also true that, in the beginning of my career, I would consult with my lawyers, my accountants, some outside specialists, including my wife and generally anyone who I thought could give me constructive input into the transaction I was contemplating.

Now that I was getting so many wins, I started asking fewer and fewer people for their opinions. In place of that, I allowed some hubris to kick-in. And I started letting myself be open to any person that wanted to talk to me about a new deal; any deal, in whatever form it may have taken—no matter how outrageous or far-fetched.

Ignoring some fading pleas from others, I became a *deal junkie* or as they sometimes describe it in kinder tones, "a serial entrepreneur." Sure enough, like 99% of the people on this type of reckless career trajectory, *"The deal that can kill you is just around the corner."* (And so it was.)

It did come. And, as hindsight is 20/20, looking back from this point in my life, I would now *never have gotten into this type of deal.* But at the time I decided to go for it. And it was something of a miracle that it did not bank-rupt me.

When things slowed down a little, and I had a little time for some ret-rospective thinking, I reached the point where I could ask myself: "What happened?"

Once I asked that pivotal question, I realized just how far I had strayed from those early business principles that I used to apply on my path—the ones that in fact had combined to make me successful in the first place. In studying a lot of business disasters and careers that ended in bankruptcy—with lives being shattered, never more to recover—I recognized enough of the patterns to see a natural flow of events.

In fact I saw it so many times that I felt that I should name this malady something—so that anyone in the future could watch for those signals show-ing that you were getting symptoms of this Syndrome.

So I dubbed it: *King Arthur's Disease,* because this was the man who had it all: A shining kingdom on the hill, a beautiful, loving wife, a loyal "best friend," and nobles who adored him. Unfortunately, he came to believe that nothing could destroy him—that he could go into (business) battles and never be defeated, while ignoring all the collective wisdom that had made him great in the first place.

I tell you this cautionary tale here, because if you are the type "A" person-ality that usually jumps into this kind of risk mentality, you are just as suscep-tible as I to catching King Arthur's Disease.

So learn from the legend of Camelot—and the Book of Peter Thomas—don't leave behind the basics that got you your dreams in the first place. Don't ignore those *wise Merlins* who are there to give you sage advice. And don't go rushing into battle against a foe you have neither researched nor vetted.

Hidden dragons are out there…everywhere. And unless you're onto them all, they can torch you at any time. So, you need to come prepared.

CONCLUSION

DOES THE REWARD SATISFY THE RISK? Managing risks is an integral part of the journey towards the Dream Factory. By understanding risk and reward, conducting risk assessments, making calculated moves, embracing a growth mindset, building a support system, continuously monitoring and evaluating, and learning from failures and successes, you enhance your ability to navigate risks and increase your chances of achieving success.

Remember, managing risks is not about avoiding them altogether but about making informed decisions and taking calculated actions. With careful risk management, you minimize potential setbacks and optimize your prosperity even as you put the finishing touches on your own Dream Factory.

THE DREAM...
IT'S YOURS!

Now that you've got it, here's what to do with it...

CHAPTER 15

Well-Being and Ambition: It's a Balancing Act

I n the avid pursuit of our dreams, it is easy to become consumed by the "churn and burn" of our own ambition. Success can become a drug on its own and consume all our waking hours. As we feel the "buzz" of high achievement and the warm glow of recognition that comes with it, we often do so at the expense of our own well-being and occasionally even our health.

"Workaholics" often proudly claim the title when they shouldn't. And it's here that the adage so often holds true: "No one wants to be the wealthiest man in the graveyard." Doubtless *Achievement can become an Addiction,* and the need for recognition can often overwhelm your peace of mind. And yet, if we but pause for a moment's reflection, we find that it is personal Balance that ultimately makes all the difference. And *The Dream Factory,* once achieved, carries with it a certain sense of self-realization.

Nurturing and Self-care are critical in maintaining a balanced sense of self. It's true about us all—that intrinsically we all contain a physical, mental, emotional and spiritual network so intricately interwoven that each aspect affects the other in ways so few of us understand. And yet we must if we are to grow to our full potential as a Beacon of Success and a Role Model for others. A healthy diet, exercise, meditation and restful sleep form the fiber and fabric of the Dream Factory, because when they work together in perfect harmony, they help empower the *Undiscovered Self* in you.

In this chapter, you will learn techniques for nurturing physical, mental, and emotional health while pursuing ambitious goals, ensuring sustained success and fulfillment. Much more than diet, mental activity and meditation, it is a complete human being Lifestyle. And it's fun.

UNDERSTAND THE SIGNIFICANCE OF SELF-CARE: Self-care is the deliberate act of nurturing our physical, mental, and emotional well-being. It involves prioritizing activities that restore, rejuvenate, and replenish our energy. Recognize that self-care is not selfish; it is an essential component of sustainable success. By taking care of ourselves, we ensure we have the strength, clarity, and resilience necessary to pursue our dreams effectively.

CREATE A WELL-BEING RITUAL: When you develop a well-being ritual that incorporates and interweaves all your activities you discover new ways to support and nourish your fully integrated self. Dedicate time each day to engage in self-care practices such as exercise, meditation, journaling, reading, or pursuing hobbies that both delight and excite you. Establish boundaries around work and allocate periods for rest, relaxation, and quality interactive time with loved ones. By creating *a well-being ritual,* you establish a foundation for balance and fulfillment in your life. And you set up a *reward center* that restores and rejuvenates you in ways that you may not have consciously addressed.

PRIORITIZING PHYSICAL HEALTH: Physical health forms the cornerstone of overall well-being. Emphasize activities that support your physical health, such as regular exercise, maintaining a balanced diet and getting sufficient sleep. Listen to your body's needs and make adjustments to your routine as necessary. Remember, physical vitality provides the needed stamina to pursue your dreams with both vigor and resilience.

The human body creates about 330 billion cells every day, replacing dying ones with fresh ones. That means, it completely restores itself about every three months. And you recycle your blood entirely about every 28 hours. So how you replenish it also becomes increasingly important.

The human body also give you feedback and will let you know when it's wearing down; provided you listen and learn. Knowing that, your assignment becomes knowing how to love it both tenderly and toughly.

Give it plenty of rest but also help it to exercise. Fitness feeds it oxygen that fuels the system at large and also speeds up your metabolism while it chews up fat and cuts into calories. Exercise is also your Number 1 stress reducer. So a regular fitness regimen can kick you back into balance faster than just about anything else on earth. Aerobics, cycling, long-distance running, swimming half-a-mile a day and power-walking, sports that demand endurance—all combine to help you become fitter, smarter and more alert. (They've also been proven to help you sleep more soundly at night.)

For physically active people, hormones called *serotonins* become your new best friends because they help activate the body's natural dopamine *(the good kind)* to reduce pain, speed up your mental processes and slow down your heart-rate when at rest. They also work with your *pheromones* to help you to become more alert, because they interact with your hypothalamus to strengthen all those *telomeres* that keep you young, fit, intellectually active... even as they famously help prolong your life.

NURTURE MENTAL AND EMOTIONAL WELL-BEING: Like your body, your mind needs a workout—and on a regular basis. And don't kid yourself into thinking that simply by focusing on "your work" that you're giving your mind a treat. Caring for your mental and emotional well-being is equally crucial, because even as it is striving daily, your brain needs nourishment. And I don't mean mind-candy. Give it some of the good stuff—like worthwhile courses, online seminars and good books— the mental energy of fulfillment that takes place when you meditate and focus on those images that inspire.

It's true there are "brain foods." And education carries its own kind of nutrition. The mind that is being constantly fed is also growing strong in the process. Having said that the brain, like any other body part, is a muscle and at times a fragile one. So it needs rest, stress-free, restful sleep and, even more than that, thrives when it is presented with pathways to enlightenment. That's why it helps so much to engage in activities that promote mental clarity—such as mindfulness, meditation, deep breathing exercises, or engaging in creative outlets. Practice self-compassion and cultivate positive self-talk. Seek emotional support from trusted friends, family, or professionals when needed. By nurturing your mental and emotional well-being, you enhance your resilience, creativity, and problem-solving abilities. A rested mind, filled with positive thoughts and creative ideas quickly becomes the best friend that your body ever had.

ESTABLISHING BOUNDARIES AND SAYING "NO" IS A KEY TO YOUR SURVIVAL. Learn to establish boundaries and say no to activities or commitments that do not align with your peace of mind and long-term goals. (Yes! We all succumb to "guilty pleasures" but keeping them to a minimum is essential. So, make it chocolate and not a cigarette.) Prioritize your self-care rituals and protect your time and energy. Recognize that saying "no" to certain opportunities or requests allows you to say "yes" to those things that truly matter. Setting boundaries is an act of self-respect and empowers you to maintain a healthy balance between your ambitions and your well-being. (And the trope holds true: "Freedom is greatest when the boundaries are clearly defined.")

PRACTICING MINDFUL REST AND RELAXATION: Rest and relaxation are integral components in the complicated Matrix of *The Self*. Practice mindful rest and serenity techniques, such as deep relaxation exercises, spending time in nature, or engaging in hobbies that bring you joy and rejuvenation. (Treat yourself to a walk in the park. Literally, *Take a good look at the world around you.*) Allow yourself guilt-free breaks and periods of rejuvenation to recharge your batteries. Remember, rest is not a sign of laziness but a necessary part of maintaining optimal performance and well-being. It's also a sign that you've learned how to flip the switch on stress at a moment's notice.

IN FACT, IT'S A GOOD IDEA TO GET IN THE ZONE: *It's easy as 1-2-3.* And I have to admit it, this is a Peter Thomas favorite. So, I joyously share it with you. Because it's one of the best stress reducers I have ever discovered. I call it *Zone 1, 2, or 3.* And it's such a great tool particularly in today's world.

Zone 1 when you are perky, full-on and at your very best. All alpha output and on your game.

Zone 2 less than *Zone 1*, but still on point … a notch down, but still nicely negotiating your world.

Zone 3 when you are totally chill … serene, in a state of perfect bliss and nothing can stress you out.

So. when you're at the airport and things have gone all bonkers from flight cancellations, delays or whatever, slide from Zone 1 or Zone 2…and over into Zone 3. Tune out the White Noise of the world—the hassle, the stress and strain that will take place with you or without you—and slip into that *secret silence* that brings you peace of mind. You will not believe how well it works! Zone 3 takes a little cultivation, but it gets easier every time you do it.

CULTIVATE RELATIONSHIPS AND SUPPORT THOSE SUPPORT-SYSTEMS: Nurturing relationships and building a strong support system are vital for well-being. Surround yourself with "the very best people"—that means individuals who uplift and encourage you on your journey. Seek meaningful connections with those who bring you emotional reinforcement and understanding. Foster relationships that celebrate your successes and provide both counsel and reassurance during those challenging times. By cultivating positive relationships, you create a network of support that sustains and strengthens you…and that brings you back onto an even keel.

PRACTICE GRATITUDE AND CELEBRATION: *Practicing Gratitude and Acknowledging Achievements are essential aspects of self-care.* Cultivate a sense of gratitude for the journey and the progress you have made. Celebrate even the smallest milestones along the way, acknowledging your hard work and growth. By practicing gratitude and embracing joy, you build neural pathways to a positive mindset and nurture a sense of guilt-free self-appreciation. Once you do, you quite literally wake up every cell in your body to billions of *negative ions* and mitochondrial clusters of positive energy. These are virtual life-extenders in ways you never imagined—cellular gates that swing open to you every day of your life.

Learning how to do this is crucial to your overall well-being—so important in fact, that we're devoting an entire chapter to it. (The one that follows this.) That in itself should be cause for Celebration ☺

CONCLUSION

CREATING HOMEOSTASIS—THE LIFE OF THE WELL-BALANCED SELF: All this may sound like a lot of work when it's not. And it isn't because—once you've put the roof on your Dream Factory—good things become second nature. Success is like a "prosperity magnet." And you'll recognize fellow travelers along the path—those who are seekers of metaphysical balance and recognize its importance in our lives. Synergizing self-care is an integral part of the journey.

By understanding the significance of looking after yourself, creating a well-being ritual, prioritizing physical health, nurturing mental and emotional well-being, establishing boundaries, practicing mindful rest and relaxation, cultivating relationships and support systems, and practicing gratitude and celebration, you achieve a harmonious balance between your ambition and your need to grow and evolve.

The Term itself, *Homeostasis, is Aristotelian* in origin—from the philosopher Aristotle—and means *"a man (woman) in balance."* The perfectly balanced "self."

Remember, *true success cannot be measured by mere superficial gains,* but by the overall mental, emotional, physical and spiritual growth that comes from refining all the facets of who you are as a human being. Embrace self-care as a fundamental pillar on the path to the Dream Factory, and let it empower you to pursue your dreams with vitality, joy and sustainable success.

CHAPTER 16

Celebrate Your Milestones: "You Deserve it."

Congratulations! You have arrived. You've not only finished constructing, polishing, and perfecting your Dream Factory and putting the roof on top, you're now also constantly cranking out a superb product. So now you've hit a crossover point where you have to take responsibility for it all. Yes that is the hidden dragon of success, because it creates a new *Universe of Purpose* for you to engage-in and maintain.

So…learn to be good to yourself. Once you've fully formed the Dream Factory, it is important to pause and celebrate the milestones that you've achieved along the way. Celebrating milestones is not just about acknowledging accomplishments but also about fostering a sense of Joy, Gratitude, and Motivation. In this chapter, we will explore the significance of celebrating milestones and how it fuels the further pursuit of our dreams.

MILESTONES ARE IMPORTANT: Milestones come to you in many ways and in all sorts of incarnations. And each one merits your attention. First, they serve as markers of progress on your journey. They represent significant steps you've taken, each emblematic of your growth, determination, and perseverance. Recognizing and celebrating milestones is vital for several reasons. First, it provides a sense of accomplishment and boosts self-confidence. (And by now you should have plenty of that. Just look how far you have come.) Second, it offers an opportunity to reflect upon the path you've traveled and the lessons that you've learned. Finally, it ignites a new bonfire of motivation, fueling inside you the drive to continue moving forward.

SET UP SOME MEANINGFUL "NEXT STEPS" ON YOUR PATH: Meaningful milestones are those that align with your dreams, values, and aspirations. They are personal and reflective of your unique journey. When setting-up these benchmarks, consider both short-term and long-term goals. Break down larger objectives into smaller, achievable steps that can be celebrated along the way. That way, they become those little stepping-stones across the river of doubt—and help you create that roadmap to chart your progress as you forge ahead. It's another helpful way to give more meaning to your journey.

EXPRESSING GRATITUDE: Explore the importance of celebrating "reward markers" along your journey. Acknowledging all your achievements to date. *And remember to use the "G" word early and often.* Express Gratitude, and reflect on the progress made. We emphasize it here on the pages, because this is truly the one component that is most often overlooked. (It gets "talked about" but very seldom practiced.) In that regard, Gratitude is the Forgotten Virtue. When in fact it is the Mother of all others.

This also entails expressing appreciation to those who have supported you along the way, such as mentors, friends, family, and colleagues. Share your "verbal" appreciation openly and often. Gratitude can be both electric and synergistic, because it not only fosters a positive outlook but also strengthens relationships and energizes "your tribe." It cultivates a sense of interconnectedness with others you admire. It even has a season (Thanksgiving) devoted to it that should be practiced all the year.

CREATING RITUALS AND CEREMONIES: Create rituals or ceremonies to mark your milestones. These can be shared experiences but they don't necessarily have to be…because how you acknowledge your milestones is entirely up to you. Sensible self-promotion is important of course. (It's important to "your brand," if nothing else.) By the same token, temper it with those private moments, the ones known only to you: develop rituals that resonate with you, such as writing a gratitude journal, treating yourself to a special meal, or engaging in a reflection and visualization course for all the great things that come next. When it's appropriate, involve others in your celebrations, such as hosting a gathering or sharing your "recent wins" with a supportive community.

PUT ON YOUR OWN OSCARS. SET UP YOUR "SUPERBOWL": A lot of highly successful people already do this. (And there are others who should, because it's something that really works!) Once you've reached a certain pinnacle of success, you can even—and we recommend this highly—*set up a Recognition Paradigm of your own,* one that will encourage others to reach for the sky and the stars.

Money and wealth, and toys are important. But when you get down to it, it's *Recognition* that fuels the spirit, and is oxygen for the soul. It's an undeniable truth of human nature that high achievers in this life are almost always recognition motivated people. That's why there are so many awards, dinners, banquets, winner's trophies and lifetime achievement awards—Tonys, Emmys, Grammys, ESPYS, Pulitzers and Stanley Cups. It isn't just about winning; it's a validation of Self. It's a way of informing the Universe, that "I've done the best I can."

By creating rituals and ceremonies—for yourself and others—you infuse meaning and significance into your milestones. And be generous when you do it. Others can see what you've accomplished and they'll be energized by your success. And even more: they'll be motivated by your recognition of them. Without doubt, it's a form of mentoring, because you've shown them "how it's done." And that in itself is leading by example.

REFLECT AND LEARN: In whatever form they take, milestone celebrations provide an opportunity for reflection and learning. Take the time to reflect on the journey leading up to the milestone, the challenges overcome, and the lessons learned. Identify strengths, areas for improvement, and insights gained. Use these reflections to refine your strategies, adjust your course if needed, and let each milestone serve as a catalyst for growth.

RECOGNIZE YOUR ACHIEVEMENTS: Take the time to acknowledge and appreciate your achievements. Celebrate both big and small milestones, as each represents a step forward. Reflect on the hard work, dedication, and sacrifices that led to the accomplishment. Recognize the progress made, the skills acquired, and the growth you've experienced even as you've done it. Make a list if you need to. It's never a bad idea.

Acknowledging achievements allows you to validate your efforts and reinforces a positive mindset. This fosters your motivation and a sense of fulfillment. It also entails a certain level of responsibility for that success. And that—in the fulfilled self—is the greatest accomplishment of all. That is the end game. That is making sure that what comes out of *The Dream Factory* also comes with a Product Guarantee. (The final set of lessons.)

INSPIRE OTHERS: Never lose sight of this, because it's *that* important: *Your Milestones (both tangible and intangible) can inspire others on their own journeys.* Share your achievements, experiences, and lessons learned with those around you. Offer encouragement to others in the pursuit of their dreams. By sharing your successes as well as your challenges, you contribute to a culture of celebration, growth and collaboration. Becoming an example to others creates a ripple effect of motivation and fosters a community of dreamers striving for success.

For that we offer a true Solution, and that involves your newfound power to influence the Society around you…in any number of very positive ways. So many good things can spill out of everything you do and benefit everything they touch. Think of yourself as a river of both energy and bounty. And never hesitate to let it flow.

CHAPTER 17

Living the Dream: It Gets Tricky

Success! "Use it! Or Lose it! Tied together the key lessons from each chapter emphasize the importance of living one's dream authentically and sustainably. As you read this, be mindful of the fact that you need to continue applying the principles and practices you've learned. Your dreams are always within reach. And occasionally, once achieved, they can be terrifying things, unless you have a plan for what to do next. You must have unwavering belief, persistent action, and a commitment to your future success. With "The Dream Factory" as your guide, you will be empowered to turn your dreams into reality and create a life filled with purpose, joy, and accomplishments to be proud of.

It is also not surprising that with all this completion, accomplishment, newfound wealth and recognition for your achievements, you will also find yourself with a brand-new set of responsibilities.

We start with the belief that you've followed our recommendations in Chapter 14 and *Managed Your Risks* intelligently, *achieved your milestones* and solidified them with a cogent sense of direction—and that you've applied our *Decision-Making Framework: CFE (Clarity. Focus. Execution).*

Once you have (and you have or you wouldn't have made it this far) you'll quickly find that you're in a very good place. Because you already know what comes next. And that is the recognition that you have created not just a Dream...but an entire ***Dream Factory.***

And you have a choice to approach it one of several ways. The secret embedded in all of this is that you have not *One Dream But Several*. It's called "The Dream Factory" for a reason. That means it's not a one-off but the beginning of a brand. Your Brand. The one that empowers you to be an example to others. No one wants to be a "One Hit Wonder," and then never be heard from again.

STAY AHEAD OF THE CURVE: Especially if you're in technology but in all other fields as well, the boneyards are filled with this year's "hot products" doomed to be yesterday's news.

Zeitgeists of technology such as Dot-Matrix printers, 8-Track players, pagers, faxes, "calling cards," VHSs, CDs, *Sharper Image* Catalogs, Polaroid Cameras, Plasma screens and Blackberries once dominated the market, only—within a year or three—to disappear forever.

Apple didn't become the world's first $1 trillion-dollar company by stopping with the Macintosh, 5% of the computer marketplace and calling it a win. It took innovation, vision and any number of previous incarnations of successful products to achieve what is now looked up on the next step in communications and entertainment technology called "spatial vision programming": The Apple Vision Pro˚.

Bricks and mortar stores and entire shopping malls have entirely disappeared—felled before the onslaught of Amazon.com—and the "Vision" of Jeff Bezos who, by the year 2000, raised over $100 Billion in Market Cap over a "concept" of online shopping that 90% of the Wall Street pundits thought would never come to pass. (A classic example of the power of Self-Belief… one so contagious that it revolutionized an entire form of global marketing… to become one of online shopping that now constitutes 34% of all purchases made in the world today.)

All the more reason to be true to your Vision: Never stop learning and growing. Never stop innovating. It's not just important to continue to develop, it is essential to your dreams—the rest of them.

Remember you've created your own special "Dream Factory." Dreams will only come out of it as long as the wheels keep turning. Continue to study your chosen field of endeavor, keep up with the latest trends, be mindful of the pitfalls and continually be looking for ways to improve what you have created. This invariably requires creating your own "brain trust." An inner-circle, a mastermind group, a "Think Tank"—call it what you will, but call it. And call on it often whenever you want to develop new concepts and test-out new ideas. The old clichés that say, "Be new or be through," or "Publish or perish," inevitably hold true.

Actor, director, producer, composer, musician and Mayor of Carmel, California Clint Eastwood perhaps said it best: "Progress or decline…there is no in-between."

Also remember, at this point in your development, that you are going to be looked upon by others as a *Beacon*—a symbol of success for others to emulate and follow.

The great Greek statesman, Pericles of Athens (the *de facto* founder of Democracy) once created a concept called "Arete." In the strictest sense, *Arete* was an Athenian term that translates into: "*Excellence, Virtue and Fulfillment.*" Three powerful words that form into one pure philosophy: The Greek equivalent of the "cup that runneth over." And the meaning is implicit: that those who have achieved great wealth and influence innately create a bounty and level of generosity as a part of their role in society. That in sum is who you've become; and who you have the potential to be: *someone whose every gesture creates a ripple effect that benefits society.*

Give generously to be sure. Support causes and groups that you feel are worthy of making this world a better place. Whether it's the environment, worker's rights, social causes or free laptop computers and courses for children in third world countries, shelters for animals or sanctuaries for abused women and children—good, noble causes that merit both your financial and moral support as well as your focus and passion are numerous. (Just be careful not to spread yourself too thin. Pick your shots. Concentrate upon those issues closest to your core values. You can never go wrong once you use those criteria for your decisions.)

Recognize the truly successful individual becomes a beacon for others to follow, learn from, imitate and duplicate. Do not look upon this as either a threat or an inconvenience. And realize that your destiny as a "Role Model" is all a part of the Dream Factory Matrix.

For that you can enhance both your Product(s) and your Brand by providing them with something called **CEMENT (*Contribute, Empower, Mentor, Educate, Network and Train*).**

CONTRIBUTE: Now that you've created your product and established your Brand, you become something of a model that others will want to follow. To be sure it's important to Contribute…and we've covered the many ways to do that. But your contributions may also entail some level of ***Co-Creation.*** That means being open to others of like mind. Embrace those who come to you, for many have great ideas. And this is where relationships may be formed in ways that may surprise and delight.

So…remain open to new ideas. Give and take. Advise and offer insights. And very often it turns out that those who come to you with new ideas may very well become partners in a new endeavor. Being available to others is often the most rewarding aspect of all. Because once your Dream Factory is formed it becomes a hub for new energy, winning attitudes and synergistic partnerships in ways you've never expected.

EMPOWERMENT: *Empowerment* is a cost-free bonus that brings solid Encouragement. It does so much to bring others to life—to the fullness of their potential. And it costs you only your time. Mind you, you don't want it eating up every spare moment you have. But when you foster the potentials in something or someone, you empower them and you build alliances—co-creators for future endeavors. And even if you're not going to physically or financially buy into someone else's concept, you've built-in some very nice karma. And it will be returned to you a thousand fold…all in the fullness of time.

MENTOR: Well…by now we know how this works. Mentoring is Encouragement on Steroids. By now, you're being looked up to in such a way that your opinion is sought out: by groups, companies and motivated individuals in your profession. This is where you take the time to instruct, inspire and enlighten. This is where you see in others what might have once been your own…passion, energy and ambition laced with originality. Sometimes you do this on a one-on-one basis. But you can also mentor others by teaching courses at your local university, coaching a little league sports team, giving lectures to civic groups, and joining speakers bureaus in professional organizations. This is service of a different kind, because your achievements are your *passe partout*, your calling card and your reputation brought to the next levels.

EDUCATE: Education is a double-edged blade—all in a very good way. This is the sword, *Excalibur*, that you wield at the top of your game. You not only have the opportunity to educate others but also to improve, enhance and advance your own. Remember, you're not only a teacher, you are forever the student. Never doubt for a moment, that there is more for you to learn. So SELF-ENLIGHTENMENT is something you should always write in Capital Letters. Take courses, learn from the experts. Remember that no matter what you've just created, in this age of geometric changes, you—as is the case with all of us—are always on the edge of obsolescence…until and unless you stay ahead of the curve.

NETWORK: We've covered networking rather thoroughly in our Chapter 13 on harnessing the power of connections. The key element here is to recognize just how important this aspect is for anyone starting out. So, given the fact that you've already mastered much of this ability to harness connections on your own, it's even more important that you share these secrets with others.

WHAT'S MORE THERE IS A FORMULA TO IT: *Connections create conductivity. Conductivity creates electricity. Electricity powers Energy. Energy generates Synergy. And Synergy—by definition—enhances Growth.*

TRAIN: Training always sounds pedantic. Like a Marine Corps drill manual. It shouldn't because everything every successful human being or human entity on Planet Earth has been accomplished because somebody trained themselves to do so. So much of our training in life is "unreflected" but happens nonetheless. We "train" our minds to think, our bodies to get fit, our armies and teams to function as units, and our schools in the ways of productive citizenship. The same rules apply when helping others build their dreams. Training requires discipline, repetition and practice—and the results invariably arrive at a point of inflection. Well trained individuals and groups perform with measurable degrees of excellence. Poorly-trained individuals and groups get mixed performances and grades.

There are a few wild-cards in all of this: such as positive reinforcement, constructive enlightenment, encouragement and instruction. Mentors and teachers who know how to apply these things have infinitely better chances of creating an excellent product. Those who do not—those who use fear and intimidation—have far lower success horizons: 12% vs. 82% by several standards of measurement.

HARD BARGAIN WITH A SOFT TOUCH: One part of dealing with success that is the hardest to learn comes with the act of negotiating exactly what's right for you. You've occasionally heard the trope (or should) that, *"You don't get what you deserve. You get what you negotiate."* This ties into Self-Belief but also into knowing your own Value. You've worked hard to get this far, and now is not the time (as they say) to "Give up the Store." And make no doubt about it: More than one dream has been hijacked by the fear of standing one's ground.

You've worked hard, you've built up your Brand, and now someone wants to buy it for Nickel. So know your worth, and *believe* in what you've done. Because that belief carries with it an energy all its own. It's not only the fuel to get you started but also to finish what you've started—and do so with a flourish. Know your value and others will to. And remember one thing above all else: Once you truly stand for something, nothing but the best will suffice. Know your worth and others will to. Also know your "Deserve Levels!" And stick to them. Then negotiate from there. Respect will take you the rest of the way—from others and for yourself.

CONCLUSION

Never underestimate the impact you have on others. Your success informs their success. They can virtually and literally "go to school on you." As someone who's "Made it happen," you have some things to live up to.

In the end it costs so little, and it means so much…and is always something returned to you at least a thousand-fold.

CHAPTER 18

Secrets of their Success

It isn't yet a hard and fast rule, but it should be: *True Winners love sharing their ways and means of winning.* They love imparting their success to others…and, not surprisingly, they very often do so. Truly successful people tend to be generous with their time, their insights, their mentoring, their compassion and their arc of giving back—to their immediate circle, their professional associations, and their communities at large.

As it turns out, it is not only second-nature to them but also what they feel to be a mandate that, by laying out their own personal formulations, they will empower and expand the next generation of high-achievers: like teaching others how to dream, how to tap into their own Genius and channel it into a viable success-matrix, and finally how to put it all together, piece by piece

That is much of the reason why, in the final chapters of this book, we share a lot of Good News! And nothing is more life-affirming than people who have actually created their own *Dream Factory* and the Product(s) that come out of them…and are now *living the dream* on their own terms.

At this point, I confess to something of a bias, because all of the people I have included on the following pages have several things in common: First, I've worked with all of them at one level or another during the course of their progress, either as a mentor, co-creator, investor or advisor—or some or all of the above. Second, as it happens, since this book is written with every intention of inspiring young entrepreneurs and those on the threshold of breakthrough enterprises, most of our contributors are young—under 40 and youthful in their approach to all aspects of their lives. *(And those who are older have the energy of someone half their age.)* Third, these are individuals who have fully embraced the concepts of Self-Belief and confidence in their own Genius to achieve. They've risen to the level of their dreams, and done so by applying *Clarity, Focus* and *Execution* to everything they do.

Each of these remarkable young people have exceptional stories to tell, and criteria they've met along the pathway to accomplishing great things. **As A Special Note:** *Each contributor's offering will be slightly different in nature.* Some chose to answer all our questions and elaborate upon them thoroughly. Others opted to tell their own story in a more personal way. Still others cherry-picked their responses with emphasis on the issues that mattered most to them…or ones that dovetailed into their area of expertise.

All of these *Grateful 8* are unique, passionate and inspiring in every way. And it has been an honor to include them on these pages.

So, with their permission—as well as their phenomenal contributions— we proudly introduce them here. And I share their amazing stories meant to inspire, encourage, empower, enlighten, and delight. Read on…

THE GRATEFUL 8:
LIVING THE DREAM

CHAPTER 19

Meet Mikhail Naumov

Tech Entrepreneur. Author. Master Investor. Genius!

G ood day, Dear Reader! My name is Mikhail Naumov — I was born in St. Petersburg, Russia in 1989, and spent my early years navigating the exciting and volatile period of post-Soviet Russia. By a stroke of luck I got to come to New York City at age 9, and began living my own version of the "American Dream."

I chose to pursue this entrepreneurial journey, by starting my first business from my college dorm-room at age 19. Upon selling it four years later, I joined the ranks of Silicon Valley tech entrepreneurs and built several software and technology companies, where I managed to raise over $50M+ in venture capital and become an investor myself. From an early age I've always believed in the power of visualization, value-creation, and personal development. These concepts have helped shape my life into the person I am today.

Along the way, at age 23, I met my mentor, Peter H. Thomas. And for the first time in my life I found someone who was living exactly the kind of life I envisioned for myself. Through my work with Peter, I've expanded my perspectives, learned the art of investments, and adopted some life-changing habits. These lessons were all gained "from the trenches" working alongside Peter on countless deals and business initiatives.

Many of these lessons you will learn about in this book — the most important of which remains, in my opinion, the ability to live a wholesome life in clear alignment with your own personal values.

This book is a treasure-trove of wisdom and practical mechanisms to help any motivated individual to actually live their Dreams. Happy dreaming!

ON A PERSONAL NOTE

I met Mikhail about 12 years ago when I went to New York to attend a GSEA event. Mikhail made a point of speaking to me and being persistent enough that I remember walking the streets of New York together and going back to our hotel in the wee hours of the morning. From there, we created a mentor/mentee relationship that continued for several years. As the relationship developed we began what all entrepreneurs do – we started to talk about real live business deals. And soon Mikhail was co-investing with me into various opportunities as they came together. As the deals evolved, the relationship grew and now I would say that Mikhail is more of an investment partner than a mentee. In fact, on some opportunities that come up now in technology I would consider Mikhail becoming the mentor and me the mentee. And—as is more than occasionally the nature of synergistic relationships—it's a phenomenal full circle.

Impressive at any age, Mikhail is co-founder of several venture-backed tech companies, including DigitalGenius and Paylode, a leading platform for AI + customer service that is quite unique in the industry. And he has already written and published a groundbreaking book, *AI Is My Friend,* that has recently become an "insider classic" on Amazon.com.

As is characteristic of this high achieving young man, Mikhail was the very first to respond to my request for his personal insights, and his perceptions of what *The Dream Factory* represents to him—as well as his own personal recommendations for how it can work for others.

In so doing, his responses are concise and yet replete with inspiring experiential references that also include his own spins…or variations on a theme. Call him our "lead-off" hitter, if you will. And it's a perfect way to kick off this very important portion of the book.

DREAM BIG AND DEFINE YOUR VISION—
THE POWER OF VISUALIZATION

Q: **How important is it to have big dreams and a clear vision when pursuing success?**

A: Our life expands to fill up the container we've dreamed up for it. Therefore, having a big dream is basically a pre-requisite to living a fulfilling and wholesome life. People see their own "dream" differently — for some it's about creating wealth, for others it's about a happy family, and most likely it's a combination of "dream factors" that are unique and meaningful to you. That's why we must allow ourselves the time and space to let our minds stretch and dream up the kind of life we want to live. Each of us is given a special gift of life here on earth, and it's our fortune and privilege to make the most of it.

Q: **Can you share a personal experience where visualization played a significant role in achieving your dreams?**

A: Earlier on in my career as a tech entrepreneur it became absolutely necessary to convey the message of my business to large groups of people. This meant countless speeches, presentations and opportunities to speak on stage in front of large crowds. I learned to visualize my own stage-presentation in advance, picturing myself in the moment, delivering the best talk the audience has heard all day. This would build up an incredible sense of excitement for me, while eliminating any and all fears of addressing a large crowd. Communicating complex ideas to large groups became an important tool in my tool-kit as an entrepreneur, and I credit this ability to my own practice of visualizing the process and outcomes in advance.

Q: **What strategies or techniques do you recommend for readers to tap into their imagination and create a vivid mental image of their desired future?**

A: Our minds are exceptionally adaptable. We can train our minds to do our bidding and use the extraordinary energy and power of the heart-mind connection to achieve exceptional results. I've found that my imagination and visualization powers are most active when I am hiking in nature, listening to inspiring music, just after exercising, or while quietly reflecting on my life. I also keep a running document on my iPhone and iPad — which is my personal repository of dreams and reflections. So I constantly refer to it, reread, adjust and refine on most long-distance flights. It really works, because it's easier to focus in-flight without the everyday distractions, phone calls and places you need to go. Sitting in one place for a few hours, allows you to plug in some headphones, open up your "dream board" and get to the work of mapping out and calibrating the life of your dreams.

ESTABLISH YOUR VALUES

Q: How did you identify and define your core values, and how have they influenced your journey to success?

A: At age 23, I met Peter Thomas and immediately found a copy of his book, *LifeManual.* It became an indispensable guide for me during an uncertain and challenging time in my life. One of the best aspects of this book is the section on Values. There I found a helpful definition of what values are, why they are important, along with clear instructions for establishing my own set of values.

Q: Can you share an example of a time when aligning your actions and decisions with your values led to a more fulfilling and purpose-driven life?

A: Today my values are: *Health, Happiness, Freedom, and Personal Growth.* Each of them is like a lens through which I can look and evaluate any important decision in my life. Like each of us, countless times I have found myself at the crossroads of a decision. In those moments, pulling out my values toolkit helps me digest my decision and calibrate it against a clear set of directions I have committed to for my life—*my Values.* In summary I think back to the first piece of wisdom I ever learned from Peter Thomas: "Mikhail, when you know what your values are, decision-making becomes easy."

Q: **What advice would you give to readers who are struggling to identify their core values?**

A: The book, *LifeManual,* is the fastest way to identify and refine your personal values. Interestingly enough, values are allowed to evolve over time as we grow and achieve a deeper understanding of ourselves and the world around us. Ten years ago, I started with a different set of values and kept those intact for a decade, until more recently it was time for a bit of an upgrade to what my values are today.

UNLOCKING YOUR INNER GENIUS THROUGH SELF-BELIEF

Q: **How important is self-belief in unlocking one's true potential? Can you share an experience where cultivating self-confidence led to breakthrough results?**

A: If you believe in yourself, despite your circumstances, you will be unstoppable. Sometimes we get down on ourselves, especially during our most challenging times. In those moments, it becomes doubly important to harness whatever hints of self-belief you have inside you to quickly work your way out of a rut.

Q: **What strategies or exercises do you recommend for readers to overcome self-doubt and tap into their inner genius?**

A: For me the biggest accelerators of self-belief have been books and biographical stories of people who achieved great things. Somehow reading about other people's journeys, with their ups and downs, helps me to see my own life as a story unfolding in real-time—specifically with me as the main character. This means that I am responsible for my life and my outcomes, and believing in myself is the first step towards personal fulfillment.

Q: **Have you ever faced moments of self-doubt during your journey, and if so, how did you overcome them?**

A: Over the years I've encountered 3-4 instances that really tested my resolve. Mostly these were situations focused around my entrepreneurial journey, building several companies. I've had moments of deep self-doubt, coming uncomfortably close to failure. In those moments it helps to remember a handful of key lessons, one of which is to "Avoid FUD!" FUD stands for *Fear, Uncertainty, and Doubt.* Fear is natural. Uncertainty is a fact of life. Doubt is self-inflicted. But each of these blockages has an antidote. Fear can be accepted and turned to motivation. Uncertainty can be clarified through research. Doubt can be overcome by taking decisive action—the sooner the better.

SELECTING YOUR MENTORS

Q: How have mentors played a role in your personal and professional growth? Can you share a specific mentorship experience that had a significant impact on your journey?

A: Like for many of us, my first mentors all came from my books. As I learned English, I took joy and inspiration from reading biographies of accomplished people and marveling at their path in life. They became my mentors as I would often try to look at various situations through their eyes. I read the stories of Conrad Hilton, John D. Rockefeller, Andrew Carnegie and others...later followed by modern-day entrepreneurial heroes like Jeff Bezos and Elon Musk.

Q: What qualities do you look for in mentors, and how do you establish meaningful connections with them?

A: Not to be redundant, but it bears repeating: By far my closest and most beloved mentor happens to be Peter Thomas. Since meeting him 12 years ago I made it my mission to develop a strong mentorship relationship with others, and my vision for this was reciprocated. Mentors all come in different shapes. But I've found there are several parameters which qualify someone to be a great mentor to you.

1. The mentor and mentee have certain similarities between them. It may be mutual interests, personal history, upbringing, mindset or even looks. Quite often the mentee will see themselves wanting to become more like their mentor, while the mentor sees a younger (or earlier) version of themselves when looking at the mentee. This is a

powerful concept and should be harnessed for truly impactful interactive relationships.

2. The mentor is far enough along their own journey where they are ready for and looking to advance their own legacy. Often this is through the mentorship of younger people in their network. The mentor is never competitive with the mentee. Rather they are instructional, collaborative and generous when it comes to sharing their time and wisdom.

3. It is also important to note here that the mentor is not a trainer or coach. They are not there to solve a problem in your business or personal life. Instead they take on a much broader role in someone's life. A mentor is someone with enough wisdom, desire, and life experience to lead by example. On a rainy day, they gladly help to part the dark clouds around your head and help you see the light.

Q: How can someone reading this leverage the wisdom and experience of mentors to accelerate their own success?

A: *Establish a deeper connection:* mentorship takes time and depends on a deeper connection between both individuals that goes beyond the superficial. I've found that asking lots of questions and listening carefully is the most effective way to establish a deep connection with your mentor while learning a lot.

Also add value: Mentorship is a two-way street. You must seek to add more value to your mentor's life while they add value to yours. This can be done through sharing your own expertise on a given subject…and having a genuine desire to add value for your mentor. In my mentorship with Peter, I quickly became his "software guy", "his AI guy", his "venture capital guy," his deal "due-diligence go-to", and even his "hiking buddy".

Be persistent: especially at the beginning it can be hard to capture the attention and time of your mentor—especially if they are very active and involved in their own endeavors.

Don't be your own obstacle: our egos or self-doubts can often get in the way of great outcomes. Your chosen mentor might be a rockstar and living on top of the world. So, for some of us it's natural to feel like it would be a stretch to get their time and attention. As if you didn't yet earn the right to have them as your mentor. Here it's important to remember that a great mentor doesn't really care about your level of accomplishments. They are there to help you grow, as part of building their own legacy. So don't be shy, get out there, and get your mentors.

MAKING YOUR DREAMS ATTAINABLE

Q: **What is the importance of setting SMART goals that are aligned with one's vision? Can you provide an example from your own experience?**

A: Every year I do a personal reflection session where I look back at the things I've accomplished during the previous year and identify key insights. I use these insights to learn and calibrate my bigger life-vision. Then I put together a plan for the coming year which includes SMART goal setting. This, in turn, corresponds to my overall vision and the current realities.

Q: **How do you break down big dreams into actionable steps? What strategies or techniques do you recommend for tracking progress?**

A: I do an annual *reflection & planning* session, and then conduct monthly checkpoints and quarterly audits of my progress. I keep my vision, values, goals, standards and other helpful tools available to me and synced up across all my devices (iPhone, iPad, Laptop, and Notebook Planner), so I can reference them at any time and frequently enough to stay on track.

Q: **Have you ever faced challenges in achieving your goals, and if so, how did you overcome them?**

A: We all face challenges in achieving our goals. Along the way I learned that goals are a great way to organize your ambitions into measurable milestones. However, as the wise old saying goes: *"It's not just about what you do, or even how you do it ... but it's about who you become."* That means it's equally important to set out my own set of personal "Standards". Standards are clear definitions of what I will and will not accept from myself and for myself.

CULTIVATING A SUCCESS MINDSET

Q: How does belief play a role in shaping one's reality and achieving success? Can you share a mindset shift that had a significant impact on your journey?

A: You become what you believe and how you identify yourself. Believe yourself to be a winner, and sooner or later you will win. Identify as an entrepreneur, and before you know it you will have built one or several companies. Our personal identity is one of the strongest forces alive inside each of us. Some people find it difficult to wake up early. But it's much easier if you identify yourself as an "early riser". Same for daily fitness, unless you identify yourself as an "athlete." The same goes for other aspects of life. We become more and more of what we identify as. So let's be sure not to limit ourselves with an overly narrow self-identity.

Q: What techniques or practices do you recommend for overcoming limiting beliefs and developing empowering thoughts and attitudes?

A: There are at least two moments in my life when I came across a form of identity crisis. The first came when I was selling my first company. I was 23 years old, and until that time my entire identity was defined by this one company I had built. *I was the company,* and the company was me. But along the way, I grew and eventually hit a ceiling. The business was no longer challenging me to grow, and it became clear that I needed to move forward. After selling the company, and despite achieving a meaningful financial outcome, I was completely lost. What was I to do now that the one thing I had been building for years was no longer part of my life? This caused me to ask the question: *Who am I now that the business as a core part of my identity is no longer mine?* This "identity-rupture" was one of the most challenging experiences of my young adult life. In hindsight it was a blessing. And had I not found the courage and patience to overcome this temporary volatility I would not be where I am and who I am today.

Q: How do you maintain a success-oriented mindset during challenging times or when faced with obstacles?

A: During particularly challenging times I try to balance and address both sides of the human experience—the mind and the heart. I map things out logically and gain clarity about the situation and possible solutions available to me. But I also spend plenty of time outdoors, walking or hiking for 2+ hours per day, to actually clear the mind and, instead, get clarity in my heart about whichever issue might be on my mind at the time. I've found that it's much easier to navigate obstacles when engaging both your mind (logic, reason, organization) and your heart (passion, spirit, dreams, and emotions).

TURNING CHALLENGES INTO OPPORTUNITIES

Q: **How do you approach challenges or obstacles on your journey to success? Can you share a specific example of how you turned a challenge into an opportunity?**

A: Whatever your chosen lifestyle or profession — if it were easy everyone would be doing it. Hence challenges are a very natural part of any journey. By now I've learned to expect and anticipate challenges before they arise. It's much easier to deal with things you've come to expect rather than getting blindsided and finding yourself in a state of chaos.

Q: **What strategies or mindset shifts do you recommend for reframing obstacles and embracing the growth and learning that come from facing challenges?**

A: I tend to not look at challenges as obstacles in my life. They exist and are a natural fact of life. Instead I use my energy to focus on the vision, the goals and the outcomes I am seeking. This makes it easier to treat whatever challenges come up as just necessary (and sometimes fun) parts of the journey.

Q: **How do you maintain resilience and stay motivated during difficult times?**

A: Articulating your way through a problem really helps, as well as making lists and organizing options. Most difficult situations become very manageable once you clearly articulate the problem, identify the context, and clearly outline your options for moving forward. I also tend to spend more time outdoors when going through a challenging time, walking or biking generates enough physical energy to clear the mind and boost the positive hormones to deal with whatever obstacle is coming up ahead.

THE KEY TO PROGRESS

Q: **What is the importance of taking consistent action toward goals? Can you share a personal experience where consistent action led to significant progress?**

A: It was not easy for me to become an early morning riser, but it was something I really wanted to do. While "hacking my way" into becoming an early riser did not work, I found another way to develop consistency through personal accountability. I discovered the ancient energy practice of *QiGong*, which has been practiced by people for thousands of years. And after learning the basic principles I found it to be a worthwhile and enjoyable pursuit. The hidden benefit came from the fact that *QiGong* is typically performed early in the morning with guidance from an experienced *QiGong* Master. Well I found and hired a master to guide my *QiGong* sessions daily. As a result I am now an early riser, happily jumping up before sunrise to do the practice and win the day. Before I knew it, the consistency of daily practice and the accountability of a Master has completely changed my daily life and routine for the better.

Q: **How do you overcome procrastination and stay focused on your priorities? What time management techniques or strategies do you employ?**

A: I have a weekly meeting with my accountability coach. During this time she helps me refine my priorities and schedule my calendar perfectly for the week ahead. I pay particular attention to setting up protected daily time-blocks for my High Leverage Activities (HLA), and schedule them at times of the day when I have the highest amount of energy and focus. I also found that having a motivating working environment is a powerful activator for focused work. I've invested into setting up my daily work station and office to be comfortable, motivating, and tech-efficient.

Q: **What advice would you give to readers who struggle with taking action and making progress toward their dreams?**

A: Whenever I find myself struggling to take action or procrastinating, I simply remind myself that my life is a precious gift, and looking back, time really flies by fast. Who knows how much more life has in store for us. So, it's best to get out there immediately and chase your dreams.

THE MEANING OF ATTITUDE, MOTIVATION, AND COMMITMENT

Q: **How important is resilience in bouncing back from failure and setbacks? Can you share a time when a positive attitude helped you overcome challenges?**

A: The day I first met Peter over a decade ago I was a kid running a dorm-room startup. I participated in a competition called the Global Student Entrepreneur Awards (GSEA), which brings together top student-entrepreneurs from around the planet to connect, learn from older business owners, and compete on a global stage for a meaningful award. While presenting my business on stage, I caught a glimpse of Peter Thomas on the Judges Panel. Minutes later I was fascinated by his keynote speech to a room full of hundreds of business owners, young and old—from over 75 countries, all gathered for the Global GSEA Awards at the New York Stock Exchange.

There was no chance in the world that I would let this guy Peter slip past my life. Within minutes, we were cheerfully chatting in the lobby of the NYSE, where I also met Rita Thomas, Peter's sweetheart and wife of 37+ years. Well long story short, Peter and I ended up so caught up in our conversation that we wandered the streets of Manhattan until 2.00AM in the morning! Just before parting ways, Peter took off a gold pin from the lapel of his own coat jacket and handed it to me as a gift. The lapel pin had the simple letters A.M.C. Peter explained that they stand for *Attitude, Motivation* and *Commitment*—the three primary forces of an extraordinary life. "It all starts with your attitude", Peter told me. "It's the number one force for an extraordinary life"

Q: **How do you maintain motivation during difficult times or when faced with failures? What role does commitment play in sustaining long-term success?**

A: Nothing ever happens without some form of motivation. From the little things to the greatest accomplishments in history—they all started with a small spark of someone's motivation. Here it's important to study yourself and understand what uniquely motivates you. Some are motivated by competition, finances, or their family. While others are driven by the possibility of creating something new. Figure out what compels you to get off your chair and take action — and that will be a powerful tool for the rest of your life.

Q: **What strategies or practices do you recommend for cultivating a positive attitude, staying motivated, and remaining committed to one's dreams?**

A: Commitment is the third part of the AMC formula. While many of us may have a winning attitude and even tremendous motivation — we must also learn to make an iron-clad commitment to ourselves, our word, and our plan. I tend to write down my own commitments and sometimes share them with others, to create an extra layer of accountability for myself.

MAXIMIZING PRODUCTIVITY

Q: **What techniques or strategies do you employ to master time management and maximize productivity? Can you share an example of how effective time management has helped you achieve your goals?**

A: Time is one of our most precious resources, yet many of us tend to waste it away. In the investment business it's often said that "Every dollar needs a job", as there's no sense for your dollars to sit idly in your bank account when they could be out there generating passive income or new growth opportunities for you and your loved ones. Well, with time — I might suggest that "Every minute needs a job as well." So, put it to work, and marvel as you reap the surprising rewards.

Q: **How do you prioritize tasks and ensure progress toward your goals? What tips do you have for setting boundaries and avoiding distractions?**

A: For the past 15 years I've run my entire life from my own Google Calendar. It helps me stay organized, allocate time, and move efficiently through my day.

Q: **What advice would you give to readers who struggle with managing their time effectively and balancing multiple responsibilities?**

A: As a tech entrepreneur you're ultimately in control of your own daily schedule. There's no boss to report to or standard office hours to keep. Without this structure around you it's easy to slip into bad habits when it comes to time management. To solve this, I hired a personal accountability coach to help me schedule my days correctly and then stay accountable for them. She has access to my calendar, and we meet every Monday morning to set out the most important activities for the week ahead and ensure that each day is productive and fulfilling.

COMMITTING TO CONSISTENCY

Q: **How important is discipline in staying committed to long-term goals? Can you share a personal experience where discipline played a crucial role in your success?**

A: While daily discipline is important it did not come easy for me. Instead I look to others for motivation. While sailing through British Columbia with Peter and Rita on their yacht, I witnessed Peter getting up every morning prior to sunrise and immediately jumping into his physical fitness routine. Just imagine an 85-year-old guy cranking out push-ups, lunges and sit-ups at 6.00AM in the morning all aboard his yacht. He even procured a portable treadmill which he had brought aboard so he can get his 2-mile hike in every morning, even while at sea. Talk about discipline and consistency!

Q: **What strategies or habits do you recommend for cultivating discipline and staying consistent in pursuing one's dreams?**

A: It's important to surround yourself with strong people with whom you resonate. They can push you to become the best that you can be. When it comes to cultivating discipline, I find myself much more consistent with physical fitness, daily schedule, work routine, when in the company of another like-minded person. It creates mutual accountability and enthusiasm that fuels each other. So whether it's a friend, a spouse, a business partner or just a hiking buddy, I've found that it makes a big difference.

Q: **How do you overcome distractions and temptations that may hinder progress or derail focus?**

A: Getting distracted or thrown off course is easier than ever today. We are bombarded with endless sources of information, notifications, calls, texts and everything in between. Not to mention work-life which, with laptops and iPhones has become a 24 /7 experience for many of us—tangled up with some kind of social life to boot. As a positive antidote, I've used my 5.55AM daily *QiGong* sessions as the perfect anchor to ensure that I use my daytime effectively, finish up work on time, and end any social engagements prior to 9.00 PM. Missing this mark usually means having a pretty miserable morning without being fully rested. The prospective pain of this keeps me disciplined and running my daily life on schedule.

GROWTH THROUGH KNOWLEDGE

Q: **Why is continuous learning important in personal and professional growth? Can you share an example of how embracing continuous learning has propelled your success?**

A: One of my core personal values is "Growth"—the idea of going to sleep a better man than I woke up. This means approaching each day with a genuine curiosity for what's in store, what lessons could be learned, what new wisdom acquired.

Q: **How do you seek new knowledge and stay curious in your field or industry? How do you embrace feedback and adapt to change?**

A: One of my companies builds software, practical applications of machine learning, and *AI* for customer support centers. When I first started building it with my co-founders, I didn't know much about machine learning and AI, and had to get up to speed, fast. The goal was to become an expert in two areas: contact centers and machine learning. For the first one I flew to Amsterdam and convinced one of my clients—KLM Royal Dutch Airlines—to let me basically live inside their contact center for weeks, working alongside their customer support reps, meet their leadership, and quickly understand the details of their daily work. On the AI side, I quickly sought the expertise of my technical co-founder, an Oxford Masters graduate and machine learning guru. We also had the chance to hire some incredible PhDs from Cambridge and other places. And I used the interviews to learn everything I could about their latest research and inventions. After about a year I could speak comfortably on the topic to almost any AI expert, and within two years was co-authoring AI patents together with my team.

Q: What resources or practices do you recommend for readers to embrace continuous learning and stay updated in their areas of interest?

A: I look at this through two lenses — Personal Growth and Professional Growth. On the personal side, "know thyself" is the ageless wisdom, and I actively invest time and resources in personal reflection and self-discovery. I read books that challenge my thinking, attend *Cognitive Behavioral Therapy* (CBT) weekly, using it as a place where I seek out opinions of people I admire whom I perceive to be at the top of their game. Professionally I look at maximizing my value in the business world. As a tech entrepreneur, investor, board member and advisor I am constantly learning from the various interactions I have with businesses and other professionals in my field. While "specific knowledge" is mission-critical in areas like medicine and law, I am much more engaged with interdisciplinary thinking and enjoy pulling together diverse insights across various industries and even cultures to create and capitalize on business opportunities that excite me.

HARNESSING THE POWER OF CONNECTIONS

Q: How has networking and collaboration contributed to your success? Can you share a specific instance where a connection or collaboration opened new doors for you?

A: I first moved to the United States at age 9, without knowledge of the English language, or any friends or contacts in the country. It became instantly clear to me that to survive and thrive I would need to develop interpersonal skills and grow my network purposefully. Along my journey I made this a priority, and it helped lay out the groundwork for who I am today…as well as the opportunities I am blessed with.

Q: **What strategies or tips do you have for building a strong network and nurturing relationships with like-minded individuals?**

A: It's really not that difficult to build deep long-standing relationships with like-minded people. In my case, I am always open to meeting new people, and mostly use my intuition to understand if they will have synergy with me and my interests. From there, it's important to focus your conversation on the things you believe to be important to them.

Almost everyone loves to talk about themselves. By giving them a chance to do so and expressing genuine interest, you will immediately create a sense of connection with the person. Finally, forming long-term relationships takes time, effort and consistency. Be there for the person on their important moments like birthdays and weddings, and especially if they get into some kind of trouble and call you for help. Find time in your schedule to call or text. Provide value by sharing interesting ideas, new discoveries, books, and tools you think might be useful for them. Most of the time your efforts will be reciprocated. And before you know it you will have decades-long friendships and professional relationships with a strong ecosystem of fellow movers and shakers.

Q: **How can readers leverage their connections to create opportunities and accelerate their own success?**

A: Being visible helps. Telling your connections about your interests and making yourself available for collaborative projects is the easiest way to create exciting new opportunities. In the business world this often comes in the form of co-investments in interesting projects, joint ventures, and other business partnerships. On the personal side, you can travel the world with like-minded contacts and participate in exciting events. Every year my wife and I join Peter and Rita Thomas in Scottsdale, Arizona for the Barrett-Jackson Car Auction. It's an absolute blast! And as fellow car enthusiasts Peter and I get to enjoy the auction while also catching up on various business projects and new investment opportunities.

MANAGING RISKS

Q: How do you approach managing risks on your journey to success? Can you provide an example of a calculated move or decision that paid off?

A: Understanding your own level of risk-tolerance is the first step in managing risk across your life and business. It's often said that a person's risk tolerance decreases with age. A younger person can risk more since they have more time to make up for any losses they incur earlier on in their career. While an older person should be weary of risky endeavors as they most likely don't have as much time to recover should something go wrong with a project or investment. While this sounds right theoretically, I find that my own personal level of risk-tolerance has not changed at all over my 15 years in business. I still take hefty entrepreneurial risks, start and build companies, make calculated investments and so on.

The only thing that has changed is the absolute amount of capital I am putting on the line. As I built my career and grew my own pool of investable capital I am still investing the same proportions of my overall net worth in a similar mix of projects and opportunities as I did earlier in my career. The only thing that changes is the size of the projects I can take on today, compared with 15 years ago.

Q: What strategies or frameworks do you employ to assess risks and make informed decisions?

A: How do you balance taking risks with minimizing potential setbacks? Ten years ago, I learned of a simple formula from Peter Thomas while discussing investment philosophies. "Take all your capital, Mikhail, and split it in half," Peter told me. "The first half is your safe-money, which you should invest in secure and protected cash-flow projects that are guaranteed to keep you solvent, while providing you with recurring passive cash flows that should ideally cover your lifestyle expenses. Then take the other half and make that your risk-money, where you can put it towards riskier endeavors that may not generate cash flows initially and could take several years or more to return the capital, but could lead to much bigger wins in the future." I've followed this piece of timeless wisdom and find that it accurately reflects my own desire for balancing risk and reward, while having the financial security and baseline certainty to truly enjoy my life.

Q: What advice would you give to readers who are hesitant about taking risks or making big decisions?

A: I found that with any project it's important to protect your downside. Everyone usually gets excited about the big lofty vision and opportunity ahead. Fewer entrepreneurs look at the downside protection in a deal in the event it goes wrong. Warren Buffet has said that the best way to grow wealth is to not lose money. It took me a couple of times getting burned on an investment deal before I really understood the value of this mindset. In any new deal I look at the upside ahead, while ensuring that I don't lose more than I am comfortably able to should it not go as planned.

BALANCING WELL-BEING AND AMBITION

Q: What is the significance of self-care in maintaining balance and well-being while pursuing ambitious goals? Can you share a personal experience where self-care played a crucial role in your journey?

A: During a particularly stressful period of my life I was firing on all thrusters, solving problems in my business, and barely noticing how my daily heart rate was spiking. Then suddenly, before I knew it, I'd lost a lot of weight. A wellness exam delivered some bad news about an autoimmune condition that started to knock me sideways—something that had been sparked, through a combination of high-stress and other factors. I was only 29, and this was a wake-up call. I took this as an opportunity to rethink my approach to wellness—completely fixed my diet, changed my habits, and (most important) learned how to accept stress as a natural aspect of my life, rather than fighting it.

Q: How do you nurture physical, mental, and emotional health while striving for success? What practices or routines do you recommend for readers to prioritize self-care?

A: The most important thing for me has been getting control of my daily schedule. Running a disciplined daily routine gives me the time and energy to balance all aspects of my life. I'm not always perfect with it, but the routine is always there to help provide structure in an otherwise chaotic world.

Q: How do you find a balance between ambition and well-being, and how do the two complement each other?

A: Forcing yourself to work or grinding through to burn-out rarely works as a long-term strategy for success. I've found that the time it takes to recover from burn-out is longer and more painful than the time I would have spent taking a break or a short vacation well in advance of burning out in the first place. Today I am very conscious of keeping a well-formed balance between chasing my ambitions and looking after my own well-being.

RECOGNIZING ACHIEVEMENTS

Q: Why is it important to celebrate milestones along the journey? Can you share a memorable milestone or achievement that you celebrated and how it impacted your motivation?

A: At age 23 I sold my first company, and immediately went to New York City and bought myself a nice new watch. It was a small token to commemorate my first meaningful accomplishment in the business world. But my biggest celebration to date was my wedding day. We had nearly a hundred family and friends fly in from a dozen countries to celebrate this life event. Among them were dozens of top young entrepreneurs and past winners of the GSEA as well as tech entrepreneurs from Silicon Valley, London, Mexico, Russia and more. All of them are still active in the business world, and some have even taken their companies public. They all keep in touch from the 3 days they spent in Moscow for our wedding and continue to be a source of inspiration for me and for each other.

Q: **How do you acknowledge and appreciate your achievements? What role does gratitude play in recognizing success?**

A: One of the most powerful human emotions is—*Gratitude.* We are all fundamentally blessed to be alive today. And what we do today is important, because we're exchanging an entire day of our life for it. When things either get tough or you win big — remembering to be grateful will give you both balance and long-term satisfaction. Virtually all challenges and moments of joy are temporary. But *Gratitude is the Eternal Flame* that can keep us warm in any circumstance.

Q: **What advice would you give to readers who struggle with acknowledging their own achievements and celebrating their progress?**

A: Most entrepreneurs I've met are hell-bent on climbing the next mountain...and are too impatient and switched-on to pause and actually appreciate how far they've come.

I too fell into this loop earlier in my career, taking exactly a 2-minute break between selling my first business and starting the next one. However, with time I learned the importance of pause and reflection. It's easier to do this for *big life-changing wins* in your career — but it's equally important to celebrate the *little wins* along the way. Whether doing something nice for a loved one or taking a long-awaited trip to a place of inspiration, there are many ways to pat yourself on the back for a job well done.

~ MN

CHAPTER 20

Meet David Hodgson, MD:

Doctor. Engineer. Award-Winning Entrepreneur. Genius!

My name is David Hodgson and I am 30 years old. I was born the youngest of three boys, in Kingston, Ontario. My father was in the army for 35 years and thanks to him and my selfless mother, I had the privilege of living in some incredible places in Canada and beyond.

I attended high school in Heidelberg, Germany and went on to study mechanical engineering. I worked as an automotive engineer in Detroit before moving to the East Coast of Canada where I led the invention of a radioactive drug delivery device at a biomedical start-up and found my passion for medicine.

I studied medicine at Dalhousie University and during my studies founded Hollo Medical Inc. My co-founder happens to be my incredible wife, an engineer from southern Italy that I met on a cruise in the Mediterranean. Our mission is to reduce the burden of chronic respiratory illness with clever and thoughtful innovation. Just after graduating from my medical degree, I was fortunate enough to be recognized as the Global Champion of the Global Student Entrepreneur Awards in 2023. This experience shaped my passion for entrepreneurship and showed me the empowering community of change-makers like me that exist around the world.

I am now a resident doctor in Halifax, Nova Scotia, a licensed professional engineer, and the CEO of Hollo Medical Inc. A few years from now I look forward to a career as an innovator in the groundbreaking field of Interventional Radiology.

ON A PERSONAL NOTE

As the leader of the Canadian GSEA Program we are on the constant hunt for candidates who will compete in the National Awards program. David applied and won the Canadian competition and went on to compete internationally and, in 2023, won the first place for the Global Student Entrepreneurs Awards at the world competitions. As I learned more about what he has done with his life in the first 30 years (and you will read all about this in this chapter) I felt that he epitomized the exact type of person I wanted to show the world what a gifted young man with a goal is able to accomplish. As it has come to pass, this is a remarkable human being we can all learn a lot from on so many levels.

Here is an engineer who wanted to learn more about the world of medicine. So he thought, after he had acquired his engineering degree, that the best way to do that was to become an MD and Radiologist. He accomplished both of these goals in addition co-founding Hollo Medical, a group that specializes in chronic respiratory illness. Another amazing goal accomplished…he made available enough time to find not only his partner in business but also his partner in life—his wife…all before age 30.

DREAM BIG AND DEFINE YOUR VISION— THE POWER OF VISUALIZATION

Q: **How important is it to have big dreams and a clear vision when pursuing success?**

A: Dreaming (big or small) is a pre-requisite to any change in our world. Having a clear perspective of the impact of that change is what puts you in a position to be successful, by whatever measure you see fit (self-satisfaction, monetary, quality of life etc.).

Q: **Can you share a personal experience where visualization played a significant role in achieving your dreams?**

A: As a mechanical engineer first, I visualize everything, and I think there is nothing more satisfying than seeing something you imagined first in your head come to life. This applies to something as inanimate as a valve to dreaming about the life you want to lead.

Q: **What strategies or techniques do you recommend for readers to tap into their imagination and create a vivid mental image of their desired future?**

A: Don't hold back. The biggest favor we can do for ourselves when trying to make an impact in our world is to get out of our own way. Let your imagination run wild. Use that creativity to push boundaries and then take those ideas and find a way to turn them into concrete solutions that have a real-life impact.

For example, when founding Hollo Medical, we wanted to reinvent a device that defined a multi-billion-dollar market that was constructed of 7 different components and 3 different material types into a single part that was about $1/5^{th}$ the size. I started with an unrealistic and subjectively impossible dream fueled by the potential outcomes for patients, cost savings and overall efficiency of mass manufacture. This dream spawned a theoretical concept, and that concept was then dissected over time to meet mechanical, manufacturing, and patient centric goals.

ESTABLISHING YOUR VALUES

Q: How did you identify and define your core values, and how have they influenced your journey to success?

A: Core values to me are an unwavering depiction of how you act on a regular basis. I identified my core values primarily based upon other's interpretation of my actions. I find it is hard to truly assess myself, so I suggest that you ask someone close to you what they believe your strengths are and why. A few core values I identify with are *Persistence, Resilience,* and *Optimism.* To innovate and enact change in the world around you it is essential to first believe that you can, even when others don't *(Optimism)*, to believe something can be accomplished even if the road is long and unclear *(Persistence)*, and to soldier on, evolve and become more skilled in the face of failure: hence *Resilience.*

Q: Can you share an example of a time when aligning your actions and decisions with your values led to a more fulfilling and purpose-driven life?

A: I believe that many of the inward-looking exercises I did with my co-founder as a part of founding Hollo helped us accurately define our responsibilities. The biggest favor you can do for yourself as an entrepreneur is identifying the right people for the job, and that includes yourself. By focusing on tasks that align most closely with my values, I become excited, motivated, and empowered to excel. That is what we are doing at Hollo.

Q: What advice would you give to readers who are struggling to identify their core values?

A: Talk to someone close to you and ask them how they would define you. Do this in different contexts (personally and professionally) and then take the time to reflect upon what they say. You'll learn so much about yourself than you might otherwise go unaware of. (It's something some people spend a lifetime, and never address.)

UNLOCKING YOUR INNER GENIUS THROUGH SELF-BELIEF

Q: How important is self-belief in unlocking one's true potential? Can you share an experience where cultivating self-confidence led to breakthrough results?

A: Without Self-Belief I feel like we wouldn't accomplish anything. We would be frozen in our tracks. The more freedom you give yourself to believe beyond what you are familiar with, the more you will realize that you can accomplish an incredible amount in life. My breakthrough moment was when working as an engineer at a biomedical start-up. While I had no proof, I had a desire to set out and solve problems that others struggled with and gave up on. Most things aren't impossible. It is more likely that someone gave up too soon. In this role, I conceived of a radioactive drug delivery device to achieve more controlled drug delivery than ever before.

This was a task that many had tried for years, but had failed in the attempt. I had my breakthrough on a Saturday, after repeated failure, with a prototype I built in about 20 minutes. It was the simplest device I had ever designed, and it worked. A few years later, I became the lead inventor on the patent, and it has now been used to treat people around the world.

Q: What strategies or exercises do you recommend for readers to overcome self-doubt and tap into their inner genius?

A: Don't doubt yourself without any proof. We often stop before we even start. If you want to do something, give it a shot—a real shot, and reflect on the results. Either way you will grow from it. More than likely, you will realize that you are more than capable.

Q: Have you ever faced moments of self-doubt during your journey, and if so, how did you overcome them?

A: My only moments of self-doubt occurred when I realized my journey was becoming bigger than myself. When your work could impact the livelihood of others (*i.e.* those on payroll/connected to the success of your business) the stakes become significantly higher. The best way to overcome them is to push yourself to solidify a long-term plan that you and your team believe in. Nothing can be done alone.

SELECTING YOUR MENTORS

Q: **How have mentors played a role in your personal and professional growth? Can you share a specific mentorship experience that had a significant impact on your journey?**

A: I think it is important to find a mentor with similar core values. This shows you a case example of how to accomplish long-term goals in life that may seem out of reach. I found my mentor in an Interventional Radiologist when I was working as an engineer at his company. His unwavering optimism and positive energy were both contagious and inspiring. It led me into medicine and ultimately into starting my first medical device company.

Q: **What qualities do you look for in mentors, and how do you establish meaningful connections with them?**

A: A mentor should be someone you are inspired by, and naturally get along with. They should be willing and open to sharing their experiences to assist in your personal growth. If this is the case, a relationship should form organically.

Q: **How can people reading this leverage the wisdom and experience of mentors to accelerate their own success?**

A: I think it is so important to acquire data and make decisions in the context of your own goals. Respect and show gratitude for someone's willingness to share their experience—especially when they do it with the intent of supporting your success and personal growth. By the same token, by no means see someone else's advice or experience as a hard and fast rule that you must follow. It is your life at the end of the day. Learn from their wisdom and experience with openness, and let it fuel your own journey. And yet remember their journey is not yours. You are unique, and your voyage through this life is exclusive to you.

MAKING YOUR DREAMS ATTAINABLE

Q: What is the importance of setting SMART goals that are aligned with one's vision? Can you provide an example from your own experience?

A: The only way to make dreaming a little more predictable and measurable is with accountability and reflection. SMART goals are an example of this, and essential to any complex project. For example, our team breaks down overall operations into bi-weekly sprints with achievable milestones that are discussed openly, carefully set, and executed in a prescribed time frame to contribute to an overarching goal.

Q: How do you break down big dreams into actionable steps? What strategies or techniques do you recommend for tracking progress?

A: As important as dreaming big is the ability to pat yourself on the back for progress or adapt if you encounter an unexpected turn. I often start at the end and work backward, figuring out what milestones are absolutely required to succeed and roughly how long they will take. That way, I know what I am up against and have realistic expectations.

Q: Have you ever faced challenges in achieving your goals, and if so, how did you overcome them?

A: The hardest thing for me in the beginning was balancing ambition with practicality. With help from my wife who thankfully balances me out and adds some much-welcomed organization to my lofty ideas, I have learned to prioritize goals with the biggest and most achievable impact for our quality of life and those of others.

CULTIVATING A SUCCESS MINDSET

Q: How does Belief play a role in shaping one's reality and achieving success? Can you share a mindset shift that had a significant impact on your journey?

A: Belief is paramount. Doubt will stop you in your tracks before you start. Let yourself enjoy the prospect of success until you see failure occur with your own eyes. You will learn from any action, and it will make you more likely to succeed. If you don't act because you fear Failure, don't expect your Dreams to come and find you.

Q: **What techniques or practices do you recommend for overcoming limiting beliefs and developing empowering thoughts and attitudes?**

A: The biggest favor you can do for yourself is to get out of your own way. Limiting beliefs by way of your own self-doubt, or the words of others, is a dangerous thing because it can prevent you from reaching your full potential. Try and try again. And use the results to dictate your beliefs, rather than preconceived notions, often set upon you by others. No matter what, you will come out stronger.

Q: **How do you maintain a success-oriented mindset during challenging times or when faced with obstacles?**

A: At first it is hard, and I think it requires a shift in perspective. But I can say from experience that Failure is the world telling you that there is a better option. If you listen, you will realize that ultimately it does nothing but show you the way to an Opportunity on the other side of it.

TURNING CHALLENGES INTO OPPORTUNITIES

Q: **How do you approach challenges or obstacles on your journey to success? Can you share a specific example of how you turned a challenge into an opportunity?**

A: As an engineer first, I love problem solving. Obstacles are what makes the journey interesting, and solving them gives you the tools to face bigger obstacles next time. Right after graduating as an engineer, I worked briefly in Detroit in the automotive industry. I was on a mission to resolve an issue with child-seat installation. But in order to solve it, I had to redesign a seemingly inconsequential part that was used for decades.

This change impacted everyone—from the manufacturing plant to trim designers to those concerned with the ultimate safety of the vehicle. Of course, it would have been easier to stick with the status quo. After all, it had worked for a long time. And yet I knew that something better could be done. What made it harder was that, after much convincing on my part, the first costly trial failed. Discouraged at first, I stuck with it, and later figured out why we had fallen short in the beginning. Then I was able to refine the solution, and to develop it into what now exists in millions of vehicles today.

Q: What strategies or mindset shifts do you recommend for reframing obstacles and embracing the growth and learning that come from facing challenges?

A: I think we underestimate how good it feels to overcome a struggle and to go outside of our comfort zone. It's not just a feeling of satisfaction in the moment, but it sets you up for further success. My main strategy is not to get bogged down by an obstacle, no matter how frustrating. Focus on the solution: that is where you will find more joy and inspiration.

Q: How do you maintain resilience and stay motivated during difficult times?

A: I think about what could be and focus on that. Sure, it doesn't always work, none of us are perfect. But if you keep that in your core, more days than not you will make progress. And that is what will get you through the hard times. Also, don't underestimate how important it is to have someone to rely upon whether it is in a personal or professional context. It is hard to do anything alone.

THE KEY TO PROGRESS

Q: What is the importance of taking consistent action toward goals? Can you share a personal experience where consistent action led to significant progress?

A: Few things can be done in one day. Particularly some of the grander goals in life are the culmination of millions of tiny steps, sometimes in the wrong direction—as in missteps—and that's OK!

Five years ago or so, I fell in love with the impact that engineering could have in the medical field. The missing link to my life was to study medicine so that I could understand the problems that needed solving and know firsthand how to act on them swiftly. For those who have not been through it, acceptance to medical school is an arduous ordeal. And it took a massive amount of time and effort to earn my seat among some truly inspirational people. I approached this methodically. From the academic to the extracurricular to the personal story—all were just obstacles to overcome to stay on my path. Here I am, on the other side of it, and I realize how that younger version of myself set the stage for my current happiness and fulfillment.

Q: **How do you overcome procrastination and stay focused on your priorities? What time management techniques or strategies do you employ?**

A: When you are working on a start-up alongside getting through medical school, every minute counts. Prioritizing those minutes and taking actions that will add value to our overall mission is the most important strategy I employ. When there are 100 things to do, it is easy to be overwhelmed. Train yourself to take that 100 and triage the top 10 things that will make the most impact. Repeat this, and you will realize that the same few items always end up on the bottom, and likely were never meaningful in the first place. I also find that I'm most productive when I am in the right mindset. If I need to recharge to come back stronger, I know most things can wait until tomorrow and that giving myself a break can at times be the best course of action.

Q: **What advice would you give to readers who struggle with taking action and making progress toward their dreams?**

A: Start. The best way to make progress is to set a reasonable goal and get excited about it. If I am pumped about a design, I will sketch it out and reflect. Sometimes it ends right there. If I am still thinking about it a few days later, it is more than likely that I am onto something. If you're going to act, sustained passion and excitement are both important. But to figure out if it is a true dream, you have to test it and see what happens. Start with something low risk that you can crumple up, throw out and start again until you find something worth framing.

THE MEANING OF ATTITUDE, MOTIVATION, AND COMMITMENT

Q: **How important is resilience in bouncing back from failure and set-backs? Can you share a time when a positive attitude helped you overcome challenges?**

A: It is an integral part of the process. Resilience enables you to grow stronger from these situations, and this means that even when things go wrong, you are still on a path of growth and self-discovery. I employ this approach every day. We often instinctively react to problems without thinking critically, and this stifles the creative and innovative approach. When I hear a team member say that an idea I have is not going to work, my first instinct is not to be offended, but to challenge them to explain critically why they believe it is not going to work. This opens a loop of communicative problem-solving that gets everyone on the same page, and ultimately helps overcome any challenge because there is communal ownership and pride.

Q: **How do you maintain motivation during difficult times or when faced with failures? What role does commitment play in sustaining long-term success?**

A: *Commitment provides Perspective.* If you start seeing failures as the road to the best design, you accept it as a part of the process, and a part of your own internal intellectual property. Taking the time to fail and improve is another line of defense against those that might not have the motivation or determination to see it through. This gives you enduring pride in your work, whether you are celebrating a win or laughing in the face of an unexpected result.

Q: **What strategies or practices do you recommend for cultivating a positive attitude, staying motivated, and remaining committed to one's dreams?**

A: There is a time and place for everything, and it is important to recognize this. Some days I may naturally lack motivation for a certain thing, and that is okay. I acknowledge that my energy, or lack thereof, is better served elsewhere. I think this idea of freeing yourself to follow your own inspiration as it comes is what enables you to live fully in every moment. It makes for more productive, efficient, and sustainable progress toward what you really believe in your core.

MAXIMIZING PRODUCTIVITY

Q: **What techniques or strategies do you employ to master time management and maximize productivity? Can you share an example of how effective time management has helped you achieve your goals?**

A: The main techniques I have learned to use out of the sheer necessity of running a start-up in the midst of medical school are task triaging and matching tasks to a state of mind. Using these techniques, I get a sense of what tasks are time sensitive or most value added, and I can also make the most of the mental state I am in whether that matches most toward a creative or clerical task. This means that even though I may only have 2 to 3 hours of free time during a day, I can make it feel like 8 or 10.

Q: **How do you prioritize tasks and ensure progress toward your goals? What tips do you have for setting boundaries and avoiding distractions?**

A: I start with the big picture and then become more granular. I'll figure out what tasks are on the critical path to completing the project, and which are potential, "nice to haves." The sooner I get in tune with that big picture and what is mission critical, the more motivated I am to follow through. This will make each minute seem valuable, as it should be, because it is your life after all. Distractions serve a purpose, like dropping everything to go for a walk, listening to music, going see a movie (whatever helps you recalibrate). Every time I do, I just make sure "those wonderful side-steps" leave me coming back even more excited and efficient.

Q: **What advice would you give to readers who struggle with managing their time effectively and balancing multiple responsibilities?**

A: Take a step back and re-align yourself with what you set out to do. For example, the next time you are stuck in meetings all day, take a note of which ones added value and which ones did not. Do the same with your daily "To Do List." What does each activity contribute to the greater good, and is it time sensitive? Putting a little structure, and critical thought into eliminating unnecessary activities is freeing, and it lets you focus on what matters most. If you've done that, and there still doesn't seem to be enough time in the day, maybe there isn't. You might need help, so open a conversation with someone on your team to do some re-balancing and not only keep the business on track, but your overall wellbeing.

COMMITTING TO CONSISTENCY

Q: **How important is discipline in staying committed to long-term goals? Can you share a personal experience where discipline played a crucial role in your success?**

A: It is up there with Resilience. The trouble with long term goals is what's implied in the name: they are a long way away. This means you need to believe that the work you put in up front will pay off. I remember working as an engineer and believing I was meant to pair engineering with medicine. I believed it with all my heart...but not without some challenges to that Belief. As anyone who's done it can attest, the road to becoming a doctor is competitive, long, and daunting. While working as an engineer by day, I found myself by night studying for the MCAT®, volunteering as a medical first responder and providing music therapy for hospital patients. I did this day in and day out with no guarantee more than a dream. But I knew deep down that if I worked harder than most, I would get there. Now, here I am! Dream realized! And worth every step of the way!

Q: **What strategies or habits do you recommend for cultivating discipline and staying consistent in pursuing one's dreams?**

A: *Don't lose sight of the Dream in the Details.* Sometimes the road becomes muddied with daily distractions that have nothing to do with your end goal. That is of course a necessary part of the journey, a means to an end. But to get through it, you need to draw motivation from what led you down the road in the first place. Let the vision of what is to come enable you to enjoy the journey. Because the journey, no matter how long or arduous, is still your life and your story. Live it with pride!

Q: **How do you overcome distractions and temptations that may hinder progress or derail focus?**

A: Distractions and temptations are good for your mental and physical health (in moderation), and I use them as short-term goals or rewards. If it is going to refresh me and let me tackle something even stronger or with more of an open mind, even more reason to derail your focus temporarily. But if it becomes a habit to avoid doing work, and stunting progress, that is more a sign that you aren't enjoying the work you are doing or that you are systemically overwhelmed. In that case, figure out how to eliminate the non-value added or non-time sensitive tasks and replace them with time devoted to mental or physical health.

GROWTH THROUGH KNOWLEDGE

Q: **Why is continuous learning important in personal and professional growth? Can you share an example of how embracing continuous learning has propelled your success?**

A: I think the desire for continuous learning is a pre-requisite for complex problem solving. If you are not in love with solving problems, learning from, and overcoming unexpected failures you will find the whole process miserable. I employ this philosophy for innovation and product development, and especially areas I am less familiar with like marketing, for example. Keeping an open mind enables you to appreciate the strengths of others, and learning a bit about what they do lets you harness their strengths and make the greatest impact for all concerned.

Q: **How do you seek new knowledge and stay curious in your field or industry? How do you embrace feedback and adapt to change?**

A: My favorite way is to challenge a current idea that seems counterintuitive. I'll break it down and try to understand the rationale for why it was done a certain way. Then, depending on whether or not I agree, I will study unique mechanisms that I am perhaps less familiar with and see if I can employ them in a new and impactful fashion. Feedback can often be stultifying, but also an essential part of the process that I actively seek out. If you are not open to it, you will struggle to create something that serves the needs of anyone and everyone outside yourself.

Q: What resources or practices do you recommend for readers to embrace continuous learning and stay updated in their areas of interest?

A: Figure out what learning style appeals to you. The sooner you start playing to your strengths, the sooner you will make this kind of thing more enjoyable than a chore. I like to learn visually and practically, so I will challenge myself to learn actively out of necessity. Find a modality by which you enjoy consuming information (YouTube, broadcasts, podcasts, textbooks, papers, books, talking to people, etc.) and put it to work. There is no hard and fast way of learning. Just do something you know is sustainable and enjoyable and you will never stop doing it.

HARNESSING THE POWER OF CONNECTIONS

Q: How has Networking and Collaboration contributed to your success?

A: It has been instrumental. The first thing you realize when starting a medical business in particular, is how complex that process really is. It is much more than solving a health problem, and you really need people who have relevant experience to guide you. Through an accelerator in Nova Scotia (Invest Nova Scotia: Accelerate), we had the opportunity to work with Joel Liederman, an experienced engineer and business builder in the medical space. He helped us identify early-on how to add value to our company and "de-risk" our pathway to our target market. This type of guidance saves valuable time and resources, plus providing confidence and clarity to your actions. People like Joel are essential…and invaluable.

Q: What tips do you have for building a strong network and nurturing relationships with like-minded individuals?

A: Always be open to learning from new people. As a conscientious person, it is reasonable to feel that you don't want to waste the time of others. It is empowering to realize that there are so many people out there willing to help, and you need to have a ton of conversations and a bit of trial and error to find the perfect fit.

Q: **How can our readers leverage their connections to create opportunities and accelerate their own success?**

A: One of the amazing things about life is that you only get one. By learning from others' life experiences, you can make the most of a knowledge base that is much broader than what is possible for you as an individual. Then you can leverage the experience of others to avoid similar mistakes. Once you've done that, it makes it easier to pinpoint your opportunities and ultimately focus all your energy on making your journey as incredible as possible.

MANAGING RISKS

Q: **How do you approach managing risks on your journey to success? Can you provide an example of a calculated move or decision that paid off?**

A: Risks are inherent to everything we do. I first analyze the situation and get a sense of the Risk versus Reward. Then I do everything I can to mitigate those risks and ensure the highest chance of the reward.

The biggest calculated move that I made was giving up a solid job as an engineer to study medicine. The reason this was a risk was because my wife and I were just starting out our lives. I was just out of university, and she had recently immigrated from Italy. To her surprise, and at no small risk to our new life together, I proposed the idea of giving up my salary and starting to pay money to study for a vision of a life that was years away. Inherent in that is what I call *The Risk/Catch 22:* adding objectively unnecessary stress and financial instability to an otherwise comfortable life—one that I wouldn't know until I experienced it. On the other side of that, however, was the *Potential Reward:* a more fulfilling and balanced long-term vision of my life.

Q: **What frameworks do you employ to assess risks and make informed decisions? How do you balance taking risks with minimizing potential setbacks?**

A: I am all for contingency planning and understanding consequences. Much like ordering a lab test on a patient. Before you order the test, you need to know what you will do with it. If I approach an opportunity that's tied to an inherent risk, I need to know I can manage the consequences and what my next step will be if that risk becomes a reality. Most risks are not cut and dry, so there is some subjectiveness to it. But in some cases, you can use tools like a design of failure modes and effects analysis to figure out potential risk, severity of consequence, and determine your action to mitigate it accordingly. This is sort of an automatic process for smaller, more frequent and perhaps less severe risks in my life.

Q: What advice would you give to readers who are hesitant about taking risks or making big decisions?

A: Come at it with structure. Employ a relatively objective tool to help you assess the likelihood of risk, then figure out how you can mitigate the severity of it with proactive steps. When you do this, you are more likely to succeed, and you'll feel much more comfortable navigating whatever pitfalls may await you. This is important because some of the best things in life come from having the preparation and courage to take a step into the unknown.

BALANCING WELL-BEING AND AMBITION

Q: What is the significance of self-care in maintaining balance and well-being while pursuing ambitious goals? Can you share a personal experience where self-care played a crucial role in your journey?

A: Most of us are aware that poor self-care can turn even the simplest daily activity into a grueling task. It took me a while to realize it. And I had some help from my wife Sara along the way to help me realize that, no matter what, your own well-being is something that has to come first.

At the end of the day, every ambition stems from us as fallible, mortal human beings. And without protecting that foundation, it becomes precarious to say the least. When we first started Hollo, I was balancing all these new and exciting responsibilities with medical school, my personal life and sharing all of this with my co-founder and wife. Working to accomplish this pulled us in so many directions that it was hard to focus on *anything*. So we ended up mastering *nothing*. By reorienting ourselves and putting ourselves at the center of the equation, we were able to tackle every day with passion, excitement and stability. And now we do so, knowing that if all else faded away we would not be left with a broken version of ourselves.

Q: How do you nurture physical, mental, and emotional health while striving for success? What practices or routines do you recommend for readers to prioritize self-care?

A: This is something I do every day…with help. Constant reflection, discussion and re-prioritization is essential to maintain a grasp on what matters most on a daily basis. If you feel overwhelmed, don't try to grind through it. Reflect. Ask why? And give yourself time to refresh. You might be able to keep it up for a few weeks, months even, but not a lifetime.

Q: How do you find a balance between ambition and well-being, and how do the two complement each other?

A: Well-being gives you the comfort, energy, and strength to face anything in life. It is the Foundation that brings you to push yourself and pursue your ambitions. Sure, you can have one without the other, but this is a case of synergy: the Whole that is greater than the Sum of its Parts. And it is this embrace of both makes you an unstoppable force able to spend a lifetime changing your world.

RECOGNIZING ACHIEVEMENTS

Q: Why is it important to celebrate milestones along the journey? Can you share a memorable milestone or achievement that you celebrated and how it impacted your motivation?

A: The journey is long, and if you don't look up many great things will pass you by! It is so important to celebrate every milestone and acknowledge openly the work and dedication it took to get there. I recently won the 2023 Global Student Entrepreneur Awards after competing against over 1,100 student entrepreneurs from around the globe. A competition that was a lifetime in the making brought me to South Africa where I was filmed competing with the other 5 global finalists from Germany, Turkey, Mexico, Venezuela and Columbia. It was a surreal moment that celebrated all of the work that my team and I had put into Hollo for the last two years, as well as my journey leading up to Hollo. It showed us the true global impact that we are having as an Eastern Canadian start-up and has turned out to be the greatest source of validation—one that we never saw coming!

Q: **How do you acknowledge and appreciate your achievements? What role does Gratitude play in recognizing success?**

A: I make a conscious effort to stop and celebrate them, particularly with those who are close to me. Most often this is my wife and co-founder, Sara. There is a wonderful quote from the uncle of author Kurt Vonnegut, where he makes a point to acknowledge the little things in life by intentionally stopping and saying aloud: "If this isn't nice, what is?" I think we could all embrace those words.

Appreciating these moments is all about living each moment fully and completely. If you don't stop to savor your successes, you let some truly beautiful moments of self-growth and validation pass you by...ones that are very hard to get back.

Q: **What advice would you give to readers who struggle with acknowledging their own achievements and celebrating their progress?**

A: I imagine that most people who don't stop to celebrate these moments avoid it out of humility. While I encourage you to find someone to share every positive (and negative) moment in life like I do with Sara, it is just as important to do so individually. Focus on your accomplishments, and cherish each one. You worked for something, and it has paid off. Take a moment and think about nothing else but that—coupled with the fact that you are capable, and the world wants you to know it. It will, if you let it; so, let it. ☺

~DH

CHAPTER 21

Meet Renie Cavallari

Aspire® Founder. Best-Selling Author. Influencer. Genius!

Renie Cavallari is the CEO and founder of Powered by Aspire®, a globally awarded leadership development and strategic consulting firm; and the RCI Institute, an awakening human potential research and leadership development lab. Known as a "dynamo who colors outside the lines," Renie is also known far-and-wide as "the compassionate no BS coach," a label she wears with some measure of pride. Renie Cavallari is also an award-winning organizational anthropologist and is the owner of 4 diverse companies.

For over 25 years, Renie has worked with thousands of leaders and entrepreneurs around the globe to help their companies be better at what they do by providing practical action-oriented applications and proven processes to improve performance. An award-winning international strategist, speaker, and leadership expert with an inimitable grasp of business and its challenges, she has driven measurable results for businesses with her innovative solutions around the world for over 30 years.

After decades of research and working hands-on with high-performance organizations to help them unleash the human potential hidden within their employees, she found a predictable, measurable, correlation between leadership alignment and organizational success.

Tireless in her desire to share her message and mission with others, Renie has plunged into that murky, shark-infested, non-fiction water of self-help books where angels fear to tread and come up with 7 exceptional pieces of insightful literature, at least three of which have become bestsellers— most notably the "Aspire" series with her latest, **HEADTRASH, the Leading Killer of Human Potential,** becoming an Amazon.com bestseller and winner of the prestigious Hollywood Bowl "Best in Business" Award. In all her works, Renie focuses and passionately believes that the answers live in how we lead and how we inspire others to play "all-in."

Renie is a Philly girl with a serious wanderlust problem; an aspiring jazz flutist, passionate cook, and a believer in people and their endless potential.

Among her many achievements and leadership roles, Renie is a member of the prestigious National Speakers Association and was named an "Outstanding Woman in Business" by the Phoenix Business Journal. TrainingIndustry.com also named Renie as one of the Top 20 Most Influential Training Professionals. In addition, Aspire has won 18 International Stevie® Awards for Innovation in Business and their People Technology® IP ... and the list (were we to publish them all) goes on.

That's more or less Renie Cavallari's curriculum vitae. And yet it scarcely covers the range and depth of this remarkable human being. Renie's journey as a highly successful businesswoman is not always something that can be explained in a few brief paragraphs listing her considerable achievements, memberships and awards. It is something more personal than that. And her career arc has been anything but a straight upward curve. In truth, it is something only women can relate to, while coming into their own in an industry entirely dominated by men (at least at the time).

Even as recently as the 1980s, it took a particular kind of genius to navigate the halls of male orthodoxy when you were a young, attractive woman driven by the ambition to succeed.

And yet when we asked Renie Calvallari to define her own **GQ (Genius Quotient)** and how she used Self-Belief to tap into that element of herself, she kind of balked at the notion...for a moment.

"I never really thought about it. Not in those terms, anyway." Renie answered. "If I could define the underlying cause of my success it would have to be a kind of scrappiness if you will—*that* combined with a passion and a drive to succeed. I grew up a working-class kid from Philly. So I was probably *scrappy* by nature. In my youth, I was embarrassed that I didn't have nice clothes or that my family camped vs. rented a place at the Jersey shore like my peers. But my resilience was a gift that has remained ever-present in my life. When you know you can create something from nothing or figure out how to make something happen by going for it and being bold, after a while you develop a superpower.

"*Scrappy* has always served me. Now I wear it as a badge of honor. *And a message to Self for all of us:* Don't be embarrassed by the tarnished memories of your youth. That is a chapter in the past. The past doesn't determine your future. Only you can decide what your future will be. And for that you have to have big dreams and use *the power to visualize everything you want to accomplish.*"

That observation virtually dovetailed into the starting point for this book. So we pressed the question and followed it with a series of others…

ON DREAMING BIG...

Q: **How important is it to have big dreams and a clear vision when pursuing success? And how do you get there once you do?**

A: If you can't see it you can't have it and if you can't feel it, you won't hold onto it. To have any kind of success you have to be able to tap into your passion. Passion is the fuel of life. It is the engine room of energy, emotion and focus that synergizes to turn on your motivation to excel.

You really have to be driven by something that truly inspires you. Something you foresee. For me, I knew that my life's purpose was to awaken the potential in people, and this has been Aspire's vision for over 28 years. Clarity is the source of productive action. When you have a clear vision, you will work purposefully and endlessly. And that's what led me to creating Aspire®.

Most people think that because I was a strategist before I started Aspire®, I had a plan. I actually hadn't quite formulated a strategy when I started it. In the beginning, I only had *The Dream*—a dream to be independent of the chains that I had experienced in corporate America (especially as a woman) and wanted to make a contribution doing only what I loved to do. That was rather vague and, as any strategist will tell you, that is not really a great game-plan. But when you get down to it, dreams can only get you so far toward your goal. *Taking action* is what will really get you the rest of the way.

What I do know about starting a company is that you MUST understand what problems you can solve for a target audience and what about those solutions you are truly interested in. What about them turns you on, lights your fire, gets you up in the morning? As the years passed, we got far more strategic, and I can say that most failures we experienced usually were great ideas but not things we felt passionately about. In other words, for whatever reason at the time, we just weren't "all-in."

You have to feel an emotional connection to what you are doing if you are going to do something big. Otherwise, it's almost a certainty that you'll run out of gas. You'll waste your time and everyone else's as well.

This was at the heart of the risky choice I made to leave the path well-traveled (the corporate America climb) and daring to start my own firm back in 1995. There weren't a lot of resources or female entrepreneurial role models at the time. So I was virtually driving blind. In this case ignorance was helpful.

Q: Can you share a personal experience where visualization played a significant role in achieving your dreams?

A: Becoming an author: I had always been a writer but quickly learned that does not make you an author. Writers write. Authors publish. And frankly, in the beginning, I had to learn that the hard way.

When I first left corporate America, I wrote a book called *Surviving the Climb*. I never published that book. Even though I loved what I had written, I was afraid to put it out there. The usual questions dogged me (none of them valid at the time): *What would people say? How dare I share my story and maybe insult the old guard? What repercussions would impact my future? What if it wasn't interesting? What if... what if?*

Looking back, I wish I had been less worried about what others would say about me or my work. But I let my doubts get in the way. Since then, I have learned to just go for it and push through the fear. And eventually, it served to light a fire under me. So that, the next time—with my next effort—I embraced my newfound intensity and got clear on what I thought was of value to share.

From there, I just started writing. It wasn't great, but it was published. So I was officially an author, and it was a start!

My latest and 7th book, *HeadTrash,* actually became clear to me while on vacation with the Thomas's in the Bahamas. I was tossing around ideas and none were really landing for me. Then I thought about the biggest challenge we humans have, and it is by far our own "HeadTrash", those nasty little voices in our head that undermine us, suck our energy and steal our potential. When I saw *HeadTrash* clearly in my mind, I couldn't stop writing. And when you're writing like that, you're bringing in a higher aspect of yourself.

Q: What strategies or techniques do you recommend for readers to tap into their imagination and create a vivid mental image of their desired future?

A: Three come to mind:

Think: I once had a boss who said to me "Renie, I pay you to think." It was a really powerful moment for me. We are all so busy being busy. I find that when I stop and just think, I turn on my imagination and creativity.

Read: Something my father, an avid reader, used to say to me was "Those who do not read are not better off than those who cannot read." When I read my mind quickly becomes inspired, curious and often creative—especially with non-fiction as it stirs my endless thirst for knowledge.

Listen: When I take time to listen to the journey, the stories and especially the challenges of others, I find myself voraciously looking for ways to solve those problems. This opens my mind and gets my creative juices moving. Nothing like problems to turn on your mind and vision.

My firm, Powered by Aspire®, is a story in itself. It began when I started studying human behavior as a necessity to be able to help companies improve their performance. Up to that point, we thought of ourselves as a training and strategic consulting firm, but what we really did was awaken human potential. And my years of research left me with one constant fact: Performance is about the mind long before it becomes about the skills, processes or strategies.

As I would sit and listen to the challenges of performance, it started to become clear that nothing changes until your mindset is aligned with the outcome you want. So leaders aren't successful because they have the skills, processes and strategies they need. What makes truly outstanding leaders is the mindset they use to lead: how they think, and how they act and react.

This became increasingly obvious as I worked with C-Suite leaders during COVID. Those who inspired and aligned their people were able to solve problems more effectively over 81% of the time than those who were reacting based on fear and anxiety. The old saying, "What you focus on comes true," is truest when leaders are up against their greatest challenges.

Q: On Establishing Your Values…How did you identify and define your Core Values, and how have they influenced your journey to success?

A: We feel the way we think and how we act reflects how we feel. Values to me are the guardrails of life. They help us stay aligned with what matters most to us. I believe that defining my values has kept me focused on them. There are some that have stayed consistent for years, like family and freedom. Other values have come into my life because of the lessons I was learning and the mistakes I was making.

Q: **Can you share an example of a time when aligning your actions and decisions with your values led to a more fulfilling and purpose-driven life?**

A: My divorce. Divorce is not something that anyone aspires to. It is a decision in the same way marriage is a decision. But I believe our true values are in action when we have to make tough decisions and how we go about it. For me, it was about how we would navigate the next 15 years raising our daughter together with love and respect (two high values for me). This helped me on the many occasions I found myself being petty. It also allowed me to accept that I could only control my own parenting approach.

Q: **What advice would you give to readers who are struggling to identify their core values?**

A. *Step 1:* write down what you think your values are. In the beginning I modeled other people's values.

Step 2: Allow your values to evolve. Don't worry about them being either absolute or permanent. I have changed my values in my life as I have grown as a person. As a classic example, I remember early in our development when I thought Aspire needed to hire crazy, high-energy people, when in truth that was only part of the equation. What I came to appreciate was that we valued people with tenacity and ingenuity—those who are scrappy by nature, so they make things happen and play *all-in*. The real value was learning that playing all-in often had nothing to do with a person's personal energy. Over the years we hired lots of people with calmer demeanor than my crazy "high pitch" energy—thank God—and they were equally successful. Be clear on what you really value and don't think that someone else's values are the right ones for you.

UNLOCKING YOUR INNER GENIUS THROUGH SELF-BELIEF

Q: How important is self-belief in unlocking one's true potential? Can you share an experience where cultivating self-confidence led to breakthrough results?

A. If you don't believe in yourself why would anyone else? I think believing in oneself comes from a sense of inner confidence and sheer desire not to fail. For me, failing is not really failing... it is just a change of direction.

Q: That leads to a couple of questions: What strategies or exercises do you recommend for readers to overcome self-doubt and tap into their inner genius? Have you ever faced moments of self-doubt during your journey, and if so, how did you overcome them?

A. That answer really comes with a combination of ingredients. Back in the day, when I quit corporate America to start working for myself, I had no idea what Aspire was, or what it would grow to become 28 years later. What I did know was that I wanted to help people *aspire* to rise above their circumstance and that I had some skills to make it happen.

I was not a dynamic businessperson and had zero entrepreneurial chops. What I did possess was a desire to make a difference in the lives of others and their performance. That had been the prime motivation for me. And of course, I also was scared of failing, which consistently made me a *go-getter*. There is nothing like needing to pay your own bills (let alone the responsibility of your employee's bills) to make you get your butt in gear...as any entrepreneur will tell you.

I remember I was sitting with a dear friend after I had just quit my job with no real plan. She said to me that it was time for me to start my own firm. She also said something that would become a real motivator to me: "Renie if you are afraid, I would love to be your partner." *Afraid?* I thought to myself. *Well, if she sees my potential I need to believe in it too. There is no way this smart entrepreneur would start a company with me if she didn't think it would be successful.*

So sometimes "Self-Belief" needs (as the Beatles say) "A little help from your friends." And that also underscores the synergy of having mutually beneficial relationships—ones based on shared goals and a mutuality of trust.

That, by logic, led me to a series of "next steps." One is to create your own informal "kitchen cabinet or board of directors." Over the years, as I had many transitions (a polite way of saying that a lot of stuff had hit the fan), I had people to think with, gain insights from, go to for feedback, make introductions and basically be there for me during all the times that mattered. Your dreams are not delivered by you alone. They are so often derived from the people around you, and invariably shared with them. So, who you hang with matters: People of your own house. Your Tribe. Those of like mind. Your team. And that comes with a learning curve.

In the early years, I had very few entrepreneur-oriented relationships. No one in my family was in business, and most of my friends at the time were in corporate America. I needed people who understood my journey, so I started reading and applying the learning that made sense for me. I made lots of mistakes but there is nothing that can replace tenacity. Somewhere in time, I picked up a saying: *Weebles wobble but they don't fall down.* I am definitely a *weeble.*

Overcoming self-doubt is also about learning how to manage your own *HeadTrash.* When we get stuck in our fear and worry we can't awaken our inner genius. Super high levels of stress cause chaos, and chaos takes away our ability to think clearly. We need clarity to take productive action. It is a formula. This is why I meditate, do yoga and get my head in the game every morning with 5 questions that help me see clearly where I need to go today.

This has taught me that the quality of our life is based on how we think, and our thoughts are controlled by the questions we ask. And I was reminded of that recently when my COO quit after ten years together.

When I got hit with the news, I was shocked, sad, angry, confused and ran through a laundry list of emotions that fueled self-doubt and took me to my knees. But making lemonade of lemons, it turned out that the departure of my COO was the greatest gift I could have received because it drove me to make the choices I never would have made had he stayed. I think one of the disadvantages of having a company for so long is that you sometimes don't step outside of it often enough and really take a look at how it serves you.

For me, I had to get busy figuring out what was next for the company and for me. So I sat and wrote down a series of questions to give myself a framework to start thinking from. I call these shift questions: Questions like, "What is the first thing I need to do to stabilize the company?"

Shift questions literally shift you into productive action, and this gets us moving forward. Forward momentum gives us progress no matter how small (and some days it was *very* small).

The framework of these questions helped me start to chip away at where the firm would go, how it would get there, what mattered most, and ultimately led me to ask: "What do I want?" And shortly thereafter, the answers started coming.

ON SELECTING YOUR MENTORS...

Q: How have mentors played a role in your personal and professional growth? Can you share a specific mentorship experience that had a significant impact on your journey?

A: I have been blessed with amazing mentors and coaches. Some I just got lucky to have enter my world, while there were others I deliberately sought out. I have no doubt that the cornerstone of my success has been both my mentors and coaches. Their guidance, insights and ability to challenge me have proven invaluable. I always tell people, if you are lucky enough to have a great mentor or coach then thank them every time they put you to the test or kick you in the butt. They are only doing it for you ...and that is a gift in itself.

I remember my firm was going through one of its many evolutions (a polite way of saying things were going down "the Rabbit Hole"). I was feeling down, disappointed in others and myself, unclear about what I wanted and what I wanted to do. I'll never forget what my mentor said to me: "What if this was the best thing that could happen in your life? What would you be thinking about if that was absolutely the case?"

It shifted me out of my pity party and into a "zone" of massive imagination. And a new, amazing chapter of my business and life became available to me. It was a clever way of saying, "This too shall pass," and "The sun always comes out tomorrow." Two beliefs to live by…and one inevitably interlocks with the other.

Mentors are a collaboration. In a great relationship, you give and you get. A great mentor becomes a synergistic relationship. When I am a mentor, I want to truly know my mentee. I want to know their journey. I want to understand how to support them. I want to be someone they value as much as I value them. By the same token mentors can be remote or less present. They can be hands-off and still make an impact on your life.

With all relationships, what you have is based on how you participate. For me, it's *all or nothing*. So that is the foundation of my mentor relationships and how I mentor others.

A true mentor has no agenda. They want to help you live *your* dreams not theirs. I think there are 3 keys to leveraging a mentor's wisdom and experience:

1. Really listen. Be open.

2. Lean into the things you don't agree with. Be curious and push yourself to understand more. In my experience, some of the best advice I ever received I ignored because I didn't like it. Foolish!

3. Share in your success. A mentor gives their time. And their gift in the relationship is simply to watch you soar.

At this point, I feel it's important to differentiate between *Mentors and Coaches*. Because they may seem to fulfill the same function when very often they have very different roles. Don't get me wrong: both have value, and both serve a purpose. But there is a difference, and *vivre la différence!* Personally, I make sure everyone who helps me—whether they are a mentor, team member, friend, coach, or loved one—knows the depth of my appreciation for their input, direction and for putting up with my crazy self!

But by the nature of constant personal proximity, coaches have to take a deeper dive into the relationship, because *Coaching is a commitment*. Mentors can often influence you without ever even contacting you directly. They can be abstract. They can be virtual. You can be inspired by a lecture by Tony Robbins or a recording featuring Deepak Chopra without ever having met them personally. You can read a book by Napoleon Hill and be mentored by *Think and Grow Rich*. (And who hasn't?)

A coach is almost always more hands-on. A Coach is developing you: holding you accountable and helping you become a better person every day. They become a part of your family—through a shared objective or a cause all related to you and "your team." With coaching, *you* are the central force and focus.

A classic case for me was my women's lacrosse coach: Coach Hart. So appropriately named because she was just that: all heart! One of the most profound influences on my character and life philosophy when I was in high school, Coach Hart had a few simple rules, one of which happened to be the inspiration to always be *All-in*. Always show up. Always give it 100%. Her mantra was, "Give it everything you've got. Don't hold back. Commit to your team, yourself and your common goal toward achieving genuine improvement and, through that, a commitment to excellence, and ultimately to victory." She also taught me not to hold back—and when I interact with others (my teammates in this case) remember that they're counting on me to always give it my best… *to leave it all out on the field!*

Double down on that with my Music Teacher, Dr. DeLuca. As a point of reference, I've played the flute with some degree of skill for most of my life. One year, when I went to my orchestra tryout, I sight-read the Mozart Flute Concerto in G—something he noticed immediately. Even though he applauded, he called me on it: "You sight-read that, didn't you?" I confessed I I had, and he said: "Don't ever do that again. When you come to play for me, bring your best or don't show up!"

It was an imprint for my life. When we're committed to something don't be lazy. *The real trick to playing all-in is to know why you want to do what you want to do.* This turns on our internal motivational switch and the most productive actions will follow. When you take care of your "why's" the what's will take care of themselves.

MAKING YOUR DREAMS ATTAINABLE

Q: What is the importance of setting SMART goals that are aligned with one's vision? Can you provide an example from your own experience?

A. When I started Aspire® 28 years ago I didn't know SMART goals, I just knew I wanted to create a brand of substance and impact. One that would change lives (and I assure you improving performance is life changing) while giving me financial freedom.

As I mentioned earlier, I am a working-class kid from Philly. Financial freedom was a big motivator for me. When you grow up with "limited access to wealth" it's amazing what a motivator financial security is. So my organizational goals consistently fell into 5 buckets:

1. *Strategic growth:* Stay boutique in size and delivery yet powerful in brand, while growing revenues and developing new service solutions.

2. *Client retention through measurable impact:* Happy clients don't just keep buying or referring, they are easier to collaborate with and they help you understand what the next problem you can solve for them. When you are solving problems you are providing value.

3. *Innovation as a competitive differentiator:* specifically how are we shifting human behavior—and how are we innovating in the aera of personal development and performance? (I call this People Technology®.) Also, how does this give our clients a competitive advantage; how does our work stand out from the competitive clutter?

4. *Operational effectiveness:* Focusing on our culture, our people and their competencies, our waste and error costs, technology and productivity optimization brings us to a new awareness of ourselves.

5. *Give back:* Over the years we have sponsored, participated, donated, contributed to and gifted many people and organizations, and the GIVE has always returned to us in the form of so much pride.

Maybe I did understand SMART goals at some level. In the end though my single focus was truly on how to make a meaningful difference for you and your company in such a dynamic way that you want to keep working with Aspire®.

It also comes with who you are and aligning it with who you believe you are. That is, in part, why I embrace the term, *Organizational Anthropologist,* as a way of explaining what I do, and what we do at Aspire®. Over the years, we've studied thousands of people—their behaviors, mindsets, strengths and weaknesses. We've examined all aspects of societies, of cultures, of their development and human potential. At the foundation of any brand is its "Culture."

Along the way we've also accepted the fact that it's OK that we're not everyone's flavor. For us...we deal solely with the human element. And humans are complicated! We're developers. We're coaches. We're innovators in culture, organizational effectiveness and brand strategy. Personally, I am hyper-focused on people who want to make a positive impact on their world.

Q: Let's talk for a moment about turning challenges into opportunities. How do you approach challenges or obstacles so that you can overcome them on your journey to success?

A. My belief is that challenges are windows to new opportunities. I think having the right mindset is key to dealing with life's obstacles. I start each day as a new day and set out with clear objectives. Understanding how *HeadTrash* sucks our energy and steals our creativity and ability to have clarity. HeadTrash is an epidemic. For 90% of the entire planet, their internal dialogue can be self-defeating and limiting in so many ways. People tend to function in a Survival or Disconnected Mode...not a *Thriving* and *Connected Mode.* They spend their days and nights in a scarcity mindset. Not a prosperity mindset. So when we encounter HeadTrash in our lives,

I have a proven three-step process: **Own it. Shift it. Dump it.** It's simple enough when you say it. Practicing it is another matter. But once you address it, and do it every day, eventually it becomes second nature.

A classic example is one that affected us all in one way or another: That came like a bludgeon with the Pandemic in 2020 when COVID-19 managed to devastate us all. For a little perspective, from the period between March 2020 and June 2021, 43% of all US businesses had to close down for a prolonged period of time and/or lay-off most of their staff, while another 19% closed their doors for good.

For me it was the first time in 25 years that my firm lost money. But that wasn't really what kept me up at night. Fortunately, for me, I always understood that "cash is king." So I had saved my money. What made COVID a very challenging period for me was that, for the first time in two-and-a-half decades, I had to lay people off; in fact, most of our team.

I saw the pain in their eyes: their disappointment in me and their fear for their future. Aspire® had always had a clear purpose-driven culture. And it had been one of our strengths that we always retained people who cared deeply.

Knowing I disappointed them was hell. And then watching those left behind burnout and struggle with their own HeadTrash took me to my knees. I think this is where entrepreneurs and business leaders need to understand that they have a journey too. And dealing with their own feelings of inadequacy and how to rise above it requires help. We are only alone when we choose to be. I am so grateful for my mentors and especially to my husband who helped me see that not everything is my responsibility and that I can still care for people who are struggling with my decisions.

Q: What is the importance of taking consistent action toward your goals? Can you share a personal experience where consistent action led to significant progress?

A. Having goals is the easy part of creating a compelling future. The real magic lies in consistency. *Example:* We all want to lead a healthy lifestyle but actually exercising daily can be a huge challenge for any number of reasons. The clue to progress is in the discipline of being consistent.

For me having a healthy mental attitude each day has been the single biggest asset. When I learned the power of my head and heart working in tandem I found what for me would be the secret sauce of what is an extraordinary life.

Q: **How do you overcome procrastination and stay focused on your priorities? What time management techniques or strategies do you employ?**

A. Every Sunday I regroup for the following week—moving things I didn't get done last week onto this week's calendar. *And* reprioritizing my World lowers my stress and limits the impact of the endless chaos that owning a company can bring.

I block my time including my personal time: time to meditate, journal and do my yoga; time for the people I love; time for the biggest things I need to get done.

I also do a *Monthly Priorities List,* which I look at each Sunday to see where I am against the things that matter most. I start looking at what needs to get done and I start chunking it down into smaller pieces. I do the thing I don't want to do first.

Above all else, my favorite tool is my *Joy Journal* and the 5 questions that get me ready for a productive day:

I. What is *my word of the day?* (Peter started me on this question years ago, and I just love that it aligns my mind and intention in a nanosecond!)

II. What *HeadTrash* do I need to dump from yesterday? This question allows you to "own" your HeadTrash so you can start to shift out of it. (Own it.)

III. *What did I accomplish yesterday?* This question allows you to feel good about whatever small or large accomplishments you had and begins to shift you into a positive and productive mindset.

IV. *What is most important for me to accomplish today?* This question shifts you into clarity which leads to productive action. (Shift it.)

V. *What am I grateful for?* Gratitude allows us to move out of our HeadTrash and infuses us with feelings of appreciation and perspective.

Q: When it comes to maximizing productivity, what techniques or strategies do you employ to master time management and maximize productivity?

A. I think *mastering time management* is a skill every entrepreneur and leader must have to keep all the trains running. My time management is not fancy. It is simple. And if I don't do it, I accomplish significantly less.

I re-prioritize at the end of each day for tomorrow. I review my *360 for Life Plan*® quarterly. So I stay focused on the big picture. I always block 2 hours a day for my self-care regardless of what time. Everyone is different. The secret lies in figuring out what works best for you. You have to have a process as time management is a just process. Everyone can learn a process, and a repetitive process becomes a habit. Optimizing your time is a habit worth having.

GROWTH THROUGH KNOWLEDGE

Q: Why is continuous learning important in personal and professional growth? How do you seek new knowledge and stay curious in your field or industry?

A. I think that my success has been grounded in a love of learning. If you aren't a learner you aren't a grower. I find what I don't know far more interesting than what I do. One of the reasons I belong to *EO* (Entrepreneurs Organization) is for the endless learning I gain. When we learn we broaden our minds and that opens up all possibilities. I attend conferences of all kinds to learn about what I do not know—whether it be health, business, economics, leadership, self-development. You name it, I am all-in.

I was raised by 2 teachers, both marvelous in many individual ways, and they instilled in me a love of reading and learning. We were a camping family and traveled around the USA and Canada all in the delight of learning and experiencing different cultures. We watched *60 Minutes* every Sunday evening and proceeded to talk about what ever topics were presented. We talked about our day and our world every night at dinner. My parents set the stage for a love of learning and the joy you bring into your life through endless curiosity.

From the beginning, Aspire® understood that we weren't really a training company or even a performance improvement company. We knew that the only reason anyone hired us was *to shift human behavior.* This sole focus was key to my mission. This led me to study human behavior. *"What made some people successful while others never rose above mediocrity? What allowed some people to risk changing their patterns to improve while others lived in the status quo."*

This became a cornerstone of the work I focused on and quickly became a key competitive difference as Aspire's training methodologies and content were, and continue to be, original work, all of which has a proven processes and intellectual property. So, curiosity and a thirst for new knowledge was the foundation of Aspire from the beginning.

Q: How do you embrace feedback and adapt to change?

A. I think feedback is a love-hate relationship. I think that all feedback is of value, and it is how we give it that allows a person to have it. I remember I learned this the hard way. At a big Aspire® leadership meeting, we had just done 360s for all of our senior leadership.

Unfortunately, the facilitator did not understand how to facilitate the feedback process. It was delivered without compassion, felt impersonal and made people feel incompetent. And as a result, people emotionally started falling apart. This was an invaluable lesson for me as a leader, a coach and a human being. Critical feedback is hard for anyone to have unless it is put in a constructive and empowering framework. I believe that moving from a place of love and compassion must be at the heart of how feedback, especially critical or negative feedback, is delivered. People need to know you believe in them and that you care enough to give them insights that will propel them to their potential. I think we all can embrace change when we feel it is safe to make the change.

Change is easy. It is sustaining that change over time that is hard! That requires consistency and dedication to the process…bringing us all back to the basics: that in order to change you have to have the desire to change and carry with it the determination to do so. That takes work.

Q: When it comes to Harnessing the Power of Connections, how has networking and collaboration contributed to your success?

A. I believe collaboration is at the heart of all great relationships. Our entire operation is based upon helping others maximize their potential. This has been key to Aspire's success. Every program we have built over 28 years, and there have been thousands, has been built with a focus on collaboration. I believe this has been our real secret sauce and allowed us to have 90% plus retention of our clients year over year for over 25 years.

All relationships require a commitment of time, energy and exchange. They take work. There is no shortcut. If you want a strong relationship you have to make the effort. Find common ground and build on it. Be in dialogue with people. No one is interested in a monologue. You need the synergy of positive feedback and emotional engagement. I have a goal of staying in touch with 10 people per week, and I find joy in making that connection without expectation of any outcome.

Q: Balancing Well-being and Ambition is subjective for everyone. So what is the significance of self-care in maintaining balance and well-being while pursuing ambitious goals?

A. You're right, it is subjective. And I personally think *Balance is BS*. We are in balance when we are spending our life in joy, which is my definition of success. My ambition has been fueled by my contribution to others; so the two live in a healthy kind of co-existence. And that brings in a kind of *homeostasis* on its own.

I prioritized my health and quality time with my daughter at the top of my never-ending to do list. I have always loved my work so working hard was easy. And my wanderlust and curiosity took me around the world. I found ways to enjoy life without worrying about am I in balance? I think balance reflects what you value at that time in your life.

For me, I set goals every year and then map them into my calendar especially the personal one. If you don't block time you won't get things done that are not habits yet. I find that this helps me with consistency, which can be a big challenge. I often prioritize everyone over myself and often found myself with a never-ending to do list with my needs nowhere on the list!

I reflect on what habits I need to dump and what habits I want to create in my life. I also start my day with a very specific pattern. I meditate, journal and do my yoga first. And I do so with a sense of priority because these help me get my head into a productive state—what I call being on the connected side of my emotional brain. If I start my day reading email or watching the sometimes horrifying news featured on the morning shows I will likely get caught up in the swill, get annoyed or start to worry about things I can't control. This in turn puts me on the disconnected (negative) side of my emotional brain. Nothing positive comes from negativity.

For years, I have spent months at the beach. I have always worked remotely during this time, and I find that I am not just able to relax but I also get creative, productive and focused. Breathing in helps me imagine. Every book I have written as been at the beach. I have built every business plan at the beach. I find clarity at the beach. So, giving myself time at the beach has shaped me and my firms in endless ways.

Q: On Recognizing Achievements…Why is it important to celebrate milestones along the journey? Can you share a memorable milestone or achievement that you celebrated and how it impacted your motivation?

A. Personally, I find it hard to acknowledge my own achievements. I don't want to feel like I am boasting. I think the best acknowledgment of my achievements are when they're recognized through others. I remember a few years back, Aspire had their annual team retreat, and we were standing at sundown in a big circle and one of my senior leaders said she wished that there was a candle that could be lit for all the people I have impacted through my work. I was stunned by the comment. And then I thought: *Who else can I help?* So I'm not driven by recognition, or things that I have accomplished. Awards still surprise me, because the real "reward" lies in the act of co-creation when we are truly able to empower others and watch them shine.

To that degree, I've come to realize that milestones have a significance in one's life if for no other reason than they allow others to see that achievement in any profession is deserving of note. So, after all…there have been many milestones over the years and the latest one was Aspire's 25th Anniversary. I had just published my fifth book. The book came out on February 14, 2020. It was obsolete on March 20th. The shortest book launch ever thanks to COVID-19.

For us, as a team, we moved into what we had done at other difficult times: *We built our Resilience Plan.* There are four focus areas to that plan:

1. **Revenue:** What can we do to retain the business we have and who might still need us?

2. **Operations:** What do we need to cut, streamline, improve?

3. **Opportunity:** What opportunities do we now need to focus on?

4. **Give:** How can we give? How can we support others?

It was the 4th component—*Give*—that really motivated our team. We started coaching executives for free. *We did 82 free Zoom speeches to help inspire teams across the globe.* We gave our time and our minds and our energy.

I think that *Gratitude* is always the best way to celebrate. It just feels good to give. Even in the darkness, it is the light that shines.

Q: How do you acknowledge and appreciate your achievements? What role does gratitude play in recognizing success?

A. *Gratitude* is at the heart of my life, and it is what helps me when I am at my worst. When I am worried, afraid, feeling like a failure I lean into gratitude and that brings me light. This isn't just in business. This is in my life.

Every year and then every quarter within the year I build out what I call my *360 for Life Plan©*. It has 4 elements:

• My compelling vision for the next year. What will it look like?

- Clarify my values and new behaviors or habits I want to add into my life.

- *SMART Goals:* Key actions I will take by each life element: family, friends, self-care, health, business, finance, philanthropy (giving back)

I measure where I am at the beginning of the year on a scale of 1 to 10 and then check in and reflect on it all quarterly. This tool started as a Renie tool and has been so instrumental in living my dreams. It became a tool we used with all of our executive coaching work to help others imagine and create the life they dream with intention. When we are intentional we achieve.

The Intangibles of Achievement: Ultimately, watching people who have worked for Aspire® move on and live their next chapter and evolve into their dreams brings me immeasurable joy. They may not actively think of me, but I sure do love to watch them shine. Recently, I had a previous employee tell me that, "You sure know how to create outstanding teams." *Translation:* What I really knew how to do was hire outstanding people and give them something to believe in. They did the rest.

Parenthood: Nothing defines what you truly value like being a parent. It is by far the hardest job on earth, at least for me. I was 39 when my daughter, Bella, arrived in my life. It remains by far the best day of my life and the day everything changed for me. When I thought about what mattered most, the answer was not just my daughter but being the kind of mother she would be proud of—all while knowing with absolute certainty that she was loved for whoever she wanted to be. Early on, parenthood taught me the value of boundaries.

There wasn't a client that I worked with who didn't know that when I had Bella (her dad and I shared her time) I was in my garage at 6 p.m. with my phone off. I never walked in the house with my phone on or talking on it. I would take calls on the way home. And as soon as I hit the garage door remote I would say, "I have one minute before I must say goodbye and be a Mama."

I would never take calls in the evenings. And if I worked at it all, it was because Bella and I were both "doing homework" together. For the most part, I worked after she went to bed. I went to all her volleyball games, dance performances and school events; and I went with her Dad. She never had to feel pressure and she was taught that she had all the love in her heart she would ever need. It would never run out, so she didn't have to worry about having enough.

I also managed my travel carefully and only traveled when I didn't have Bella. I think Bella was solely responsible for teaching me how to lay down boundaries that reflected my values. Sometimes motivation comes from sources we never suspect.

And that in itself is a cause for gratitude.

~RC

CHAPTER 22

Meet Joe Polish

Master Connector. Athlete. Author.
Genius Network® Founder. Genius!

J oe Polish, on his own, could be the Recruitment Poster Marine for two of our Dream Factory Chapters. "Chapter 8: Turning Obstacles into Opportunities," and "Chapter 1: Unlocking Your Inner Genius Through Self Belief." And it isn't by accident that his primary company is known as the Genius Network® because that's what he's spent a lifetime teaching others how to do—and in some revolutionary ways none of us could imagine until now.

Often billing himself as, "From Dead Broke Carpet Cleaner To One Of The Most Connected Businessmen On The Planet!" Joe Polish has by 2023 become one of the most sought-after marketers alive today. Known for his ability to connect with almost anyone in the world, he leverages his networking prowess to bring together the top industry transformers and leaders from the four corners of the Planet Earth. His mission is to change the global conversation around addiction and recovery from one of judgment to one of compassion. And it starts, not surprisingly, with his own story…and in his own words:

"My mother died of cancer when I was just four years old. My father was heartbroken from my mother's death. My brother was screwed up as well.

Through it all, I felt scared and was, in every way, very disconnected. After my high school graduation, I spent three full months freebasing cocaine *every single day*. At my worst state, I weighed 105 pounds. And yet the bottom was still not in sight. Finally, in one single day, I did every drug you can think of. And as a result, I came an inch from death by overdose.

"Finally, a choice 'to get better or die,' I cut ties with all my 'friends,' moved a state away, and got sober. After a series of odd jobs, I became a failing carpet cleaner. What saved me was the discovery that I loved marketing. And very soon, I learned to apply enough sound marketing practices to explode my business into something that got the attention of people and places that mattered…From there, I branched out to teach others how to do the same. As a networking spinoff, my idea for Bill Phillips's 'Body of Life,' raised the most money ever compiled for Make-A-Wish® Foundation. And by 2004, my *Nightingale-Conant* Marketing Course became the 'top seller in the world.' So there I was in a matter of a few short years, going from being dead-broke to making millions and helping others to the same. A great success story if there ever was one. And yet I felt there were still a few pieces out of place in my life.

"Around this time, I still found myself living a double life: successful in my forward-facing business, but privately in a lot of pain and turmoil. Toxic relationships, embezzlement by an employee, my father dying, workaholism—addictions…of a different kind, but addictions nonetheless. Navigating this treacherous emotional terrain, the only guiding light at the time were those golden hours, those special evenings, I spent sitting around in circles, sharing with others in recovery groups…and feeling the unbridled honesty that came from them all.

"Recovery circles showed me one indelible Truth: *Everyone has pain* (and addictions in whatever form they may take). No matter how successful or famous people may become, we all have hidden dragons. This is especially true of Entrepreneurs who are often addicted to work. But no business groups were ever addressing an Entrepreneur's pain and suffering. Partly because success can be an illusion in itself. Unless you balance the rest of your life, it can easily become just another drug.

"Anyhow, one day in 2004, a Client, Robin Robins—who just paid me $6 K for 2 hours of consulting—suggested that I start a year-long business group where I would bring together the brightest marketing minds and the best entrepreneurs from various sectors of the marketplace. From that point, I asked her how much she'd pay for such a group and she told me: '$25,000.' So I took her suggestion *and* her check, and Genius Network® was formed.

"It's powerful right out of the gate. Abundance360 was started inside Genius Network®. (Peter Diamandis sold it for millions in 2018.) We birthed Arianna Huffington's marketing campaign for her book *Thrive,* and it debuted at #1 on the New York Times Non-Fiction Bestseller List. Richard Branson spoke at my first Genius Network®. I started Entrepreneur trips to Necker Island and raised millions for *Virgin Unite.* So here I was: curating Genius. And a lot of big stuff was happening!

"STILL I FELT SOMETHING ESSENTIAL WAS MISSING FROM THE GROUP

"That's why, in 2015, I took the Genius Network® stage and—at great risk—revealed all my own personal "stuff." Because I was hoping it would help the group evolve. So I took a deep breath, walked out in front of thousands of people, shared all aspects of my 'very private self,' and revealed ALL my addictions…*Every Single One.* **In so doing, *I took the lid off the box of "Me," and I laid it all out there.*** In front of all my peers.

"That's the day Genius Network® up-leveled to a place where people not only could grow their businesses, but also recover their health, save their marriages, become better fathers and mothers, more reliable friends and even mentors.

"MY MISSION IN TODAY'S MARKET IS TWO-FOLD:

1) To help build a better Entrepreneur through an E.L.F.® *(Easy, Lucrative, and Fun!)* life and business; and…

2) Help change the global conversation about how others view and treat addicts.

"Yes, I love marketing, ***but I'm driven to help reduce human suffering, and I know connection is the way.***

"Any problem can be solved with the right Genius Network®. In addition to building a better Entrepreneur, we build-in solving the addiction problem... ***When it comes to dealing with dependencies... let's focus on the pain that causes the problem, over the addiction itself.***

"Addiction means something different to everyone. For Entrepreneurs, it usually means workaholism to escape life's other problems... or another addiction to escape work!

"THE GENIUS RECOVERY MISSION IS TO CHANGE THE GLOBAL CONVERSATION AROUND ADDICTION AND RECOVERY.

This is the place where you exponentially grow your income, get solutions to EVERY ONE of your personal and professional challenges, nurture your most critical connections and wake up Your Own True Genius."

~ Joe Polish

In 2023, Joe Polish and Genius Network® have achieved levels of success beyond even his wildest imaginings. The Networker's Networker, his podcasts and broadcasts have featured such world-famous self-empowerment gurus such as Sir Richard Branson, Tony Robbins and Jim Kwik. His books, *The Average Joe's MARKETING BOOK* and *What's In It For Them?* are Amazon.com bestsellers. And his audio/video lectures are fan favorites to hundreds of thousands of listeners and viewers. His Genius Network® concept, along with his own remarkable story has been shared on the pages of such national publications as *The Huffington Post, Forbes, Fortune, Entrepreneur, SUCCESS Magazine, INC* and ABC Network.

Since Joe is the consummate expert on all aspects of both Networking and Marketing, it is only appropriate that we tap into his genius here: on the subject he has virtually mastered over any other...

HOW "NETWORKING" CAN MAKE YOU MORE SUCCESSFUL

The secret to success in life and in business is learning how to connect and form relationships with other people. "Networking" has come to mean shallow conversations, transactional relationships, and the anxiety of impressing other people so that they'll do something for you, or give you something you want. Setting this kind of intention spawns the classic acronym: WIFM (What's In It For Me?). And it ultimately brands the entire concept as exploitive and self-serving.

But that's not what Networking has to be. In fact, when you change your perspective on how you interact with others so you can make the right connections with the right people in the right way, in any situation, it can create a paradigm shift that can alter your life forever.

How do you do this? By asking one simple question: **WHAT'S IN IT FOR THEM?** By asking this question, you shift the focus off "You" and onto the ways "you can be useful to others." *You get out of the transactional networking mindset and start to form transformational, meaningful, and collaborative relationships.*

Asking the right question over and over lets you connect with people by figuring out what they need, helping them get it, and making their lives better. In a very real way, by forming the right kind of Q&A matrix, you're finding ways to reduce other people's suffering...and helping them create "Wins." By reducing others' suffering, you become a magnetic and valuable person— someone other people highly regard and want to collaborate with.

ONE CONNECTION CAN CHANGE YOUR LIFE

At the outset, I started my working life as a dead-broke carpet cleaner in Chandler, Arizona. I set up my own carpet-cleaning business with all my savings—$1,500—because I wanted a better future, but also because I didn't have any better options. I quickly learned that carpet cleaning is dirty, hard work. Over time, I moved away from doing the actual cleaning, shifted my business toward selling carpet-cleaning services, and eventually moved into selling and marketing products and services— billions of dollars worth—for businesses of all kinds. As my business grew, there were moments—lessons and relationships—that helped propel me forward. I think of these as "dominos," because like dominos falling, each experience leads to the next one in a chain reaction that keeps going and going—all in very positive and magical ways. In fact, one of these first dominos was what I've titled *"The Jet Ski Millionaire."*

HERE'S THE STORY: When I was a dead broke carpet cleaner living off credit cards, I found myself questioning my decision. It seemed like no matter how hard I worked, I was sinking deeper and deeper into debt. My strategy changed after a friend of mine invited me to go *jet skiing* with a couple of guys up at Saguaro Lake. He said that a successful real estate investor would be there, and I thought I might learn something from him (even though I was so broke that taking a Saturday away from work was hard; hard enough to be highly distracting).

At the lake, I explained my situation to this man sitting on the tailgate of a pickup truck—how I wasn't making money in carpet cleaning and wondered if there wasn't a better business to go into. "Does anybody in your business make money?" he asked. I told him that a few people did. "Then the business isn't the problem. You're the problem."

As I drove home that evening with a bad sunburn, I came to the conclusion that he was right. I was just as capable as anyone else. Surely, I could make a carpet cleaning business work. After reading more books about business and systems thinking, I learned about systematizing the best parts of a business to make it work more efficiently. With that, inspiration struck. I would optimize the part that made me money: MARKETING. And, from a business point of view, it worked.

Within six months, I went from grossing $2,100 in an average month to grossing $12,300. At that, I stopped thinking only about cleaning carpets and shifted my focus to messaging and marketing...and my business continued growing from there.

The point is the meeting I had with that "Jet Ski Millionaire" was a connection that opened a new way of thinking to me and changed my life.

HOW YOU CAN BUILD YOUR OWN GENIUS NETWORK

Years ago, I heard someone say that if you can't write an idea down on the back of a napkin it's probably not worth doing. Later, I heard a line from the late copywriter Gary Halbert: "Any problem in the world can be solved with the right sales letter."

I'm going to add to that wisdom and say: "Any problem in the world can be solved with the right Genius Network"—which is simply a network of people who have skills, capabilities, and genius you can access whenever you need a connection, idea or solution—*People who can help you solve problems, meet challenges and develop opportunities.*

Connecting with other people is almost always about relieving pain on some level, even if that pain is relatively slight in the grand scheme of things. On the extreme end, think of two lonely, sad people who happen to meet, get along, and become friends. They now have a two-person "network" that helps alleviate their loneliness. While a friendship of proximity is definitely not a Genius Network, a Genius Network still operates by some of the same principles.

In a Genius Network, everyone in the group is well connected, wants to give to others, and probably has some other external markers for success—*whatever that means to them.* On the surface, it may seem like those people aren't in much pain or don't have problems—but that's simply not true. Sometimes their problems are smaller by comparison (the "pain" of not knowing how to hire a great employee for their business, for example). But sometimes the problems are as big as they come (such as the pain of hiding a fatal illness from your family and the fear that comes with it).

In other words, an average network and a Genius Network are not all that different in terms of the underlying motivation, because both can help you solve problems and create better experiences for yourself and others. The main difference is that a Genius Network is much more intentional—with people who come together to solve specific problems with the shared intention of giving to one another rather than simply taking.

When I want to solve any problem in the world, or reach any opportunity, or overcome any challenge, I ask myself who the very best people would be in whom I could invest my time, money, and energy. To do that, I use a Genius Network® tool and mindset to force my brain to search for solutions.

The idea of Genius Network® isn't something that just falls into your lap. It's about becoming a *Genius Networker* who does Genius Networking so each and every person in your realm of experience can eventually have a Genius Network.

That declaration is pretty categorical. So it inevitably prompts the question: What do I mean by that? An easy way to think of it is with a simple exercise:

1. Take a piece of paper and draw a circle in the middle.

2. Draw eight smaller circles in a ring around it.

3. In each of the smaller circles, write the name of one of the eight most important people in your life.

4. Under their name, describe their skills and capabilities.

5. Now think about how you can help each of those people. And think about how they can help you.

As this exercise helps show, Genius Networking starts with being thoughtful and learning how to be valuable to the people around you. After that, it's about connecting and spreading that value across a network—and finally, it's about using that network to solve problems. The right Genius Network is always the best tool for solutions.

To use the tool, first identify an area you want to improve: a relationship you want to grow or a problem you want to solve. Next, identify the most valuable relationships you have in your life, what they want, and the capabilities they have. Finally, determine how you can be most helpful to them.

In essence, the "My Genius Network®" tool forces you to consider the following:

1. Who are they?

2. What do they want?

3. What capabilities do they have?

4. What do I know and what can I do to be most useful to them?

This capability only works long term with someone who has developed their character and good intentions and who follows through with congruent action. It is a tool that works to the degree you involve yourself with it authentically and engage with it from there. If you are willing to do that, it will be very valuable to you.

INVEST IN RELATIONSHIPS THAT MOVE TOWARD ACCELERATING YOUR SUCCESS

You've heard the saying: "Time is money." To me, and to anyone who defines true success as being happy and accomplished in the world, *relationships are money*. The distinction is important, because many people who are financially successful are incredibly disconnected from others—and they're some of the unhappiest people you'll ever meet as a result.

In many ways, building businesses and wealth and building relationships go together because the best thinking behind them is so similar: You have to be a long-term investor to see real results.

Creating great relationships, like creating great wealth or big impact, begins with your mindset. People who view relationships as transactions act like they are in the transaction business. People who view relationships as having long term value behave like they're in the relationship business.

Another way to think of *transactional versus transformative relationships is the difference between spending and investing*. They may sound similar, but they are completely different. *Spending* refers to the necessary costs of an undertaking, costs that are often unpleasant. *Investing* is adopting a long-term mindset and accumulating positive, generative energy.

A "spending mindset" doesn't work when you want to meet and befriend the right people. Burning through relationships via short-term, transactional exchanges leaves you depleted. The only way that pattern can sustain itself is by finding greater and greater numbers of people *(i.e.* victims) to take advantage of. But, sooner or later, it almost always catches up with the person doing all the taking.

When people act this way, it's as if they're treating every interaction with people they meet like an overnight stay at a cheap motel they were forced to stop at on a road trip. Life may be a journey, but at least some of the people we meet along the way should become our traveling companions.

Adopting the investing mindset is like frequenting the local restaurant where the owner knows your name, knows your family, and all the staff are your friends… and you don't even need to look at the menu because the server knows your order.

Investing time, money, and energy in relationships means looking at everyone as an investment, not a cost. It's nuanced, because being too stingy or unwilling to spend your time, attention, money, effort, and energy won't result in the rich life and deep relationships you want, but neither will be spending those resources thoughtlessly on anyone who crosses your path.

As in all things, you need a good framework to be effective. Fortunately, when it comes to relationships, the framework you need is just one sentence long.

THE ONE SENTENCE SOLUTION FOR GROWING YOUR RELATIONSHIPS...

In 2000, Ben Hunt-Davis captained the British national men's rowing team. Ben gave the team a question to ask before every decision made and every action taken in and out of practice: "Will this make the boat go faster?" If the team considered going to the pub the night before training, they asked themselves, "Will this make the boat go faster?" If the answer was "No!" They did not go. (Here's a tip: *If you have to ask, the answer is usually no.*)

With the difference that one question made in their behavior, they won gold at the 2000 Sydney Olympics. To go for gold in your relationships, you can use the same strategy.

Before doing something, ask yourself: ***Does this grow the relationship?***

Establishing a connection is great, but good relationships are also about growth. After you've planted a seed of time, attention, money, effort, and energy, you can't just walk away. To see it grow into a tall tree with a thick trunk, you need to keep watering and tending to it.

The caveat, of course, is that not all growth is created equal. You can grow a mighty oak tree. Or you can grow a cancer that subdivides in geometric progressions and invades every vital organ. Not all growth is progress, and not all growth is helpful. The key is to make sure, after you pour in your resources, that your relationships are mutually beneficial, rather than destructive. As you dedicate yourself to growing trees, you'll have to routinely check to see whether or not they are actually producing fruit.

The lesson for how you deploy your time, attention, money, effort, and energy is simple: Relationships have a built-in feedback mechanism called growth. Any relationship, positive or negative, will develop and grow as you invest more and more.

The question is, are you growing together in the right direction? Or are you spiraling off into the darkness? What are the by-products or fruits of your relationship? What internal and external transformation is it producing? Ignore the feedback that growth offers at your peril.

The lesson is: *Make the choices that make the boat go faster. Your relationship will keep growing. And so will you...*

~ JP

CHAPTER 23

Meet Bronwyn Bridges

PragmaClin Co-Founder/CEO. PhD. Psychologist. Genius!

H i! My name is Bronwyn Bridges. Born and raised in Summerside, PEI! I was brought up alongside my older brother Blaize by my mom Patti, a full-time long-term care nurse and my dad Phil, a sports fanatic who always took on new endeavors. From an early age, I fell in love with volunteering and spent a lot of my time at the long-term care home with my mom. I began sitting on boards as a youth representative, where I learned that, regardless of age, my opinions mattered.

I was 14 when I was diagnosed with PTSD, and although a tough time in my life, it allowed me to learn valuable lessons about perseverance and to help raise awareness on suicide prevention, mental health and to push the boundaries for equal and efficient access to health care. My drive to be able to give back over the years ended up in my receipt of Youth of the Year, the Terry Fox Humanitarian Scholarship, the National Impact Award, and numerous others acknowledging my strides within the community.

I took a Bachelor of Science in Biology and Psychology to explore the space I enjoyed most and fell in love with —Parkinson's Disease (PD) research. I went on to begin a Masters of Pharmacy in PD, which transitioned to a PhD when I met Gord.

During the COVID-19 pandemic, I co-founded PragmaClin, a revolutionary MedTech company. We designed a cutting-edge digital assessment tool targeting neurological conditions, particularly Parkinson's Disease. Through sheer determination and a flair for entrepreneurship, I've been successful in securing over one million dollars in non-dilutive government funds and over half a million dollars from pitch competitions. I am grateful to have been given the opportunities to present at numerous prestigious conferences, winning the grand prize at international competitions, and in 2022 was recognized as one of Atlantic Canada's *30 Under 30*.

Today, I stand tall, proud of my journey, and ever passionate about driving change in the healthcare landscape. As I move forward, I hope my story inspires others to follow their passions and make a lasting impact in the fields they are truly passionate about.

AN AUTHOR'S NOTE: I had the opportunity to watch Bronwyn do her live "pitch" as she competed for the 2023 Global Student Awards. Bronwyn became passionate about working on tools to diagnose and treat Parkinson's decease. She had earned her Bachelor of Science in Biology and Psychology and was enrolled in a PhD program.

Bronwyn was polished, professional, in charge, had a fully operating company, PragmaClin, and a revolutionary Med Tech company with several employees. She had already learned how to file for and receive government grants—a difficult thing for anyone to navigate—and knew how to line up mentors; all this before age 26. Bronwyn has so much to teach us, I felt she just had to share both her philosophy and her personal path to achievement on the pages of *The Dream Factory.* And she has graciously consented to do just that...

DREAMING BIG AND DEFINING YOUR VISION— THE POWER OF VISUALIZATION

Q: How important is it to have big dreams and a clear vision when pursuing success?

A: There's this idea floating around that you've got to have this super clear, step-by-step roadmap if you want to be successful in life. But honestly? That's not the whole truth. What really matters? It's the dreams we hold onto, the big, wild, "shoot-for-the-stars" kind of dreams that keep us going.

These dreams are the reason we wake up each morning, excited to make a difference in whatever way that is. Without those dreams, even the most meticulously plotted journey can feel like you're just going through the motions. The big and ambitious dreams are the ones that keep us up at night, thinking about all the ways we could make them happen.

Embrace those wild dreams, visualize them, chase after them, and let them light up your way. Visualizing the "dream" and not just the pathway to get there lays a foundation for how we are able to build our own version of success. The more we manifest the dream, the more we live it each day.

Q: Can you share a personal experience where visualization played a significant role in achieving your dreams?

A: Growing up, anxiety was a constant companion for me—often making me worry about whether things would turn out as planned. Pursuing my bachelor's degree was punctuated with challenges, particularly a series of major concussions that weighed me down during exams. My aspiration was to delve into occupational therapy, yet I faced rejection from five Canadian universities. However, when one door closed, another opened: I was presented with a fully funded opportunity in a province I never imagined moving to, but that aligned with my passion in the medical space that I adored.

That's when I had a paradigm shift. Instead of fixating on every single hurdle, I focused on the bigger picture: my burning desire to contribute meaningfully to healthcare. I vividly visualized moments with people with Parkinson's Disease, filled with genuine connection and laughter. That vision underscored that the journey's specifics mattered less than the destination itself. Embracing this mindset, I took bold strides forward, transforming my "what if" worries into optimistic possibilities, always open to the wonder of the unexpected. Had I become fixated on the negative "what ifs," I wouldn't be where I stand today.

Q: What strategies or techniques do you recommend for readers to tap into their imagination and create a vivid mental image of their desired future?

A: One of my go-to techniques for manifesting a desired future is affirmations. When we remind ourselves daily that we are beautiful, over time, we begin to genuinely see our beauty. When we confidently state our aspirations, like earning a salary bonus, it motivates us to work towards that goal. Every morning, dedicate a moment to three affirmations that resonate with your dreams and aspirations. Visualization, paired with unwavering action and determination, becomes an unparalleled force. By consistently affirming and visualizing your dreams, you're setting yourself on a trajectory to achieve them.

Q: Could you please tell me a story as an example?

A: One of the most impactful techniques I've embraced is the use of affirmations, particularly before high-pressure situations like pitch competitions. In the hours, or even just moments leading up to my presentation, I would immerse myself in a vivid visualization exercise. I'd picture the audience, not just as passive listeners, but as engaged participants, hanging onto every word, nodding in agreement, and eventually erupting in applause. I would delve deeply into my aspirations, visualizing not just the immediate success of the pitch, but also the broader dreams they were tied to. Whether it was the launch of a revolutionary product, the building connections with industry leaders, or achieving a personal milestone, these visual exercises made them feel tangible, right at my fingertips. This practice not only calmed my nerves but also filled me with a confidence and purpose that shone through during the actual presentation. During the GSEA 2023, this exact moment happened, and the visualization felt so real, it brought pure and raw emotion to this very moment on stage. Never underestimate the power of visualization.

ESTABLISHING YOUR VALUES

Q: **How did you identify and define your core values, and how have they influenced your journey to success?**

A: Honestly, figuring out my core values wasn't like flipping on a light switch. It was more like piecing together a puzzle, where every experience, be it a win or a face-plant moment, added a piece. The late nights, challenging decisions, and even those 'oops' moments at the start of it all, has taught me what mattered most. I realized that integrity wasn't just about honesty but standing by your word even when it's tough. Empathy wasn't just understanding others, but genuinely rooting for their success. Over time, these values became my compass, shaping my decisions and guiding PragmaClin's direction. Success isn't just about the end game; it's about how you play. And these values? They've been my playbook.

Q: **Can you share an example of a time when aligning your actions and decisions with your values led to a more fulfilling and purpose-driven life?**

A: There have been a few crossroad moments for PragmaClin. A few of these situations were similar in which through conversations with investors ended up in them wanting to know what other diseases we were planning to tackle. Stating that "Parkinson's wasn't a big enough market." Investors want you to pivot to more "profitable" demographics for a better exit. The numbers made sense, but my gut was doing this weird flip-flop thing. My values screamed at me: We'd built this company on the premise of Gord's life experience, the lack of Parkinson's care, and making a genuine difference. It wasn't just about profits for us; it was about purpose.

So, I took a deep breath and explained that, although in the future it may be on our roadmap, we were not focused on becoming a unicorn by tomorrow. We wanted to make a true difference in a space we knew needed it most. We have shut down conversations with investors and chased the much more tedious non-dilutive funding routes that were more aligned with our mission. That decision not only validated our company's direction but also reminded me that when your actions mirror your values, you don't just chase success; you live a story that's so much richer and fulfilling.

Q: What advice would you give to readers who are struggling to identify their core values?

A: Defining core values isn't like choosing a new pair of sneakers. But here's a bit of wisdom from my playbook, so take it with a grain of salt.

First of all, think about the moments in your life that made you super proud, or conversely made you cringe. Your reactions in those situations provide massive hints about what truly matters to you. Then, have real raw conversations with yourself. Forget about what's "trendy" or what others expect from you. Dive deeply. Be willing to take risks. Find out what lights a fire in you? What's non-negotiable? Engage in introspection, and maybe even jot down your thoughts. It's okay if your list changes; we're all works in progress. But as you navigate this journey, remember: Your core values are your compass. They guide your actions, decisions, and define your personal brand. So, take the time, do the work, and trust in the process. Embracing your values will make your journey – whether in business or life – so much more authentic and impactful.

UNLOCKING YOUR INNER GENIUS THROUGH SELF-BELIEF

Q: How important is self-belief in unlocking one's true potential? Can you share an experience where cultivating self-confidence led to breakthrough results?

A: In this vast world of business, self-belief is everything. Let me dish out a story that paints the picture. There I was, fresh-faced and ready, meeting a seasoned contractor in his 50s. You could see the skepticism in his eyes from a mile away. Our initial encounter was a test of my self-confidence; every gesture and word from him seemed designed to put me in my "place."

Admittedly, I wasn't as self-assured as I'd have liked to be during that first meeting. Yet, my core belief in myself and my capabilities remained unshaken. As our meetings and check-ins over time continued, it became clear that his respect for me was not on par with the value I brought to the table. In the end, prioritizing my self-worth and to continue being at the forefront of the company, I confided in my co-founder that I was uncomfortable continuing to extend our work with them. This decision wasn't just about business; it was about knowing my worth and setting standards for how I deserved to be treated. Your belief in yourself can shift the energy in the room, breaking barriers and overturning biases. So, for anyone out there doubting themselves, remember: the belief you hold in yourself isn't just a guiding light; it's your north star. And when situations or people don't align with that, sometimes the best power move is to walk away.

Q: What strategies or exercises do you recommend for readers to overcome self-doubt and tap into their inner genius?

A: Let's get real; every one of us faces self-doubt, especially in this hyper-competitive world. But, you've got this untapped genius inside, and it's about time you unleashed it. First up, remind yourself that you are kind, smart and able to take on the world. It's not some fluffy self-help tactic; it's daily armor. Whisper to yourself, shout it out, or plaster it on your mirror: "I am unstoppable!"

Trust me, it works! And remember, it's okay to seek out a mentor or join a peer group. Their external perspective can often spotlight your hidden strengths you may not be able to surface on your own. Lastly, embrace continuous learning. The more you know, the more confident you become. So, go ahead, sign up for that workshop, or pick up that book. And always, ALWAYS remember, your genius isn't about being perfect; it's about harnessing your unique strengths and daring to show them to the world. Stay fierce!"

Q: Have you ever faced moments of self-doubt during your journey, and if so, how did you overcome them?

A: As a 25-year-old scientist turned CEO of a health-tech company, the weight of expectations, combined with the intricacies of leadership, often feels overwhelming to me, I couldn't count on two hands the amount of time my capability was questioned with a condescending "kiddo." That word has echoed, casting a long shadow of self-doubt through many meetings and conversations. Instead of accepting that's what I would always be to some, I did some serious self-reflection and recounted every achievement, every hurdle I'd overcome, and every milestone that I had met in time. Through that process, I came to realize that leadership wasn't about showcasing invincibility but about resilience, learning, and drawing strength from those who believe in your vision. My team knows I am not perfect, and I don't pretend to be. But remember, if you don't believe in yourself, then who will?

SELECTING YOUR MENTORS

Q: How have mentors played a role in your personal and professional growth? Can you share a specific mentorship experience that had a significant impact on your journey?

A: Navigating the complexities of leadership often felt like I was drowning in a sea of responsibilities. While participating in various accelerators expanded my horizons and introduced me to an array of influential experts, it also posed the challenge of mentor saturation. It became crucial that I started to determine who not only aligned with PragmaClin, but also with me on a personal level.

Among the mentors who've left marks on my journey, two stand out: Jonathan Rezek, who transitioned from mentor to advisor, and Thomas Arena, a mentor from an incubator in the USA.

Jonathan, with over three decades in business development, faced an unexpected challenge one day on stage. This incident would foreshadow his Parkinson's Disease diagnosis years later. His stories encompass not only his battle with PD but also invaluable lessons from his vast professional experience.

Thomas, on the other hand, is a Chief Growth Officer with a 30-year legacy of spearheading growth strategies. His expertise has been a treasure trove of wisdom for me, transforming his experiences into lessons I could internalize and learn from.

Their guidance has transcended mere business exchanges. Through countless interactions, both Jonathan and Thomas have celebrated my victories and bolstered me during challenging times. Their approach, always marked by respect and empathy, ensured that I never felt inadequate. They emphasized the uncanny equilibrium that exists to balance logic and intuition. Their mentorships went beyond corporate tactics; they were lessons in resilience, personal growth, and the silver lining in every setback. Thanks to them, I've recognized mentorship as a CEO's anchor, providing clarity in the midst of confusion and a shoulder to lean on in any moment.

Q: What qualities do you look for in mentors, and how do you establish meaningful connections with them?

A: Choosing mentors isn't just about ticking off boxes of expertise; it's a deeper connection. First and foremost, I look for authenticity. I need to know that their guidance comes from genuine experiences, not just textbook lessons. Empathy plays a colossal role. A mentor who cannot step into my shoes, albeit momentarily, may not grasp the unique challenges of leading a startup in today's age and in my realm of knowledge. Additionally, adaptability is key. The world I'm operating in isn't static; it's dynamic, changing at lightning speed. Establishing meaningful connections? That's an art form unto itself. It's about open conversations, mutual respect, and a shared vision of growth. It's less about structured meetings and more about candid coffee chats where vulnerability becomes the bridge to genuine understanding.

Q: How can readers leverage the wisdom and experience of mentors to accelerate their own success?

A: When utilizing mentors, it's not just about absorbing their knowledge, but about understanding their failures, their victories, and the nuances in between. Each story, each advice, is a lesson you don't have to learn the hard way. So, engage actively. Ask questions, the deeper, the better. But equally, listen intently. Their experiences are a goldmine of shortcuts to success. Also, a little reminder here: while mentors light the path, it's up to you to walk it. Take their wisdom, mold it to fit your narrative, and then stride forward with the kind of confidence that only comes from standing on the shoulders of giants.

MAKING YOUR DREAMS ATTAINABLE

Q: **What is the importance of setting SMART goals that are aligned with one's vision? Can you provide an example from your own experience?**

A: Turning dreams into real accomplishments begins with SMART goals—those that are Specific, Measurable, Achievable, Relevant, and Time-bound. These aren't just buzzwords; they're a roadmap to success. By adhering to SMART goals, you clear away the fog, creating a straight path towards your ultimate vision. I've learned this the hard way. Early on, without such clear goals, I often felt like I was running in circles, unsure of my progress and how my daily tasks fit into the bigger picture. This isn't just about business; it applies to personal aspirations too. Imagine wanting to lose weight; setting a goal to shed 50 pounds in a month isn't just unrealistic—it's unhealthy. However, by breaking that larger goal into smaller, SMART steps, like aiming to lose 4-5 pounds a month through diet and exercise, progress becomes clear, measurable, and motivating. This way, every step feels purposeful and takes you closer to your grand vision.

Q: **How do you break down big dreams into actionable steps? What strategies or techniques do you recommend for tracking progress?**

A: Laying out your journey starts with pinpointing crucial milestones, then diving deeper into specific tasks and even sub-tasks. Leveraging goal-tracking tools can be a game-changer, helping you stay motivated and accountable. It's about finding what resonates with you; there's an incredible number of fantastic tools out there, waiting to be explored. Our team, for instance, swears by Notion for its seamless tasks and goal-tracking without feeling overly micromanaged. On a personal note, my calendar and side to-do list are my lifelines. There's an unmatched thrill for me in ticking off a task, knowing that I'm one step closer to a grander goal. Embrace that feeling; it's the heartbeat of progress.

Q: **Have you ever faced challenges in achieving your goals, and if so, how did you overcome them?**

A: Facing challenges head-on is a principle I've always believed in. My science background has always taught me to be resourceful and question the clear. When a tough situation arises, my first instinct is to dig deep inside myself for a solution. However, I've learned the value of stepping back momentarily. A break, a session at the gym, or even a short nap can be incredibly rejuvenating and provide fresh perspectives. I'm hesitant to immediately involve my team, not wanting to divert their focus. Yet, if I find myself at a standstill, I turn to them for insights. Time and again, they've come to me with their innovative ideas and solutions. It's a testament to the collective strength and wisdom that lies in collaboration.

CULTIVATING A SUCCESS MINDSET

Q: **How does belief play a role in shaping one's reality and achieving success? Can you share a mindset shift that had a significant impact on your journey?**

A: Pantsuits. I began wearing bright and colorful pantsuits. I always thought that wearing suits was a thing that women didn't do as often. But I started wearing my "power suits," and I instantly started to notice a change in my confidence. Instead of being seen as a "cute" little girl, I was suddenly being taken seriously. People started to look at me as a successful woman. It wasn't merely the fabric or the tailoring but the profound alteration in my psyche when I entered a room. I exerted a whole other level of confidence—one in which I felt heard, seen and listened to; and considered important by a room of people who looked nothing like me. The day I started to wear pantsuits is the day everything changed for me; a true paradigm shift in my career.

Q: **What techniques or practices do you recommend for overcoming limiting beliefs and developing empowering thoughts and attitudes?**

A: "Celebrate Small Wins" is more than just a mantra; it's a philosophy that enhances the importance of acknowledging and appreciating the tiny milestones on our journey to success. In a world that often places emphasis on grand achievements, it's easy to overlook the smaller steps that pave the way. Those steps, no matter how seemingly insignificant, are the foundational blocks that create a path toward our larger goals and help us to overcome moments of self-doubt and empower our thoughts and attitudes.

Each small victory is an affirmation of our progress, resilience, and dedication. By celebrating them, we not only boost our confidence but also fuel our motivation. It's a reminder that success isn't just about the destination but the journey in itself. Each small win is a testament to our perseverance, a lesson learned, or a challenge overcome. It's a way to keep the momentum, maintain enthusiasm, and cultivate a positive mindset. In the grand tapestry of our ambitions, every thread counts, and every small win weaves into the larger picture of success. So, embrace every achievement, big or small, as they collectively shape our journey and define our stories.

Q: **How do you maintain a success-oriented mindset during challenging times or when faced with obstacles?**

A: Find your anchor. It could be a partner, a close friend, a colleague, or a family member—someone you can lean on during challenging moments, a presence that ignites a spark when all seems dark.

For me, that anchor has always been my mom. She's my steadfast listener during tough times—not always offering advice but also just a caring ear to my thoughts and emotions. She adeptly transforms negatives into lessons and keeps my success-driven mindset alive, even in moments of darkness. She gently reminds me that a difficult moment doesn't define an entire life.

TURNING CHALLENGES INTO OPPORTUNITIES

Q: **How do you approach challenges or obstacles on your journey to success? Can you share a specific example of how you turned a challenge into an opportunity?**

A: Every sunrise I'm reminded that with a new day comes with new challenges. But here's my secret sauce: I don't view challenges as roadblocks but as detours, taking me on paths less traveled, often leading to unexpected discoveries. My approach to challenges is twofold: First, I pause, breathe, and detach. It's easy to get lost in the immediacy of a situation, but perspective is everything. Next, I dissect the challenge, understanding its core and seeking hidden opportunities within. It's not about conquering or sidestepping obstacles, it's about integrating them into my narrative, allowing them to shape and refine my journey to success. Remember, it's the grit and grind that gives the diamond its shine. Challenges? They're just part of the journey.

One of the biggest obstacles I faced was in balance and letting go. Balancing my PhD comprehensive exams, while simultaneously being on the ground to launch our first clinical study in Dubai seemed insurmountable. Juggling academics, office responsibilities, and the prospect of traveling felt like an uphill task. This compelled me to relinquish some control, entrusting a significant chunk of the responsibility to a team member. Such moments of vulnerability reshaped my perspective on leadership and control, teaching me the invaluable lesson of placing trust in others. This approach not only lightened my load but also catapulted our collective progress to unprecedented heights and has now opened up many more opportunities within our team for leadership growth.

Q: **What strategies or mindset shifts do you recommend for reframing obstacles and embracing the growth and learning that come from facing challenges?**

A: Every challenge, no matter how tough it seems at first, has a silver lining waiting to be revealed. Instead of seeing them as giant roadblocks, why not think of them as life's quirky detours? Whenever I hit a bump in the road, I take a breath and wonder, "What's the Universe trying to tell me?" Just this little shift in thinking can turn a tough day into a chance to learn and grow. Connect with people who think differently than you, keep soaking up new knowledge. And hey! Always remember: the best stories often come from the hardest journeys.

Q: **How do you maintain resilience and stay motivated during difficult times?**

A: I've learned that resilience isn't just about weathering the storm but dancing in the rain. When times get tough, I anchor myself to my "Why?"—the very reason I ventured into this roller-coaster of entrepreneurship in the first place. I take moments to reflect, breathe, and reconnect with the passion that ignited my journey. It's equally important to surround oneself with a tribe—people who uplift, challenge, and remind you of your strengths when you're on the brink of forgetting. And yes, self-care isn't selfish. Whether it's diving into a new novel, going to the gym, or savoring a cup of coffee, it's those little acts that rejuvenate the spirit. Everyone faces challenges. The difference lies in how we rise after a fall. Embrace failures as mere detours, not dead-ends, and let them fuel your motivation to build, iterate, and conquer.

THE KEY TO PROGRESS

Q: What is the importance of taking consistent action toward goals? Can you share a personal experience where consistent action led to significant progress?

A: In the thrilling, ever-evolving world of startups, I've come to understand that dreams don't just manifest overnight, but things can move at a fast pace. I think back to the beginning of PragmaClin and sitting at the same coffee shop with Gord, every single day, working on proposals and business plans. He would talk. I would type. We would discuss. We were building day by day, but at the time it seemed like a long and tedious process. In truth it was so much more than that.

It's not the grand gestures but the daily, deliberate efforts that create empires. Each small step might seem insignificant when viewed in isolation, but collectively, they pave the road to our visions. That business plan managed to secure our first government grant, and shortly after set us up for our first public presentation. It's easy to get swept up in the allure of "big moves," but it's the quiet, consistent grind that compounds into monumental success. I often remind my team, and myself, that success isn't a sprint—it's a marathon. Breaking things up into smaller tasks and looking back on how those actions all contribute to the larger goal is incredibly important. So, lace up, set your pace, and cherish every step of the journey. The magic lies in the momentum.

Q: How do you overcome procrastination and stay focused on your priorities? What time management techniques or strategies do you employ?

A: Reverberating from this digital age's constant buzz, where distractions lurk behind every notification, makes mastering focus an art form. For me, procrastination isn't a sign of laziness, but rather an indicator that I'm either overwhelmed or unclear about the next step. So, what is my go to? Sometimes it may be a nap. (I really love a good nap.) And afterward, I feel refreshed and ready to realign myself.

About that time, I break tasks into digestible chunks, making them less intimidating. I've grown fond of the *Pomodoro Technique,* the one that Peter Thomas recommended earlier in this book: *working intensely for 25 minutes and then rewarding myself with a 5-minute breather.*

It really works. Because it's like a rhythmic dance between focus and relaxation. To shield my priorities from the daily onslaught of demands, I rely on digital tools, but there's an old-school charm in handwritten to-do lists that never fades. Sometimes, the simplest techniques are the most transformative. Prioritizing is an ever-evolving skill, a delicate balance between the now and the next and focusing on what is urgent and, or, important.

Q: What advice would you give to readers who struggle with taking action and making progress toward their dreams?

A: Looking back on my life these past few years, I've realized dreams aren't distant stars, but luminous gems waiting to be unearthed. If you find yourself paralyzed at the threshold of your aspirations, remember: *Action is the antidote to doubt.* You will never achieve your dreams if you don't try. Starting is always the very first step, and talking about it won't get things started. Take actions. Don't let the fear and uncertainty about your dreams intimidate you. Begin with one small, tangible step. Create a ritual, whether it's jotting down your daily progress or celebrating tiny victories. For in these moments, momentum is born. Your journey isn't defined by leaps, but by the footprints of consistent effort. Embrace patience and resilience, and soon, those hesitant steps will evolve into strides of unwavering confidence. Your dreams await, not at some distant horizon, but in the magic of today's action. So, ignite that spark, and let it blaze the trail to your destiny.

THE MEANING OF ATTITUDE, MOTIVATION, AND COMMITMENT

Q: **How important is resilience in bouncing back from failure and setbacks? Can you share a time when a positive attitude helped you overcome challenges?**

A: From skyscraper highs to unexpected setbacks, my life's journey has been a roller-coaster of emotions.

The power of resilience has played a starring role both personally and professionally. At just 14, I faced one of life's harshest tests: discovering my grandfather after he tragically took his own life. The PTSD diagnosis that followed might well have held me back, but I chose to face it head-on.

Professionally, even before PragmaClin, challenges came my way regularly. But those setbacks? Those heart-wrenching moments when everything seems against you? They shape and sharpen us. Each misstep teaches us and each setback reminds us of our humanity. But true resilience isn't just about getting up; it's the spirit that drives us forward after the fall, the whisper that says, "I'm still here, and I'm not backing down." Sure, success is dazzling, but resilience is the steady flame that lights our way through life's darkest hours, leading us to new beginnings. And here's a piece of wisdom I hold dear: resilience is more than a trendy term—it's the heartbeat of every journey.

Q: **How do you maintain motivation during difficult times or when faced with failures? What role does commitment play in sustaining long-term success?**

A: The real battle isn't in achieving every goal, but in the persistence of chasing them, especially during the tumultuous times. There were moments I sat in the PragmaClin office at 2 a.m. with the weight of perceived failures weighing heavily on my shoulders, questioning if the climb was worth the fall if it didn't work. But here's what I've learned: Motivation is like the ever-changing weather: sometimes sunny and at other times stormy. Commitment, however, is the compass that remains unwavering. It's the silent promise I made to myself that regardless of the obstacles, my eyes would remain set on the horizon—for my dreams, for the hope of those living with Parkinson's Disease, but most importantly for Gord.

The sparkle of long-term success is not just in the heights achieved, but in the relentless spirit that refuses to be dimmed by transient storms. Because while motivation might wane, commitment to one's purpose turns challenges into life lessons, leading us closer to our envisioned success. To see Gord, who is tackling his Parkinson's Disease head on, but still grinding out proposals each and every day, I owe it to him to be his light as well.

Q: What strategies or practices do you recommend for cultivating a positive attitude, staying motivated, and remaining committed to one's dreams?

A: In the ever-evolving world of entrepreneurship, the energy you carry sets the tone for your journey. Early in my journey I realized that success isn't just about strategies and plans; it's equally about the mindset you foster. I have been told that I have a magnetic personality. But here's the thing: Cultivating a positive attitude is a habit, much like watering a plant daily. It starts with nurturing the mind with positive affirmations and self-talk. The way I see it…if I can make others laugh or be the reason someone smiles today, I have motivated myself to keep going. Find what drives you, be it a past experience, a future goal, or a cherished loved one. Let these motivations be your guiding force and push you to achieve your dreams.

MAXIMIZING PRODUCTIVITY

Q: What techniques or strategies do you employ to master time management and maximize productivity? Can you share an example of how effective time management has helped you achieve your goals?

A: Mastering time management became an absolute necessity for me when I found myself juggling the demanding responsibilities of running

PragmaClin full-time, while simultaneously preparing for my PhD com-
prehensives. To navigate these two commitments, I integrated tools and
techniques that were both efficient and enjoyable. To-do lists became my
daily guide, laying out tasks in clear, achievable chunks. I supplemented
this with a detailed calendar system which I used for all of my bookings,
allowing meetings only when there was capacity. However, it wasn't just
about rigid scheduling; it also ensured that my tasks were infused with
activities that brought me joy, which served as a motivation booster. For
me, a morning surprise drink from Starbucks may have been my motivation to go in on weekends to study. I also set up those tiny rewards when
smaller milestones were achieved. Setting clear goals, imposing self-imposed deadlines, and prioritizing critical tasks formed the backbone of
my strategy. This disciplined approach not only kept me on track but also
provided a sense of accomplishment and purpose.

**Q: How do you prioritize tasks and ensure progress toward your goals?
What tips do you have for setting boundaries and avoiding distractions?**

A: Learning to say "no" is one of the most empowering decisions one can
make in the quest for effective time management. While it might seem
counterintuitive, especially in a world that often glorifies the "yes-man"
mentality, it's a pivotal tool in ensuring you stay focused on your priorities. Every "yes" to a task or commitment that doesn't align with your primary goals is a potential "no" to something more valuable. By consciously
choosing where to invest your energy and time, you guard against being
spread too thin and ensure that you give your best to the tasks that truly
matter. It's a lesson I had to learn the hard way, because none of us likes to
come off as selfish or uncaring, but it's transformed my productivity and
focus. When you can confidently decline tasks or opportunities that don't
fit into your bigger picture, you free up invaluable time and energy for the
projects and commitments that resonate with your vision and purpose.

**Q: What advice would you give to readers who struggle with managing
their time effectively and balancing multiple responsibilities?**

A: Listen, I get it. At 25, I was struggling with the weighty crown of a startup
CEO while trying to maintain a full-time PhD, semblances of a social

life, personal growth, and well…sanity. If you're feeling like you're in the center of a whirlwind, here's my two cents worth: Time isn't just money; it's gold. Prioritize ruthlessly. Not everything yelling for your attention deserves it. Break those colossal tasks into digestible chunks. They're less intimidating and easier to tackle. And here's the hard pill—learn to say 'no'. It's an art, really. Spreading yourself thin won't do you any favors. Say no to tasks, people, events – anything that doesn't help in your path to self-discovery and growth. If it doesn't bring you joy or fulfillment, it's a no. Find tools or methods that resonate with you, whether it's a digital app or a classic planner. And remember, it's okay to take a breather when you need to recalibrate. The empire can wait for a moment; make sure you're in the right headspace to rule it.

COMMITTING TO CONSISTENCY

Q: How important is discipline in staying committed to long-term goals? Can you share a personal experience where discipline played a crucial role in your success?

A: From my earliest memories, discipline has been my anchor. While my parents offered unwavering support, they never swayed my choices, ensuring that my actions were always my own. Rather than veering off-course, I held firm to my core values and moral compass.

The essence of my relationships has always been depth over breadth. Despite numerous adventures and challenges, I've been blessed with steadfast friends who've been my pillars through it all. This bond was partly built on my commitment to focus. Often, it meant turning down outings to keep my eyes on the prize, choosing purpose over fleeting pleasures.

My family, though comfortably middle-class, did their utmost to give me all they could. Inspired by their sacrifices, I started working at 14, driven by a single-minded goal: to ease their financial burden and stand on my own two feet.

For several consecutive summers, my days began pre-dawn, traveling the province to tutor for the disability council. Then, I would head into the city for a stint in bookkeeping and cap my evenings juggling roles as a waitress and bartender. Those long hours took a toll on my rest, but they forged in me an unyielding spirit of determination and discipline.

By channeling this discipline, I earned scholarships that funded both my degrees. Today, not only am I self-sufficient, but I'm also able to save for the future and occasionally pamper my parents.

My journey has imprinted on me a pivotal lesson: Motivation might light the initial fire, but it's discipline that keeps the flame alive, guiding us towards enduring success.

Q: What strategies or habits do you recommend for cultivating discipline and staying consistent in pursuing one's dreams?

A: Here's my Golden Triad for instilling discipline: First, initiate your day with a morning ritual, something as simple as meditation or journaling, to center yourself. This anchors your intention and paves the way for focused action. Second, create micro-goals: smaller, daily objectives that ladder up to your larger ambitions, this could be as simple as making your bed. Celebrating these mini victories can become the fuel propelling you forward. Third, and perhaps most crucially, engage in regular self-reflection. Set aside time weekly, away from the noise, to evaluate your path, ensuring you're not just busy but effective. Discipline isn't about rigidity; it's about aligning your daily actions with your desires and goals, making sure every step, however small, is a step forward.

Q: How do you overcome distractions and temptations that may hinder progress or derail focus?

A: In today's digital whirl, distractions are more than abundant—they're enticing. Yet, as a young CEO, I've realized the power of fiercely guarding my focus. Here's what I practice: Prioritize to Thrive. Each dawn, before the day's chorus begins, I set my Top Three Tasks: I carve out dedicated, undisturbed time for these, treating them as non-negotiable commitments. While digital detoxes can be tough, they're vital. I periodically mute notifications, immersing myself in creativity and productivity or rest if needed. When distractions beckon, I refocus by picturing the broader vision, my overarching dream. Know this: each focused moment builds your legacy. Don't let transient diversions weaken your foundation.

GROWTH THROUGH KNOWLEDGE

Q: **Why is continuous learning important in personal and professional growth? Can you share an example of how embracing continuous learning has propelled your success?**

A: In our fast-paced world, relying on past achievements can quickly make even top performers feel left behind. As a young CEO, I've learned that constant learning isn't just a bonus; it's essential. It's my anchor to ensure I'm always on the leading edge. I have dived into several podcasts, books, and programming to learn the skills I may not have had on my own. It drove home a simple truth: every skill learned, every insight gained, paves the way to new horizons. In the journey of success, a mind that's always learning is always thriving.

Q: **How do you seek new knowledge and stay curious in your field or industry? How do you embrace feedback and adapt to change?**

A: In the fast-moving business world, there's no room for complacency. To stay ahead, I maintain an unquenchable thirst for knowledge and a ceaseless curiosity. I see myself as a detective, always searching for the next ground-breaking insight or trend. My shelves are filled with the latest industry reads. Webinars fill my hours—and lively debates with both allies and competitors keep me sharp. But more than all this, I value feedback. It acts as a clear mirror, showing both strengths and shortcomings. While it can be tough to hear where I've faltered, that momentary discomfort signifies growth. By welcoming feedback and being agile, I've not just adapted to change but thrived on it.

Q: **What resources or practices do you recommend for readers to embrace continuous learning and stay updated in their areas of interest?**

A: In this age of information, there are countless ways to keep learning and stay updated with little to no cost. Personally, I swear by podcasts. They're perfect for multitasking. I can be on the move and still soak in new knowledge: platforms like Coursera and Udemy offer fantastic courses across a plethora of topics. Also, don't sleep on "the good old book." Whether physical or digital, they're still gold mines of information. But honestly, the game-changer for me? Engaging in communities of like-minded people. The real-time discussions, diverse perspectives, and resource sharing in these spaces are invaluable. So, dive in, stay curious, and remember: "Every day is a school day," if you let it be!

HARNESSING THE POWER OF CONNECTIONS

Q: **How has networking and collaboration contributed to your success? Can you share a specific instance where a connection or collaboration opened new doors for you?**

A: Networking and collaboration have been cornerstones of my success journey. One of the most memorable networking stories began not at a big conference, but within the close-knit environment of an accelerator. When starting a business, these programs can be incredible platforms to broaden horizons, gain industry insights, and even secure funding. On one occasion, a mentor from the accelerator shared a unique opportunity—a women-only mission, exploring the Asian Healthcare markets in Japan.

Admittedly, I didn't initially meet all the set criteria, but as fate would have it, I was chosen. While delving deeply into Japan's healthcare system, I crossed paths with a dynamic business leader. The surprise twist? She lived just five minutes away from me back home! It's a testament to how the world can be so vast, yet so intimately small. This serendipitous connection blossomed into more than just a professional relationship. She opened doors to multiple markets, imparted invaluable advice on both local and global healthcare landscapes, and became a comforting, "motherly" presence for me, especially since I was miles away from my own family. The trajectory of my professional journey has been profoundly shaped by such moments, showing that when you put yourself out there, the universe often conspires in your favor.

Q: **What strategies or tips do you have for building a strong network and nurturing relationships with like-minded individuals?**

A: You are who you surround yourself with. A motto I started to live by over the past few years. Being in the company of positive, uplifting individuals can inspire you to chase your dreams, to maintain a positive attitude and grow beyond perceived limitations. These individuals often act as mirrors, reflecting the best versions of ourselves and encouraging us to see our own potential. On the other hand, surrounding yourself with negative or toxic individuals can drag you down into a cycle of pessimism, self-doubt, and stagnation. In essence, the company we keep acts as a compass, either pointing us towards our true north or leading us astray. Being mindful of this can be a key determinant in the trajectory of our lives.

Q: How can readers leverage their connections to create opportunities and accelerate their own success?

A: Connections can be the secret sauce to supercharging your success journey. Think about it: when we nurture genuine, heartfelt relationships, we create a web of mutual support and growth. It's less about collecting contacts and more about forming bonds. Reach out to those who've walked the path you're eyeing; their wisdom can be your shortcut.

Remember, it's a two-way street. Be that person who lends a hand or shares a resource. Stay in touch. Maybe drop a friendly update, or share a coffee chat. Seek collaborations; two heads often do better than one. Dive into professional groups that resonate with your goals. Most of the time, they're treasure troves of opportunity and growth. And if you're eyeing a connection someone you know has, politely ask for an introduction. Embrace feedback with open arms; it's like having a compass that ensures you're on the right track. Finally, use technology to your advantage; platforms like LinkedIn are fantastic bridges. And through it all, wear your learner's hat. Stay curious, stay connected, and you'll find doors opening where you didn't even know they existed.

ON MANAGING RISKS...

Q: How do you approach managing risks on your journey to success? Can you provide an example of a calculated move or decision that paid off?

A: Navigating the path to success, especially in a startup company with limited resources, often feels like walking a tightrope—each step demands careful thought, balanced with the courage to move forward despite the risks below. A crucial aspect of this journey is understanding and managing those risks and being able to quickly weigh the pros against the cons in a situation. Being able to find the balance of making a rash decision, and making a quick counter-decision based on facts sets apart the trailblazers.

I vividly recall a pivotal moment on our journey. An opportunity arose to move to the US for a potential investment and the chance at a crucial trial. On the surface, the decision was filled with risks—financial, logistical and personal. It wasn't just about relocating; it was about uprooting our established foundation and stepping into unfamiliar territory. But success isn't achieved in comfort zones. We took a deep breath, evaluated our options and, leaning on both instinct and insight, made the move. It was challenging no doubt, but in retrospect, that gamble was one of our most crucially important business decisions. The investment and trial are currently paving the way for unparalleled growth and solidified our belief in the power of calculated risk.

Remember: *risks are inevitable*. It's the ability to discern, decide, and dive in, even when the waters seem uncertain, that can transform those risks into game-changing rewards.

Q: What strategies or frameworks do you employ to assess risks and make informed decisions? How do you balance taking risks with minimizing potential setbacks?

A: Making informed decisions when evaluating risks demands more than just a keen intellect; it requires a blend of structured thinking and intuitive understanding. Listing down the pros and cons of each choice serves as an essential framework, painting a clear picture of potential outcomes. This systematic approach helps in weighing the benefits against the drawbacks, while looking through a logical lens to view the situation.

However, while structured thinking lays out the landscape, the compass that often guides us through is our gut instinct. This instinct, honed by past experiences, emotions, and the subconscious mind, sometimes captures nuances that might escape even the most rigorous analysis. Balancing the tangible insights from a pros-and-cons approach with the subtle nudges of our intuition creates a holistic strategy, ensuring decisions are both informed and in tune with our innermost feelings.

Q: **What advice would you give to readers who are hesitant about taking risks or making big decisions?**

A: Trust your gut instinct. This inner voice, shaped by experiences and the wisdom of our subconscious, holds an uncanny ability to sense the unseen. While logic and analysis are valuable tools, there's an innate power in trusting that instinctual pull, that gentle nudge from within. Taking chances based on this trust isn't about blind leaps into the abyss; it's about recognizing that sometimes our soul discerns truths our minds may overlook. Embracing this intuition can lead to unanticipated adventures and rewards. In a world full of white noise and clusters of subjective advice, acting on our gut instinct can be our GPS, guiding us toward paths we might never have imagined but are destined to tread.

BALANCING WELL-BEING AND AMBITION

Q: **What is the significance of self-care in maintaining balance and well-being while pursuing ambitious goals? How do you nurture physical, mental, and emotional health while striving for success... and how do you find a balance between ambition and well-being, and how do the two complement each other?**

A: In the race of ambition, we often find ourselves sprinting toward our dreams, fueled by passion and a clock that never seems to pause. Yet, amidst this exhilarating chase, there lies a profound truth: our journey toward success is as much about the resilience of our spirit as it is about self-care and recognizing when to seek help.

Think of yourself as an intricate machine, designed for greatness but requiring regular care. I've walked this path and faced moments where the weight of my aspirations clouded my clarity. It was during such times that I understood the immense power of pausing, seeking mental health support, and even embracing medication. I learned that voicing my need for a break, asking for guidance, or simply leaning on another's strength wasn't a sign of weakness but a testament to my self-awareness.

I am still trying to find this balance each and every day. So, as you actively chase your dreams, remember to intertwine your ambition with moments of reflection and self-care. The support of those around you—

therapists, friends, family —are there. Don't be shy about asking for help. Within this blend of drive, self-care, and vulnerability lies the authentic path to success. Remember: it's not about reaching the peak but enjoying the climb to get there.

RECOGNIZING ACHIEVEMENTS

Q: **Why is it important to celebrate milestones along the journey? Can you share a memorable milestone or achievement that you celebrated and how it impacted your motivation?**

A: Celebrating milestones along the journey is essential because they serve as markers of our progress and affirm our capabilities. Each milestone achieved is an acknowledgment of our hard work, dedication, and resilience. It acts as a pause button, allowing us to reflect on our achievements, bask in the glow of our efforts, and gather momentum for the challenges ahead. Celebrations infuse us with positivity, reinforcing our belief in ourselves and our mission.

Recalling the time when I won my first pitch competition as the CEO of PragmaClin offers a profound illustration of this concept. The stakes were high, $25,000, our first funding to support our hard work we had already put in. I felt the weight of the responsibility to make my co-founder proud. When PragmaClin was announced as the winner, the elation I felt was indescribable. Not only was it a validation of our business idea and strategy, it was also a profound affirmation of my ability to lead, to articulate our vision, and rally support. This win was more than just a trophy or a title; it was a milestone that provided me with a newfound confidence. It made me believe, more than ever, in my capacity to steer PragmaClin to success. Such milestones, when celebrated, don't just remain as memories; they evolve into pillars of strength and confidence that continue to uplift us throughout our journey.

Q: **How do you acknowledge and appreciate your achievements? What role does gratitude play in recognizing success?**

A: Honoring yourself both physically and mentally is a cornerstone of success. I've often pushed myself too hard, so taking intentional breaks has become crucial for me. Whether it's indulging in a spa day, getting lost in a book while relaxing in my hammock, hitting the gym, or simply catching some extra z's, these moments of pause rejuvenate me. Embracing gratitude, mentally, is a way of whispering a heartfelt "thank you" to oneself. It shifts the focus to the positives in our journey, attracting even more goodness. Remember, true success flourishes when you're at your best, so always prioritize your well-being. Cherish your achievements, and let gratitude light up your path!

Q: What advice would you give to readers who struggle with acknowledging their own achievements and celebrating their progress?

A: Recognizing and celebrating your own achievements is an essential practice, yet it's one that many of us overlook, often overshadowed by our own internal critics. First and foremost, it's crucial to appreciate the baby steps. Not every accomplishment is a grand ceremony; sometimes, it's the quiet moments, like completing a task or learning something new, that deserve our applause. Sharing your victories with someone you trust can also provide a fresh perspective, helping you see your progress through a different lens. If negative self-talk tries to diminish your accomplishments, challenge it. Ask yourself: "Would I diminish a friend's achievements in this way?"

However, perhaps the most pivotal lesson is understanding the uniqueness of our individual journeys. It's tempting to look sideways, measuring our progress against someone else's. I've been there, with others placing my journey side-by-side with another's, as though they were comparing apples and oranges. But remember, each path is as distinct as the individual walking it. *Your milestones—your pace, your challenges—they're unique to you.* Celebrate them, cherish your progress, and always remember: your journey can't be measured by someone else's ruler.

~ BB

CHAPTER 24

Meet Yarden Zilber

Jet Pilot. Businessman. Family Man. Genius!

Yarden presents himself as "an evangelist" of celebrating the gift of life and living it well. An entrepreneur with 30+ years of corporate leadership, deal-making and business development experience in various sectors, as well as front-line military experience as a combat jet-pilot in the Israeli Air Force, Yarden Zilber belongs to that new breed of businessman who has been able to make a thriving career out of his innate drive and adventurism.

Born in Israel, Yarden moved to Canada in 2015 after more than 12 years in China. While there, he was the first Israeli to complete an executive MBA in the top Chinese MBA school: China Europe International Business School in Shanghai. He also has a BS degree in Electronic Engineering from Tel-Aviv University and is a graduate of Harvard University's Venture Capital and Private Equity Investments program.

Most recently, after three years of being Chairman of the Board and lead-investor of Niricson Software, an AI, SaaS, Infrastructure Inspection Company, Yarden stepped down as part of his move with his family to Barcelona, Spain. Before that, he joined my group at Dogtopia—the leading Doggy daycare in North America, as a Board Member and Managing Partner of Dogtopia of Seattle and a Board Member and Partner in Dogtopia of Canada.

Meanwhile, he has also become the Founder and Chairman of Sheng-BDO Ziv Haft, an Investment Banking and Business Development firm specializing in cross-border transactions. As part of his role, he initiated and led the $2.5 billion Shanghai Bright Food acquisition of *Tnuva,* the largest food conglomerate in Israel. He is also the Managing Partner and Chairman of Sheng Enterprises Canada, an investment and advisory company in Real-Estate and Venture Capital.

A key member of EO (Entrepreneurs Organization) Network, Vancouver Island Chapter, Yarden Zilber chairs the Canada GSEA (Global Student Entrepreneur Award) program, and he is a board member of the THOMAS GSEA FOUNDATION to promote students' entrepreneurship. A happily married father to three kids and one Goldendoodle, Yarden enjoys family activities with his lovely wife that include hiking, boating and reading.

I was the keynote speaker at a business conference when I first met Yarden. He also spoke at the same meeting. And as I listened to his talk, I felt he was a very interesting man who delivered an excellent message about life. As I got to know Yarden, I learned that the difference between him and most of us is that he is very disciplined. Unlike many others, he sets his goals and always gets them done.

That's just for starters. In the years I have known him, Yarden has proven time and again that he has what it takes to succeed and, having built his own Dream Factory, would now like to share some of his professional insights with you. So he was more than happy to participate as one of our contributors for this book...

THE IMPORTANCE OF BIG DREAMS AND CLEAR VISION IN ESTABLISHING YOUR GOALS

Q: **How important is it to have big dreams and a clear vision when pursuing success?**

A: To address the question, we first need to clarify what we mean by "success" and "big dreams." For me, success is about meeting your goals. The pinnacle of success is living life to its fullest. Thus, "big dreams" align with those ambitions that propel us towards that fullness of life. Given this perspective, having big dreams is of paramount importance. They guide you to your desired destination and empower you to make a lasting impact.

The real challenge? Determining how you want to live your life. After my military service, I embarked on an exploratory journey, keen on discovering diverse lifestyles. This was my way of broadening my horizons, understanding what resonated with me in terms of culture, food, music, habits, relationships, and more. My initial thought was to settle in New York. As someone who grew up in a small village, New York City epitomized the vastness and allure of the world as most of us know it. However, this is where the tale took a little twist…

A close friend returned from a business trip to Shanghai, raving about the city's dynamism. Concurrently, my newfound interest in Chinese philosophy, a subject formerly alien to me, began to grow. In the midst of this, a thought emerged: Why not dive deeply into the unknown? A place where I'd be a complete stranger, where every facet of life would challenge my perceptions. The idea felt audacious, and perfectly aligned with my thirst for exploration. While many in my circle deemed my aspirations to be far-fetched (an opinion I rather enjoyed), I weighed the risks against the potential rewards.

Taking inspiration from an old Chinese adage: "The journey of ten thousand miles begins with a single step," I started preparing for this new adventure. My determination was unwavering, and no obstacle felt insurmountable. The outcome? An exhilarating decision I'll forever cherish.

AS TO VISUALIZATION…Visualization has always been my tool to render grand ideas tangible. Whenever a novel business idea strikes, for example, my initial step is to give it a name. This act alone, in my view, breathes life into the concept. From there, I imagine its success and then ponder the necessary steps to actualize that vision.

I believe in the structural harness of imagination. *Constructing a methodology* helps you to vividly conceptualize an ideal future. Begin by tackling straightforward questions such as, "Describe a day or week in a perfect life under [a specific scenario]." The essence or qualities of this vision are crucial. More so than the granular details, these qualities frame your aspirations and establish benchmarks for your ambitions.

For instance, prior to relocating with my family to Barcelona—a move intended as an experiment in adaptability and mind expansion—I visualized what an exemplary week there would be like. This was not a vacation, but a typical week: my children in school, and my wife and I immersed in our daily routines.

An ideal day would unfold something like this: morning with my children, a dedicated two hours for physical activity, followed by any of the subsequent activities—work, networking, Spanish lessons, or touring Barcelona's myriad attractions. I'd ensure that I would be home when the children returned from school, with occasional evenings dedicated to outings with my wife, new friends or business engagements. Weekends were reserved for family pursuits. The vision felt right. Playing with the vision in my mind helped me to clarify the qualities – I'm interested in family life, human interactions, culture and business while maintaining healthy exercising routine. Can I build a plan that covers that?

To further this plan, I tasked ChatGPT with the creation of a year-long itinerary based on our interests and the city's offerings, factoring in weather, local festivals, and holidays. The resulting blueprint was compelling (very compelling), making the dream seem all the more feasible. It was merely a matter of refining the plan and setting it into motion.

As I pen these words from Barcelona, I'm elated to share that reality, as it mirrors the original vision I had conjured.

ESTABLISHING YOUR CORE VALUES

Q: **How did you identify and define your core values, and how have they influenced your journey to success?**

A: Defining one's core values is an evolving process, mirroring the complexities and shifts of life itself. When you've crystallized a set of values and subsequently encounter a divergence, it demands introspection. The crossroads often present two paths: either recalibrate your journey to align with those values or reevaluate and adjust the values themselves. This could be because your values have evolved over time or perhaps the initial ones didn't genuinely resonate with your essence. If you approach this with authenticity and recognize your decisions as manifestations of your choices, these values become an invaluable compass for decision-making.

At this juncture in my life, my cardinal values are: *Love (relationships), Purpose, Pleasure, and Health.* The first trio is centered on living life in its entirety. Meanwhile, Health isn't merely a value—it's a foundational pillar. Every endeavor, every aspiration is pursued with our body, mind, and spirit. By prioritizing and optimizing our health, we inherently elevate the quality and impact of our endeavors.

Q: Can you share an example of a time when aligning your actions and decisions with your values led to a more fulfilling and purpose-driven life?

A: Following the completion of my multi-billion-dollar deal, doors open with more opportunities to broker similar agreements. However, the inherent challenge with these intricate cross-border transactions is not just their complexity, but the frequent travel they entail. Around this time, my twins were born, making me a proud father of three incredible children. While I relish striking deals (I still do), the prospect of constant travel meant sacrificing invaluable moments with my family, especially during their formative years. It was not aligned with my values!

For me, the window to be an active, present father was fleeting. Given that fatherhood held a loftier place in my value hierarchy, the choice became self-evident. I opted to prioritize my role as a father. As I reflect upon it, this decision stands as one of the most fulfilling ones I've made.

Fatherhood, with its myriad challenges and opportunities, has been the most demanding and rewarding journey, presenting unparalleled opportunities for personal growth and forging deep bonds with my children.

This experience further reinforced my belief: when decisions are rooted in genuine values, they lead to contentment and fulfillment. It's a conscious acknowledgment that choosing one path often means forgoing others. Yet, when choices are anchored in core values, they're devoid of regrets.

Q: What advice would you give to readers who are struggling to identify their core values?

A: Recognizing and defining one's core values is an evolutionary process, one that should be revisited and refined as life unfolds.

If you're embarking on this introspective journey, I recommend the following approach:

1. **Reflection:** Analyze past decisions. What values influenced your most fulfilling choices? Conversely, what values seemed absent in decisions that led to regret or dissatisfaction?

2. **List and Prioritize:** Compile a list of values derived from your reflections. Don't hesitate to borrow values that resonate with you from others. From this list, prioritize and narrow it down to 3 or 4 that truly complement your current life phase.

3. **Implement:** Embrace these values and let them guide your subsequent decisions. If you find yourself dissatisfied or conflicted about a decision made based on these values, it's a cue.

4. **Re-evaluate:** Such dissatisfaction signals a potential misalignment. Perhaps your selected values don't genuinely reflect your priorities or your life has transitioned to a new phase. Return to the first step and recalibrate. I would strongly recommend re-examining your values every year.

Remember, the key is continuous reflection and adaptation. Your values should serve as trustworthy compass points, steering you toward decisions that resonate with your true self.

UNLOCKING YOUR INNER GENIUS
THROUGH SELF-BELIEF

Q: **How important is self-belief in unlocking one's true potential? Can you share an experience where cultivating self-confidence led to breakthrough results?**

A: Self-belief is deeply intertwined with authentic alignment to one's identity and the courage to face potential failures. At its core, self-doubt is often a manifestation of the fear of failure. Yet, embracing the reality that failure is an inevitable part of the journey can be liberating. While failure is painful, when viewed through the lens of personal growth, it's just a chapter in the grander narrative. After every stumble, you are presented with a choice: to learn, recalibrate, and either strive harder or redirect your course. When living authentically, each failure becomes a stepping stone, rather than a dead end.

Regarding the deal I alluded to earlier, I recognized my limitations—lacking the experience, expertise, or connections to see it through. Yet, my intrinsic motivation dwarfed these barriers. With failure as an anticipated outcome, what did I have to lose? I pondered: Is there a way around my shortcomings? If so, why not embark on that endeavor? At worst, I'd expend time and effort, which I was prepared to invest.

Q: **What strategies or exercises do you recommend for readers to overcome self-doubt and tap into their inner genius?**

A: When one defines ultimate success as the pursuit of living life on one's terms, self-doubt becomes almost paradoxical. True failure doesn't come from stumbling along the way but in refraining from chasing the life you desire. Consider this: given our finite time and capacity, while we can indeed pursue anything we're passionate about, we can't possibly chase everything. This necessitates making choices and setting priorities anchored to our core values.

Performance is a culmination of innate talent, persistent effort, and deliberate action. When these elements converge towards what truly matters to you, they magnify your potential. Remember, while we can control our actions and intentions, the outcomes often rest in the universe's hands.

For those seeking tangible strategies, I've personally benefited from a unique physical exercise to confront and manage my fears. In the controlled environment of a swimming pool, where I could stand with ease, I would submerge and hold my breath. As the seconds ticked away, the initial discomfort would escalate to genuine fear and even panic. Yet, amid this internal alarm, I recognized I had a choice: I could stand up and breathe whenever I wished. Over time, this exercise conditioned me to distinguish between situations that were genuinely threatening and those that merely felt so. It helped me to accept fear as it is—a signal (an important one) that I have a decision to make. However, a word of caution: such exercises carry inherent risks and shouldn't be attempted without appropriate safety measures in place.

Q: Have you ever faced moments of self-doubt during your journey, and if so, how did you overcome them?

A: A memory from my military service underscores this perspective. During one arduous training, we were tasked with climbing a mountain, our backs weighed down with heavy loads. Gazing up at the daunting ascent, a sinking feeling settled-in and a bundle of doubts with it: *There was no way I could conquer this peak.* The sheer enormity of the task seemed overwhelming. But then, a mental shift occurred. Could I take one step forward? Yes! There I just did…. And another after that! Certainly, instead of being intimidated by the entirety of the mountain, I fixated on the immediate task—one step at a time. Miraculously, by dawn, we stood atop the peak, feeling a renewal of confidence and a kind of rebirth as well.

Life often presents itself with *boxes of paradoxes.* There are moments we assume we're equipped for a task, only to realize we aren't. Conversely, we sometimes underestimate our capabilities, assuming we can't achieve something, only to discover we can. Continuously testing these assumptions refines our understanding of our potential and capabilities. And confidence, in the end, only comes in the doing.

SELECTING YOUR MENTORS

Q: **How have mentors played a role in your personal and professional growth? Can you share a specific mentorship experience that had a significant impact on your journey?**

A: It's crucial to distinguish between a coach and a mentor, even though both have an important role: A coach offers structured guidance centered on honing specific skills and techniques. In contrast, a mentor shares wisdom drawn from personal experiences, prompting the right questions that steer you toward independent learning and decision-making.

The essence of mentorship lies in empowering the mentee to chart their path. Recognizing that a mentor's experiences are uniquely theirs, a mentee should not simply adopt the mentor's answers but should seek guidance in framing the right questions that one shall answer.

I vividly remember an encounter early in my career that underscores the power of mentorship. After presenting a business idea to a seasoned businessman, he challenged me with a simple question: "Why aim for $10M? Why not $100M? Why not $1 billion?" Initially, I was taken aback by the audacity of those figures. But he prompted me further: "What's the difference between pursuing a $10M venture and a $100M one, besides an extra zero?"

This question was revelatory. I realized the primary shift was in perception and accessing different networks—the $100M investors operated in a different realm than the $10M ones (I also concluded that a $1billion dollar venture was not the right first step). Motivated by this insight, I secured my first $100M deal…

This transformative question continues to guide me, and I often pose it to those I mentor.

Q: **What qualities do you look for in mentors, and how do you establish meaningful connections with them?**

A: Mentorship can manifest in both formal and informal capacities. At times, an individual might play a mentoring role without even being aware of it. Regardless of the format, the impact of such relationships can be profound.

When seeking a mentor, it's essential to identify someone you genuinely respect, especially in the domain of the mentorship. This respect is crucial, not just for their achievements, but also for their perspectives, opinions, and the wisdom they can share.

The linchpin of a successful mentor-mentee relationship is sincerity. It's vital for both parties but becomes even more pivotal for the mentee. A sincere mentor equips you to evaluate their insights critically. This reflection allows you to gain from both points of agreement and disagreement, enriching your learning and growth trajectory.

Q: As to Making Your Dreams Attainable...What is the importance of setting SMART goals that are aligned with one's vision? Can you provide an example from your own experience?

A: I firmly believe that setting SMART goals is the only effective way to realize your vision.

Sun Tzu, in *The Art of War,* once said, "Strategy without tactics is the slowest route to victory. Tactics without strategy is the noise before defeat." This wisdom aptly applies here. A vision without a specific SMART plan resembles a strategy devoid of tactics.

On my 40th birthday, my doctor delivered two pieces of news. First, he mentioned, slightly in jest, that references to "young people" no longer included me. Thanks for that, doctor! More gravely, he informed me that my triglyceride levels were elevated and needed monitoring. Given my previous health status and our family's medical history, this was unsettling for me, especially with the recent birth of my eldest son. While I was determined to normalize my blood work, having a vision wasn't enough. Without a specific plan, it would remain just that: a vision.

To turn this around, I needed to take a deep dive into understanding my health and set actionable goals. I identified my main challenges and tackled them systematically. First, I aimed to improve my metabolic health. Second, I wanted to enhance my physical activity levels. Each primary goal was then subdivided into more granular objectives. For instance, one of the sub-goals to better my metabolic health was to cut my sugar intake. Upon assessing my consumption habits, the first SMART step I took was to eliminate sugary drinks, allowing only one alcoholic beverage a week for social interactions. Most of us naturally implement this goal-setting approach in our careers. So, why not apply it to all of life's priorities?

Q: How do you break down big dreams into actionable steps? What strategies or techniques do you recommend for tracking progress?

A: If you're at point A and aspire to reach point B, the pivotal question to pose is, "What's preventing me from getting there?" Typically, multiple obstacles exist, necessitating prioritization. So the essential query becomes, "Which is the most impactful bottleneck?"

Once identified, channel your efforts toward resolving it. After addressing the primary bottleneck, or if there's a lull in the process, shift your focus to the next pressing issue. By consistently and methodically pinpointing and tackling these bottlenecks, you'll navigate efficiently toward your goal. A crucial aspect of this strategy is continuous assessment and prioritization of these bottlenecks.

Peter (Thomas) once imparted a piece of wisdom to me: "You're just one person away from solving any problem." This sentiment rings profoundly true. That vital individual might be you, or someone else. So, once you've spotlighted a pressing challenge, determine the right person to address it. If you haven't met this individual yet, seek them out!

Q: Have you ever faced challenges in achieving your goals, and if so, how did you overcome them?

A: This question brings a smile to my face. I can't recall any meaningful goal I've set that didn't come with challenges. In fact, a goal without a challenge is merely a task. If a goal truly matters to you, aim higher and challenge yourself to achieve your dreams. When chosen carefully, these goals will make you live your life in full. This also means you'll need to prioritize your goals – as the saying goes: you can do anything, but you can't do everything!

CULTIVATING A SUCCESS MINDSET...

Q: **How does belief play a role in shaping one's reality and achieving success? Can you share a mindset shift that had a significant impact on your journey?**

A: At a biological level, influenced by evolution, our beliefs deeply shape our behavior down to the cellular level (Dr. Lipton's *The Biology of Belief* delves into this subject). *The power of belief is undeniable.* Yet, many of us unknowingly inherit our perceptions and prejudices from our surroundings rather than consciously choosing them. That, to be sure, leads to a point of self-examination: *Given their significance, shouldn't we challenge and select our beliefs based on our core values?*

I was raised in an ideologically driven family with steadfast beliefs on various matters. A pivotal mindset shift for me was realizing that while my story began in the chapters written by my parents, it's now my responsibility to pen my own. My upbringing not only endowed me with valuable insights, but also with some that don't align with my personal values and life choices. To truly live my life to its fullest, I've learned the importance of examining, challenging, and redefining my beliefs. While we can't change the past, we have the power and responsibility to shape our future narrative. After all, it's our life story, and what could be more crucial than that?

Q: **What techniques or practices do you recommend for overcoming limiting beliefs and developing empowering thoughts and attitudes?**

A: People evolve their value system through various processes—be it logic, spirituality, or other methods. Identifying and embracing your own method is crucial to the journey of refining your beliefs. Change can be challenging, but is undeniably worth the effort. At times, some deep-rooted beliefs and behaviors are hard to shake off. In such situations, recognizing these automatic reactions and consciously choosing a response can make all the difference. Consider them as additional voices in your internal orchestra.

To offer a personal example: As I was striving to improve my metabolic health, I came to understand the potential benefits of fasting. Yet, I had a psychological resistance rooted in the belief that we should eat two to three times a day, lest we affect our energy and functionality. Eager to challenge this notion, I delved into research and decided to conduct a three-day water-only fasting experiment.

With a Continuous Glucose Monitor (CGM) to track my glucose levels and my wife observing any behavioral changes, I embarked on this journey. Contrary to my expectations, it wasn't as grueling as I had feared. My old belief, which had been a hurdle in achieving my goal, was debunked.

That said, the echoes of that old belief persisted. Every time I'd initiate a fasting period (roughly once a month), a familiar voice would whisper doubts and reservations in my ear. But now, I'm equipped to recognize and counter it with my newfound understanding. I've found out that revisiting scientific materials by highlighting the benefits of fasting while I'm fasting helps me overcome the doubts in my early fasting days (the "power of WHY?").

I offer a note of caution here: This is not an attempt to recommend fasting to everyone. (That's a deeply personal thing.) This is just an example offered from my own experiences.

Q: How do you maintain a success-oriented mindset during challenging times or when faced with obstacles?

A: When that occasion presents itself, I always return to my personal definition of success: To me, success means achieving your goals. The pinnacle of success is living life to its fullest. If you resonate with this perspective, then the very act of pursuing it is success in itself. The challenges you encounter along the way are inherent to the journey of living life to the fullest. True failure would be to abstain from striving for a fulfilling life.

Victor Frankl said: "Between the stimulus and response, there is a space. And in this space lies our freedom and power to choose our responses. In these responses lies our growth and our freedom." What wonderful, liberating wisdom!

Delving a bit further into the physiological understanding of the sequence of stimuli – *attention* – *emotion* – *thoughts* – *action* (or in the reverse direction: our actions stem from our thoughts, which originate from our emotions, which in turn arise from where we direct our attention as a reaction to internal/external stimuli) provides us with a powerful tool. Fortunately, we possess the power, to some degree, to determine what we pay attention to. Cultivating this ability to regulate our focus can have a transformative effect on our actions. I found that *The Power of Why?* has a profound impact in helping me direct my focus. I can intentionally create stimuli by reminding myself "Why?"

While we as human beings naturally wish for a smooth journey, the Universe (call it what you wish) often has other plans. It's essential to permit oneself to experience emotions such as sadness, frustration, or anger when things aren't going exactly as planned. Emotions are crucial indicators of our internal state and provide important input. By the same token, it's vital to understand that these emotions are transient. When you center your attention on the broader objective of living a full life, your emotions, thoughts, and actions will eventually align.

I've found that meditating on my life motto helps me to keep it in my attention and call upon it in times of need (again, tapping into the "Power of WHY?").

When you get right down to it, *it's all about Balance.* You learn to prioritize. Life takes on so much more meaning when you do. Accomplishing your goals is only a part of living your dreams. Sharing them and helping others partake is also part of the gift.

This journey is also about Legacy. What you want your life to be: In the best of all possible worlds, it will be an example to learn from and follow—one that enables you to inspire others and mentor them as well if and when the occasion presents itself. Just as you have benefited from that same marvelous circle of contact: those of like mind and high ideals…as well as a sense of "giving back" and leading a life of purpose.

~ YZ

CHAPTER 25

Meet Marcia Meyer

CEO/Founder The Be Kind People Project®.
Educator. Genius!

M arcia Meyer is living proof that if you're going to be CEO and founder of something called *The Be Kind People Project®* you had better be willing to walk-your-talk. And so she does. In essence, The Be Kind People Project® is a non-profit 501-c3 that focuses on delivering youth-relevant learning opportunities that inspire humanity, academic achievement, civility, and healthy living so our student generation will grow into respectful, responsible, and caring citizens and leaders.

Starting out as a secondary Spanish teacher in rural and at-risk urban schools, Marcia switched over to take on her role as a senior executive at PetSmart™ during its growth from a regional start-up to a multi-billion-dollar national category leader. She followed that with fifteen years in leadership positions in services, international business, procurement, product and brand development, operations, and marketing. Throughout her career, Marcia has earned recognition for her remarkable skills in strategic planning, concept development, change management and customer engagement. That impressive compilation of experience has led to her expertise in growth strategies for organizations and providing the foundation for people to develop personally and achieve success.

Using the combination of an extensive business background and her own strongly developed personal values, Marcia has redefined what being a full-time volunteer after retirement can look like—all done through her work with *The Be Kind People Project®*.

Beginning from a community effort she led to thank teachers, Marcia has seen to it that the The Be Kind People Project® now reaches hundreds of thousands of students annually with innovative creative arts, academic, health, and character education programs. The Be Kind People Project® has also scaled effectively nationwide, with over 8 million student contacts since 2012. The impact of the programming that links academic, health, emotional wellness, digital safety, and character education has provided *a significant reduction in bullying and cyberbullying,* while also showing *academic improvement* for the schools and students involved.

Marcia believes strongly that bringing together people who want to work collaboratively to enhance the lives and positively impact the personal values of our children, our schools, our families, and our communities is one of the biggest personal investments one can make in America's future. (And the lovely little chart on the left perfectly defines her "kindness" mandates.)

When we asked Marcia to add her contribution to this splendid mélange of hearts and minds, she took a little longer than the rest—simply because she is meticulous in "wanting to get it right." So, when she finally came through, we were delighted and want to share her lucid insights with you…

DREAMS AND DEFINING VISION
KEYWORD: COURAGE

Our personal dreams generally come from within...from our hearts. Great dreams are almost always based on personal thoughts or aspirations. Just like we do with our REM sleep dreams, many dreams will come, and many will go. But the dreams that persist and/or move to us into a more conscious existence are those that could evolve into something more tangible and real. I think people should spend dream-time focusing on personal ideals and even carve out time to do so.

Just a hint that works for me: *When a dream occurs, write it down!* You wouldn't want to forget a great dream. And we can all have multiple great dreams. I take note of experiences or thoughts that start in my mind as, "I wish...."

A *Vision* generally involves a plan and actions that work toward the vision. As such, our dreams can evolve into a purpose, an action plan or even an enduring meaning.

In addition, visions can be for events, for projects, for a career, for a partnership or a person. All in all, a vision is something that is highly likely to modify slightly—even as the plan associated with it evolves. At the same time, it gives us focus. I think that visions, like the capacity to love, can expand to meet personal growth and life experiences. Everyone could (and should) develop a personal vision. As such, it can be many things—material, relationship-based, experiential, philanthropic, career-oriented, even philosophical; it's whatever resonates for an individual.

My life's vision has always been *to be a conduit of good for the benefit of others*. That's plain and simple; and yet it took several decades to develop. And yet even now, it is ever-evolving and constantly expanding. To me, that means how I honor, respect, communicate with, and treat people will always be with the intention to edify them in some way. Inevitably, it involves actions rooted in kindness.

But visions can be both immediate and tangible! In fact, I think having visions for things that are important in life helps a person to understand the power of *dreaming – visioning – planning* – and experiencing something aspirational. Like most things, skills get better with practice. Building visions from dreams is an important life skill.

One of the things I enjoy is watching people compete in sports, always giving it their personal best. I especially like the Olympics because they represent a combination of personal excellence and physical achievement that can result in both individual and national acclaim.

In 1988, the summer Olympics were held in Seoul, Korea. I enjoyed watching my children follow the successes and failures of the athletes with great interest—even as they developed an extraordinary sense of national pride. "I wish we could go to the Olympics someday to be there to cheer for our country," became *the vision that manifested into a dream* of our family being at the next Olympics and experiencing them in person.

We kept that dream alive and worked to find out how that could happen for ordinary people. We asked questions. We made phone calls. We carved out time. We pre-planned events and times we wanted to see. We stated that *we were going to do it.* And we did it!

As a result, our family of four attended the 1992 Olympics in Barcelona. Not only was it an amazing first-time experience, but it was also fulfilling because everyone had put forth the effort to turn the vision into reality. As the dream evolved...the Barcelona Olympics were followed by Atlanta in 1996, Sydney in 2000, Athens in 2004, Beijing in 2008 and London in 2012. So, that dream created a vision, and that vision created a plan—for how family vacations could include some of the most memorable milestones any human beings could experience.

ESTABLISHING YOUR CORE VALUES
KEYWORD: GRACE

I don't think that values "just happen." They're a combination of observations, experiences, environment, and influences on one's life. I firmly believe that if there is anything that defines a person, it's one's set of values. In other words, I think that defining one's life is more about *how* a person lives than *what* that person does. I believe that values drive someone's decisions. And those decisions determine their impact on others. So, it invariably holds true that values—or a lack thereof— are at the core of one's thoughts, words and deeds.

Doing work and study in the last decade on the importance of building a foundation for personal values for children, I've learned that one's basic values, *i.e.* a sense of right and wrong, are established very early in life—often in the first five years. Think about it: A child learns about what's acceptable and what's not and what happens with *good behavior* (smiles, approval, affection… even rewards) and the consequences of *bad behavior* (a stern voice, "no", or maybe even the classic "time out corner")! Those early childhood years are critical in a human being's development.

Research has clearly shown that between the ages of 5-13, a child often learns by mimicking other people—first their parents, but also in school, especially in peer groups and even more emphatically with their teachers. Teachers are constantly reinforcing our notions of "right and wrong," all with their own set of values. And peer groups are demonstrating different types of behavior—again, built by each child's personal experiences and value sets. So it is inevitable that when a child is in school, the application of that child's values evolves.

In building a strong foundation of basic core values through strong character education that is both definable and actionable, the net has been cast to both teachers and children in school environments. If school culture and climates can have a basis in common sense and respectful interpersonal values, the resultant decisions improve the overall school climate.

Why is that important? Because, children are constantly mimicking and applying those values to their own lives…hopefully wholesome ones.

I look back and use the word "wholesome" to describe the formation of my values. My father was an economics professor and basketball coach in Christian liberal arts colleges. My mother worked in administrative positions, always in education; my paternal grandmother was a teacher until her 90s; and everyone contributed to family farming. My siblings and I had strong adults and the foundation of a Christian belief system that helped mold our behavior. Our peer group in a small Kansas community, even in school with teachers and friends, had a similar background and values.

But values also come with building blocks. One of the most important components for me has been to value diversity and people or experiences who are different than what one knows. I remember clearly when one of my father's basketball players was chosen to be in a Junior College All-Star game.

This was in the early '60s when racial tension in the US was high. My father's player, Clem, was an African American. Our family was happy for Clem and drove him to the tournament to share the experience with him. When we went out to dinner with Clem in a southern Oklahoma restaurant on the way to the game, the manager told us that he could serve my father, my mother, and me – but that Clem would have to leave the restaurant and wait outside without food. Well…that was a deal-breaker if there ever was one.

I remember my mild-mannered father slapping his menu on the table, raising his voice, contorting into an angry face I had never seen before, ignoring the disapproving looks of the other patrons, and yelling in a tone that everyone in the restaurant could hear, "If you won't serve this young man who is with us, then you won't serve any of us." He probably said more that I don't remember, but I can fully recall walking out with my father's arm around Clem—even as I knew that what had happened was the right thing to do.

Today, I'm living the decision to align my values with my work/life purpose. Following Winston Churchill's statement of "we make a living by what we do…we make a life by what we give," I started a non-profit after my corporate career with the intent of helping children form the foundation for enduring life values, especially those in underserved or at-risk communities, wherever and however they learn.

This decision, in large part, was influenced by my granddaughter, Grace, who was entering school as a child with special needs. Her diverse learning and personal abilities were embraced in every way inside her family. Stemming from that, my dream had been that other children and teachers at her school would form a culture of responsibility and respect for others. Everyone would benefit, including Grace.

That single wish my heart made, *the dream* turned into a vision of a nationwide non-profit that has as its Prime Directive: *building generations of respectful, responsible, healthy and caring citizens and leaders.*

"Grace"—the person (with a capital "G") has been our family's great teacher. Her uniqueness, self-acceptance, and always trying to do the best she could inside the scope of her abilities taught our family so much about honoring differences, selflessness, and acceptance *based in love*. This evolved into the concept of "grace" (small "g") shaping how we live. A treasured friend and pastor, Jamie Rasmussen, defined the concept of "grace" perfectly: *It means showing kindness, being present, and inspiring hope.* Grace was only with us for 16 years, but her lessons as our teacher *in the true concept of grace* live on—amplified daily in our family's actions and words.

UNLOCKING YOUR INNER GENIUS THROUGH SELF-BELIEF KEYWORD: HUMILITY

I think that self-belief comes both from proactive recognition from others and from personal resilience. But there are underlying contributors to both components.

Recognition and encouragement from others can be for something personal ("I like your hair!")...or from recognition for actions and efforts ("Your work on that report was excellent."). Both feed self-confidence. And both paths can be parallel.

Just as important as improving on a natural talent or attribute is having confidence to learn and try something new. That may be even more important in building self-confidence and self-belief. There is great growth when one learns something new and achieves competency in acquired skills. The more often new things are undertaken, the more likely it is that the self-confidence to learn and do new things will spring out of it.

Learning how to learn may be the single biggest component of self-confidence. To learn, one must be curious, open-minded, and draw upon the wisdom or established facts of others. When a person realizes that he or she can "figure it out," it becomes a fundamental indicator of self-confidence.

Humility must be the counterpart of self-confidence. Humility is personal: It's something a person develops through self-awareness and self-realization. It's also a trait that people learn through failure. When one is humble, there is a greater propensity to pursue learning and explore how to improve. Humility also asks for help when needed and considers the opinions of others as valued and accepted. Humility can expand one's self-confidence because it allows an openness for discovering how to improve.

Can humility and self-confidence co-exist? Absolutely! Humility is inclusive. The lack of humility is self-focused, and can become self-obsessed. One could say that the inclusion of others in accomplishments is a trait that requires great personal self-confidence. The humble person will acknowledge others and express gratitude for accomplishments and/or let a simple "Thank you, I appreciate you," indicate that even the person recognizing them is included.

I encourage people to understand that talent and abilities are personal. Not everyone will be good at everything they attempt. Making those decisions for oneself isn't always easy. But building upon the decisions for achievement will result in having self-confidence in the right things; the things that matter.

At the end of the day, there is absolutely nothing I do better than other people, yet there are many (most) things I do worse. I'm okay with that and understand that I'd rather be known as a person who provides support for others to achieve their goals and dreams than someone who works to bring attention to oneself and/or tries to be the best at everything.

SELECTING YOUR MENTORS
KEYWORD: ACCEPTANCE

I always fumble for words a bit when people ask about mentors. I've learned from so many people but have never had a "true mentor."

When starting in the department store retail business in the mid-'70s, I was placed in the men's division at a time when there were not many females, and I'm not sure that the men in the specific areas were happy to have "a girl" among them rather than in the women's fashion areas of a department store.

I discovered early that I was considered a curiosity, and one that received a disproportionate amount of scrutiny from the (male) senior managers. I worked hard to do my best, and there were two men who took a gamble on helping me achieve my potential: One person, Harry C, asked to have me promoted very quickly into a high-profile role in a leading branch store. Those were the days of leisure suits, and nothing was hotter in the retail world than men wanting to buy *qiana* shirts (yes, that's a silky nylon material without a "u" following the "q") in dusty rose or other muted almost pastel tones to wear under their pale blue matching polyester jackets and pants…and then buying enough other colors for each day of the week. (Flashback to John Travolta's *Saturday Night Fever* breaking onto the scene!) No female had ever managed such a large business opportunity for the company in any area. And here I was: five months pregnant in the men's department, supervising only male employees. Harry's faith in me was an encouragement and a sign. In so doing, he taught me how to do the job, patiently pointing out each mistake, while demonstrating how to act when others would question me.

Although not a mentor who offered guidance beyond a short position stint, Harry taught me to trust in myself, not to take things personally, not worry about what others thought, and to realize that my value was in my ability, and not in gender or any other perceived limitations. As I look back on it, I realize that experience in my mid-twenties, built the foundation for not ever thinking about male/female differences or ANY difference—and to always accept people for exactly who they are. That includes *everyone,* regardless of their abilities, gender, preferences, or beliefs.

One could say that Harry was a pioneer in demonstrating and teaching the power of what we today call diversity, equity, and inclusion. That personal experience deepened my commitment to value each person as unique and important. It is a thread that has continued throughout my life experiences.

When I entered a corporate start-up years later, I found myself as the only female in a team of six males and then as the only female in the boardroom with over twenty men. When taking a CEO position in the UK ten years later, the same thing happened. The interesting thing is that other than never having to wait in line for the ladies' room (!) I never viewed myself as different. I had a role, like others, and my responsibility was to do my best to achieve that goal. I never succumbed to the "women's lib" movement; I didn't understand it. Be yourself as a valued individual, and just be *who you are.* Don't try to adapt to "stereotypes," or other's attempts to put you into a peg.

MAKING YOUR DREAMS ATTAINABLE
KEYWORD: FLEXIBILITY

Goals give direction. In fact, I would say that big goals are seldom achieved without small goals inside the process.

I always think about goals like following a map (GPS or otherwise!) to get to a destination. The best route is established, and there are always milestones to track progress. You can rate anticipated speed and time, plus what is needed along the way. If all goes well, the desired destination can happen.

To no one's surprise, as you're going through this, changes invariably come. Finding something of interest that shifts your focus, discovering a better route...or even changing direction as to where one is going, based on information you've gathered along the way—these are the things that matter. My personal life goals have changed so many times! Never has my vision changed, but the goals to live to that vision have altered. Family, life unexpected events, societal or cultural shifts, even something like COVID, and more can change goals. In fact, if goals don't change occasionally, I would wonder if maybe even the establishment of a more flexible goal might actually be in line!

I graduated from university as a trained secondary Spanish teacher. Teaching was wonderful, and pouring my mental and emotional energy into young lives was fulfilling. However, as life got more complicated, it became clear that the salary of a teacher wasn't sufficient for daily living. (*Why hasn't that changed??* is a very good question.) I had to take a part-time job in a department store—nights, weekends, and summer. The value of hard work was certainly at play here.

Quite surprisingly, because I had done a good job (of counting, nothing very special!) during a summer inventory, I received an offer to pursue a full-time position in retail management—a consideration that had never entered my mind! However, the financial incentive of providing a better quality of life made the offer a viable option. I had confidence that I could learn what was needed to be effective, and I had a contingency plan in mind. (I could always go back to teaching.)

That decision turned out to be a major unexpected detour in my life route. Not only did I meet people who had an impact on my personal confidence and self-acceptance, I had the opportunity to learn how the retail business operates and (through that learning) acquire new skills. It changed everything both short term and long term. All my goals had to be re-established, yet life values and my personal mission were never altered. When you think about it, there are times when walking away from something and starting over may be a hidden contributor to achieving one's dreams.

My father is so wise. When I turned forty, I was distraught at being "so old." My father told me, "This is the decade when your life experiences and values will combine. You'll explode. Enjoy every minute." He was right.

When I turned fifty, his advice was, "Look at what you've accomplished and where you are. If your life and career goals have been met or are in reach, start giving things away." Of course, those "things" weren't material; they were responsibilities or roles in life. My father told me, "When you have the courage to give things away at the right time, there will be parts of your brain and soul that will emerge that couldn't be active while your life was developing. You have no idea what could be ahead of you." Again, he was right. I left the corporate world at the age of 52. It was a great chapter in my life, but the chapters that have followed with entrepreneurship and philanthropic contributions have been even more richly wrought. That never would have happened without the combination of having a life vision, a sense of self-confidence, and the courage to be flexible to change. Well….and without my father's timely advice!

CULTIVATING A SUCCESS MINDSET
KEYWORD: POSITIVITY

Having a "success mindset" is intentional. Success, like dreams, can be big or can be small. But it's seldom accidental. I think small successes are the most important thing to recognize and appreciate. Small successes happen more often in life, and they also let a person look at various elements of success. Success is so highly personal in how it is perceived, yet it can sometimes be institutionally established. That's when it gets hard, and when self-confidence enters the equation. For instance, if a person looks for it, he or she can find success every day. Acknowledging daily life successes can develop the habit of appreciating the good parts of a day. This attitude also fosters self-improvement, even if not consciously doing so.

Intentionally practicing daily appreciation, fostering a positive approach, and having a *Grateful Mindset* can overcome self-limiting beliefs and attitudes. Often, we are placed in institutional mindsets of success. In my experiences, institutional success values, such as obtaining a big client, achieving a stock share price, or winning a game or championship in sports overshadow individual success points. That's when we need to have the sense of self-confidence and resilience to do better next time, the maturity to value accomplishments for what they really are, and the discernment to separate one's own values as an individual from institutional standards.

I have always struggled with the tendency to put my own self-worth in connection with institutional paradigms for success. If professional goals or successes aren't achieved, I ask myself, "Did I work hard enough? Give the right direction to others? See all the opportunities?" In other words, institutional successes sometimes is based on the expectation of perfection rather than recognizing efforts and/or important achievements that are included within success.

This is where learning to be *intentional* is important. I've learned to internally recognize the small successes and be sure to acknowledge them in others. Not only does this create a realistically positive mindset; it also helps others to do the same.

TURNING CHALLENGES INTO OPPORTUNITIES
KEYWORD: RESPECT

Obstacles always exist in life. Some are in our control to overcome, and others are not; but our reaction to life's obstacles are completely in our control. We can choose how we react to anything—and what influences those reactions? Values. Decisions. Behavior.

This is probably the right spot to interject that obstacles can sometimes be other people. We can only change ourselves, not others. Also, obstacles can be in various segments of your life, both personal and professional. I've encountered those people, probably more than I'd prefer, but this is where another life belief comes into play.

When there's an obstacle, I take the "High Road." Always. Invariably. Selflessly. Respectfully. Taking the High Road means rising above situations, resisting the temptation to complain or be petty, and to give time for situations to resolve themselves. I've found that on the High Road, the metaphorical traffic is lighter and the road is smoother. Taking the High Road doesn't "fix" obstacles, but it certainly gives you time to look at the situation and assess what must happen to change issues, if any, and plan next steps. If the obstacle adjusts short-term goals and doesn't compromise one's long-term values, then it is good to give a chance to unfold.

However, one should not live under compromising situations that violate core values. For me, extreme obstacles that have violated my core values have involved lying or altering results (cheating) for the benefit of an institutional or individual goal/success. I've encountered that type of obstacle – and have removed myself completely and permanently. Conflict is inevitable, as are hard decisions and the courage to make a change. Take time to reflect, but don't let the obstacles defeat you. Obstacles that are met and managed can build resilience and future success.

THE KEY TO PROGRESS
KEYWORD: PERSISTENCE

When things are easy and moving forward per one's expectations, progress can be taken for granted. People will either drift away, keep grinding, refocus how work is done, or lose focus by avoiding how to work through difficult times. The loss of focus is often manifested by means of procrastination.

Procrastination happens to everyone! Peeling away the reasons for procrastination will lead to overcoming it. There are reasons I explore when trying to figure out why things are being left to the last minute: 1) Is the task even important? 2) Do I feel equipped to complete it? 3) Am I afraid I might not do it well? 4) Do I have other more pressing things (or preferred things) that are conflicting with my time priorities? 5) Is the task just too big?

There are doubtless other reasons to procrastinate, but those are my top five. My most common reasons for procrastinating are because there are conflicting priorities and/or the task is just too big. That's when stepping back and assessing the issues one faces—down to the details needed to complete the task—can help. I resort to the good old-fashioned form of writing down what must be done and then going back and prioritizing everything that needs to happen from there. I sort things (on Excel) so it's easy for me to evaluate and shift priorities and then administer triage.

Doing things, one step at a time, can help achieve results and accelerate momentum. The combination of knowing both importance and timing priorities breaks down tasks into manageable steps – and procrastination becomes easier. The examples given were for tasks, but they can work on both *getting started* and *making progress*.

ATTITUDE, MOTIVATION, AND COMMITMENT
KEYWORD: INTENTIONALITY

One can determine attitude, create motivation, and develop commitment. Each of those attributes are personal and intentional decisions. Making intentional decisions about how to react to situations give a sense of empowerment to a person. The only decision needs to be how to ACT, which cuts short the need to REACT in times of challenge.

One's attitude affects everything. Showing grace to others and grace to oneself is a wonderful start to accepting a realistic attitude.

Motivation and commitment are often intertwined. They both start with having a clear plan and objective. Motivation tends to be either internal or external and can be a set of experiences, situations or even words. Coaches provide motivation, for instance, that are tied into rewards and benefits from a team or player's actions. Commitment is always personal. It involves a person understanding what he or she considers important and having the perseverance to move towards that goal. Motivation might be the instigator of actions, but commitment provides the momentum.

One of my values in extending good to others is to care for my family in the best manner I can. The ways to do that have been to spend time with the family, provide good education opportunities for my children, and enable their lives at home to be comfortable, safe, and accepting. In very simple terms we all understand that personal *commitment* to family is the primary *motivator* to work hard to earn a living and then steward the money I have earned responsibly and with a supportive *attitude*.

MAXIMIZING PRODUCTIVITY
KEYWORD: PRIORITIZE

Time can be considered an obstacle – or a gift. I choose to look at the day as a gift to do my best for the betterment of others and how can I best do that? Productivity increases with several key truths I've found that work. First, take care of the most important things right out of the gate. Use discernment for what can wait and what needs your attention—and learn how to do the important things well.

I'm going to use cooking as an example. For Thanksgiving, a traditional meal has a great turkey as its centerpiece. An accomplished chef would say that the time to roast and present a proper turkey meal will dictate the rest of the preparation of the dinner. For example: Knowing when a Thanksgiving turkey will be ready helps the cook know when to start the mashed potatoes close to serving the turkey so they will be hot and steamy, put the cold dishes in the refrigerator in time for them to be refreshingly cold, and bring other items to room temperature as needed. It takes making a schedule and following it.

My single most disastrous entertaining experience happened when I didn't take time to plan and execute a Thanksgiving dinner for 12 people. The turkey didn't thaw in time, the new method I was using to cook it (first time ever… no practice) was missing directions and trying to raise the heat higher and higher in the oven made for erratic cooking. The turkey was late—and with red uncooked flesh around the bones. The mashed potatoes were hard and cold. The salad had wilted by the time the rest of the food was served. I was mortified because our guests had to wait so long for an awful meal. And the disaster left in the kitchen from preparation took hours to clean.

What happened? I didn't prioritize the most important thing: the turkey. (So my turkey was a "TURKEY." And not in a good way.) Neither did I prioritize my skills at preparation. And everything else just tumbled out of place—a ripple effect and not the kind that benefits others in the slightest.

Lesson learned: Nowadays, to handle personal and life productivity, I keep a running record of notes and things to be done in the same notebook. Therefore, I never have to look for lost files or points of reference and can keep things on track with a personal system of "do this first" or "delegate".

I like hiring people who are much smarter and better than I am! When that happens—and if they understand their role and the vision— then others can take responsibility, cutting down the pressure on you to "juggle too many balls."

Setting boundaries returns to one's values. As a working mom, I set boundaries for what was important to me based on my values. I had commitments at my church. My children had teacher conferences, plays and sporting events. I didn't miss them. In fact, at one point in time, I was commuting from London to Phoenix frequently. I learned that I could take a direct flight from London that would arrive in time to see my son's game on a Friday night, be with the family on Saturday, participate in the church orchestra on Sunday mornings, and then fly back to London on a Sunday night.

I think that every person needs to look at their own life regularly and allocate time: 1) to do the important things first and do them well, and 2) to spend time every day on something that aligns with their values.

COMMITTING TO CONSISTENCY
KEYWORD: RESPONSIBILITY

Consistency boils down to understanding the value of responsibility. When developing a goal, either professional or personal, how you implement it will often determine the make-or-break achievement of that goal. That means having a plan and sticking to it.

In any complex goal, after breaking it down into achievable milestones, you'll also need a process for understanding milestones. Whether it's an important business objective, something that will make a difference in a neighborhood, or losing ten pounds before a class reunion, having a plan with benchmarks along the way is essential.

Very few of us can do things alone, and if we try, we lose the richness of the input from others. Having accountability to someone in reaching a goal is very important. I would urge you to write down steps along the way that need to be met, establish the rules of engagement (*i.e.,* what will and what can't happen), review them frequently, have honest conversations about how you're progressing, *and* be sure to listen to others along the way. There also needs be ongoing communication—and inspiration—to work toward keeping the goal alive. One can over-communicate with others, or even with oneself. (Don't "talk it to death.") Keep it basic. Trust in others. And don't try to micromanage.

GROWTH THROUGH KNOWLEDGE
KEYWORD: CURIOSITY

I once went to a professional conference where one of the activities was to take a "brain health physical." I expected it to be the adult version of the SAT – basic knowledge. Instead, it was a test of both critical thinking skills and multi-tasking abilities. As it was, I never could have predicted the results: We definitely compromise our clarity of thought when we try to do multiple things at the same time.

The takeaway from that brain health physical was two-fold: *1) do one thing at a time and 2) do something new every single day.* Both are harder to do than meets the eye. However, I think about them every day and take time to internally reward myself when there are no distractions or when I might take a different route to a familiar location—or when I try a new puzzle, or even take time to visit someplace new. Eliminating conflicting brain stimuli or doing something new and different tends to calm my compounding of multiple daily thoughts or worries even as it builds curiosity for what to do next.

Ongoing learning is different for every person because people learn differently. I learn by doing; my husband learns by reading; and skilled listeners learn by hearing information. Therefore, what a person does must fit both their interests and their learning style. There's a side benefit to ongoing learning and curiosity: They are feeding ground for new dreams! Do something new every day – and be intentional about it. Listen to your "I wonder if.." or "I wish…" thoughts. There might be a new dream or vision on the horizon.

HARNESSING THE POWER OF CONNECTIONS
KEYWORD: INTEGRITY

Integrity means that one's words and actions support each other. A true relationship cannot be developed without honesty of intention and integrity of character. Connections, networking, and collaborations evolve from your being genuinely interested in other people.

Authenticity and vulnerability are important in building relationships. Genuine interest in another person is something you really can't fake (nor should you). People can instantly spot someone who is *truly invested in them and present in the moment.*

I have a good friend, Bo, who has worked with building character through education—non-profit work from the beginning—who has proven to be the best relationship builder I've ever known. Bo doesn't consider people as strangers, just as people she doesn't yet know. She genuinely cares about learning other people's stories. And she leaves others feeling good about themselves. I've heard her wonder, "Do I have a sign on my forehead that says 'tell me your story?' Even people in the grocery store do that."

Bo's secret? She smiles and acknowledges people. She makes positive comments about others—intentionally always looking for the good. She works at remembering things about each person, follows up, and always recalls things learned about the person in subsequent meetings. She genuinely cares about others and makes each person feel like the most important person in the world.

THERE'S AN OBJECT LESSON HERE: People spend time with and do business with other people they both trust and like. That in mind, I encourage you to take the time to learn what you can about others—and especially care about who they are as people.

MANAGING RISKS
KEYWORD: ANALYZE

One might say that if there were a path without risks, there may not be enough innovation. Often the simple notion of "change" can be considered a risk.

I think the best thing to do is to expect risks along the way; they're going to happen. I always tend to have a contingency plan (and sometimes multiple plans) if things don't work out as expected. Probably worse than having risk is to not recognize it! Having a plan and course (the roadmap) to follow, plus checking milestones, will help avoid that error. Before deciding the change of course actions and/or adding to an overall project at hand, analyze the facts before making decisions. "My gut says…" may work on minor decisions, but true risk requires analysis before taking those next steps.

Of course, there are personal risks and professional risks. There's a different thought process for personal risks that requires *awareness and competency*—and often those risks happen with a split-second mental analysis *(i.e.* the flames are jumping out of the grill and the lid is open). Those types of analyses rest heavily on past experiences and general self and situational-awareness.

There's a saying: "Subjective opinions go out the window when facts come in the door." Find the facts. Compare them to the plan, the end results desired, and the progress to date. From there, a foundation for a good decision is formed.

Self-confidence enters the equation when managing risks. That means that one must have had both success and probably failures in similar situations. I would strongly suggest not ever attempting risks that could possibly endanger someone or oneself…or would otherwise violate one's personal values. Even risk can be managed responsibly.

Once, as a single mother in my mid-thirties seeking an opportunity (and with two children to support) I was faced with moving from one city to another I knew nothing about to pursue a career I needed…despite the fact that I had challenges facing me I'd never had before. Stepping into the "unknown" was terrifying…and filled me with questions for which I had no answers at the time: Could I buy and maintain a home by myself? Could I find childcare? Could we find a support system in the new city? Would I do well in my job? It was a big risk. But I took it. And as I was determined to make a go of it, the solutions came.

I spent literally four months researching details that would support my value of honoring and caring for my family. Even doing that was a risk. I had to advise the company as to the time I would need to research the facts before making the decision. They agreed. During those four months, I analyzed my finances with various scenarios, found good schools, researched neighborhoods for where to buy a home, found a church nearby with an active youth program, and interviewed caregivers. I even found places for our dog and cat to stay in the new city while we were moving. Then we made the move only after analyzing all the facts.

It wasn't an easy move, and there were surprises along the way; however, the important things were handled by relying on solid information. By the way, there was a contingency I hadn't planned for…the selection of the neighborhood and school led my son to being in a t-ball league with his school friends. I met the man who has been my husband for over 30 years on the ball field. And that's a good risk-reward benefit all its own!

BALANCING WELL-BEING AND AMBITION
KEYWORD: CHOICES

The balancing act between ambition and self-care goes back to the importance of values. Ambition can result in *what* a person does and accomplishes. Self-care—physical, mental, and emotional—represent *how* a person lives. Just like other issues we've discussed, self-care and balance don't come without understanding one's own values *and being intentional* in one's decisions and actions. Achieving balance involves personal choices that benefit you as an individual…as well as others.

I enjoy working. For me, work is the combination of determination and intellectual growth. I can't even remember all the times that people have said (almost always without being asked), "You work too hard. You should slow down." I always listen and then make my own decisions about how to spend my time. This is easy to do if other important values of faith, family, and being a conduit of good for others are not compromised. The point is not about me. It's about the fact that each person can make their own choices for what is right.

One can make choices every day about what makes each of us thrive physically, emotionally, and mentally. Nurturing oneself spiritually, physically, and emotionally is an important part of every day. One's values are invariably reflected in behavior.

My own values of self-care revolve around being active, relying on my faith to give me purpose, eating healthy foods, avoiding smoking and substance abuse, restricting alcohol use to an occasional glass of champagne, wine, or a rare indulgence of a chocolate martini, enjoying the benefits of the acceptance of my cat and her quirky personality, and always giving myself freedom to laugh daily, even at silly things. A sense of humor and laughter helps to buffer the sharp edges and you with a release from pressure at the very time you need it. Sleep is my super power. I always prioritize rest and recovery from sleep.

Mental healthcare is real. Stress is real. Burnout is real. And relationships take time. Just realizing that life is likely to contain pressure on one's physical, mental, and emotional health can help a person not feel alone or inadequate. There are things that we're all just not prepared to handle by ourselves. In addition to being oneself, accepting who you are, the other important thing for balance is recognizing when you need help and finding it. Help can be with life challenges, with medical issues, with mental or emotional confusion or pain, or navigating relationships. Have the confidence in yourself to make the choice to ask for help, listen, and then do what's right for YOU.

RECOGNIZING ACHIEVEMENTS
KEYWORDS: APPRECIATE OTHERS

The keywords for recognizing achievements again go back to my guiding vision of *being a conduit for extending good to others*. Achievements never happen in a vacuum, even if a project is done alone. Expressing gratitude for people who supported you along the way and/or contributed to one's success can be some of the most meaningful times of your life—whether you're giving acknowledgment or receiving it. As with good teachers, people usually remember how a person makes them feel more than specific details.

Our company recognizes accomplishments, big and small. In fact, there are weekly "shout outs" to others. "Thank you" is always appropriate and welcomed, regardless of the situation. So many people deflect personal attention for achievement, and it's sometimes hard. Again, I think the best thing to do is be humble and always acknowledge others who have both recognized and helped you.

What we do with professional milestones should be multiplied in personal relationships. Personal relationships have so many opportunities to show gratitude and to celebrate. Look for them.

Working hard to cultivate and develop personal relationships is important. I intentionally do something kind for my husband every day; sometimes it's a favorite meal, sometimes it's just listening; sometimes I take great care to acknowledge who he is. Sometimes I like to surprise him with a card or a note. He's a self-confident person…but I know that it makes his day just a little bit better. And what happens? He reciprocates, although we've never talked about it. It's just the way we live. It's the little things (unnamed and unmentioned) that often make all the difference.

THE "G" WORD REMAINS A STAPLE OF OURS: *Expressions of Gratitude are the ultimate State of Grace. Gratitude* is like a full circle: the more you give, the more it comes back to you in a thousand different ways.

~ MM

CHAPTER 26

Meet Daniel Dubois

ShareShed™ Founder. Athlete. Entrepreneur. Genius!

Hello, world. My name is Daniel Dubois, and I believe that loving relationships and growth are at the core of a well-lived life. One filled with intention, discipline, spontaneity and adventure. Allow me to introduce you to my universe.

Raised near Granville Island in Vancouver, BC, I have always been a young entrepreneur at heart. At just five years old, I'd gather moss from beneath the Burrard Street Bridge and sell it door-to-door—a passion for creating something exciting out of virtually raw material that was hardwired into me. My early days were filled with entrepreneurial ventures like clothing lines and Kool-Aid® stands, all backed by my incredibly supportive parents who instilled in me the tools of self-awareness and confidence.

During my first semester of college in 2010, I discovered the burgeoning world of "Collaborative Consumption," now known as *The Sharing Economy*. I soon founded *ShareShed™*—a marketplace for outdoor adventure gear, an endeavor that opened my eyes to future possibilities. Selling ShareShed™ in 2017, I joined *Airbnb*, realizing a dream, only to leave two years later with a vision to transform real estate into a source of freedom and prosperity through a venture called KEY.

Entrepreneurship is my calling. I've built a powerful network with thousands of EO and YPO members, investing tens of millions annually in groundbreaking ideas. My belief in fostering youth entrepreneurship led me to non-profit boards and interviewing some of the world's top investors and entrepreneurs. These experiences, filled with insights from industry leaders, have shaped my understanding of innovation, which I am eager to share.

Now at 31, I'm enjoying the time of my life, raising our one-year-old daughter, Kay Marigold Dubois, with my amazing wife, Lucy Born, my partner of 14 years. Together, we plan to grow our family and continue embracing life's adventures.

Solving society's toughest challenges requires intense intention, discipline, self-awareness, and resiliency. I hope that my journey and the lessons I share with you will inspire you to live a life by design, not by default. To swing for the fences, to dream big, and to find purpose and passion in everything you do.

~ DANIEL DUBOIS, 2023

ON A PERSONAL NOTE: Everyone who has participated in writing a chapter in this book are some of the most special people on this planet. Daniel fits that description in spades.

It is rarely that I say "that man could really attain any predetermined goal he sets for himself." But I say that about Daniel with no small amount of confidence and as the beneficiary of considerable experience. In truth, Daniel was an entrepreneur before he could spell *entrepreneur.* His answer to any task you ask of him is to say "yes", and somehow find a way to get it done.

As a bit of a backstory, one afternoon, in Victoria, BC a small group of us were involved in raising the profile of the Global Students Entrepreneurs at a conference that was being held that evening. We only found out about the opportunity at noon on the day of the event. Daniel came up with the idea of "making some calls" and inviting a few people to come and meet me aboard my yacht, so I could explain what our goals were. My crew wondered if there would be 10 or 12 people coming and I positively advised them to prepare *hors d'oeuvres* for 12.

A short time later, I looked at the gate of the marina at about 3:00 p.m. and found myself somewhat astounded at a rather massive group of people who were laughing and having the best time—all of whom were apparently coming directly our way! At first, I did not realize that they were all heading for the boat. The line just kept coming and coming.

Eventually, there were over 100 people who swarmed aboard and literally became a danger to possibly capsizing the yacht. So we had to make adjustments, like docking before they did. (And when you think about it, what a wonderful problem to have!)

That is perhaps the best way to illustrate Daniel's enthusiasm for life: He is a natural energizer. He just makes things happen. You become infused with his enthusiasm and feel that you also can do anything…as you will soon discover when you read the following pages:

DREAM BIG AND DEFINE YOUR VISION— THE POWER OF VISUALIZATION

Q: **How important is it to have big dreams and a clear vision when pursuing success?**

A: Everything starts with a vision that represents your core values and the life you aspire to live. In my experience, having a big and audacious vision can often act like a magnet, attracting world-class talent who want to be part of something grand and meaningful. I've seen firsthand how dreaming big can open doors that might otherwise remain closed.

In my early 20s when I was just starting my entrepreneurial journey, I managed to gather support from leading investors and even hired talented individuals who had achieved great success in their past ventures—such as someone who had just sold his last company for $40 million. This wasn't merely due to my ambition. It was because of a clear and compelling vision that resonated with others—a big dream that created the type of world others wanted to see brought into fruition.

However, it's essential to recognize that success doesn't always mean building a big company. Whether it's a small local business or a global venture, what truly matters is aligning your dreams with your values and working relentlessly to mold them into a reality. Both big and small dreams can be fulfilling if they reflect who you are and what you believe in. From my life experiences, the bigger the dream, the easier it is to attract amazing talent—mentors and investors who will get in the trenches with you to make that big dream into something both tangible and solid. But what makes any dream truly powerful, regardless of its size, is the alignment with your core values and the relentless pursuit to turn it into reality. That's the essence of entrepreneurship and the key to fulfilling success.

Q: **Can you share a personal experience where visualization played a significant role in achieving your dreams?**

A: In high school, outside of building a clothing line, basketball was my life. I would wake up before school and train with the legendary late Harlem

Globetrotter, Mel Davis.[5] Mel focused 80% of his time teaching me about life, while we only spent 20% of the time on basketball. To him, basketball was a human development engine disguised as a physical sport.

Mel brought hard love, respect, and showed me the power of visualization. Nearly 7 days a week, I would stay at the courts of Granville Island until the lights went out at 10:15 p.m. My vision was always to play college basketball. But, after totaling my motorcycle at the age of 17, I was left bedridden and on morphine for months. I wasn't able to get out of bed, even to go to the washroom without my body going into shock and shaking uncontrollably.

I back-packed Australia for six months instead of pursuing basketball, and upon my first semester of college, entrepreneurship consumed me. For physical activity, I played rugby football since it was much easier on my ankle, which was still severely compromised from the trauma of my accident.

Three years after totaling my motorcycle, I called a friend to say we should get back into basketball. He said he was playing that night at Capilano University and invited me to join. At the time, I didn't even own any basketball shoes. So he said he'd bring an extra pair. I'm a size 12 and he said he had a size 15 but they fit small. I doubled up my socks and a few hours later I walked into what I thought was going to be some friends playing pickup ball. Instead, it turned out to be summer tryouts for the Capilano University men's team. There were 80 people in the gym, all trying out to become a walk-on to a team that was already decided. I was not anywhere close to being in anything resembling game shape. As I labored up and down the court in a cut-off rugby t-shirt, one of the coaches made a comment that I was a rugby player trying to play basketball.

---

5   The Harlem Globetrotters were an "all black" All-Star basketball team officially formed in the late 1930s that performed "exhibition basketball games all over the world." Since no blacks were allowed in the NBA until the early 1960s, the Globetrotters featured some of the most phenomenal players to ever play the game—and that made them international ambassadors for this uniquely American game long before pro basketball became popular in the USA. The Harlem Globetrotters featured such basketball legends as Mel Davis, Goose Tatum, Connie Hawkins, and Wilt "The Stilt" Chamberlain...the latter two of whom went on to become NBA Hall of Fame players.

I had the most humbling sport experiences of my life as I struggled to find my footing after three years without touching a ball. At the end of the tryouts, the coaches had everyone sit down on the court. The head coach gave a lecture, similar to one of the many classic Mel Davis lectures I experienced early in my career. Assistant coach, Aaron Greystone said, "At CapU, basketball is about becoming the best version of yourself … You can only be in one place at one time. So why not make the absolute most of the moment you're in?" I felt deep inspiration to surround myself with this kind of coaching philosophy. My plan was to transfer to UBC to play rugby but after one lecture on CapU's vision for this team, I was set on joining.

It felt like I was hit between the eyes with a vision of playing the best I'd ever played in my life at subsequent CapU tryouts…and at the end, having the coaches call my name, singling me out as someone special. The coach then said this was the first of two tryouts and that they were scheduling another one a few weeks later. I started to train with intensity. I saw my cousin and with great excitement, told him that I was going to show up at the tryouts, dominate, and have the coach at the end call me out to learn who the hell I was.

Three weeks later, I had the tryout of my life. One of the top players in the country was there—not to try out for the team, since he'd already committed to another school, but to dominate and generally make a fool of everyone else. That prompted me to go after him. I full-court pressed him when he went to run point guard and ripped the ball right out of his hands. I blocked his shots, and it wasn't long before it seemed like his soul was stolen. At the end of the tryouts, the coaches didn't sit us down as they had the previous time. Instead, they said that, due to the considerable number of people still there, they would only be notifying anyone that made the team.

As soon as we were excused, the head coach yelled, "Dubois!" I smiled, knowing exactly what was coming. As I approached him, he had a big grin—the first smile I'd ever seen from him. "That was one hell of a show you put on out there tonight. Where did you play in high school?" Before I knew it, I was on a full scholarship to Capilano University where I soon became Captain of the men's basketball team. And shortly thereafter, I also became the Recruitment Poster Marine for the business program: a dream come true after a visualization that felt like reality.

SUMMARIZED: *That experience taught me a profound lesson about The Power Of Visualization.* My dream had been broken, yet through visualizing success, aligning my actions with my inner vision, and embracing a relentless pursuit, I turned that dream into reality. It was a clear affirmation that seeing is not only believing but also achieving. Visualization isn't just a tool; it's a bridge between dreams and reality, and it's available to anyone willing to take the journey.

Q: **What strategies or techniques do you recommend for readers to tap into their imagination and create a vivid mental image of their desired future?**

A: The strategy that I've used was introduced to me by Brian Scudamore of 1-800-GOT-JUNK. Write out exactly what a day in your life looks like 10 years from now: *Where are you living? Who are you living with? Conversations that are happening as you walk into the office.*

This "painted picture" or "vivid vision" exercise is a tool you can use to create a detailed mental image of your desired future. And the technique that comes with it can be a powerful way to align your team, spark innovations, and drive motivation. Here are some sample questions that can help guide you in this exercise:

1. **What Does Success Look Like?**
   - What are the specific goals you want to achieve?
   - How will you know when you've reached success?
   - What will your organization/product/life look like when successful?

2. **What Values Guide Your Vision?**
   - What core values or principles are at the heart of your vision?
   - How do these values manifest in your daily operations or lifestyle?

3. **How Does It Feel?**
   - What emotions do you associate with your vision?

- How will you feel when you reach this future state?
- What emotions do you want your team/customers/community to feel?

4. What Are the Key Milestones?

- What are the critical steps or stages along the path to your vision?
- How will you celebrate or acknowledge these milestones?

5. Who Is Involved?

- Who are the key players that will help you achieve this vision?
- How will you engage and inspire them?

6. What Challenges Will You Face?

- What obstacles or challenges can you foresee?
- How will you overcome these challenges?

7. What Impact Will You Make?

- How will achieving this vision impact your industry, community, or the world?
- What legacy will you leave?

8. How Will You Stay Aligned with Your Vision?

- What practices or rituals will you put in place to keep yourself aligned with your vision?
- How will you remind yourself and others of this vision regularly?

9. What Will You Avoid?

- Are there any paths or practices that are not aligned with your vision?
- How will you be able to ensure that you can avoid these traps?

10. What Resources Do You Need?

- What tools, skills, people, or funding will you need to achieve this vision?
- How will you acquire or develop these resources?

11. How Will Your Vision Evolve?

- How might your vision change or grow over time?

- What mechanisms will you put in place to revisit and revise your vision?

12. What Does the Daily Reality Look Like?

- What will your day-to-day life be like when living this vision?
- What practices or activities will be common?

13. What are the Key Performance Indicators (KPIs)?

- How will you measure progress towards your vision?
- What metrics or indicators will you track?

HERE ARE SOME OTHER TOOLS:

1. **Identifying Core Values and Goals**: Before visualizing success, individuals must have a clear understanding of what success means to them. Defining core values and setting specific, meaningful goals is an essential first step in forming a clear mental picture.

2. **Embracing the Power of Visualization**: The story demonstrates how visualizing a goal as if it's already achieved can be a motivating force. Readers should take time to close their eyes and vividly imagine achieving their desired future, engaging all the senses in the process.

3. **Creating a Vision Board**: A physical representation of dreams and aspirations can help solidify a mental image. Creating a vision board with pictures, quotes and symbols that represent the future they wish to create can be a potent visual aid.

4. **Finding Role Models and Mentors**: Connecting with people who embody the success or the values the readers aspire to can provide both inspiration and practical guidance. In my story of college basketball, working with mentors and coaches played a vital role.

5. **Committing to Regular Practice**: Just like training in a sport, the regular practice of visualization can make it even more potent. Establishing a daily routine where visualization exercises are performed can enhance its effectiveness.

6. **Aligning Actions with Vision**: Visualizing the future isn't enough; it must be followed by actions that align with the vision. The story

shows a commitment to practice, training, and taking opportunities that align with the visualized future.

7. **Being Adaptable and Resilient**: As my story illustrates, life can throw any of us unexpected challenges. Being adaptable and resilient in the face of setbacks, and continuing to hold the visualized future in mind, is essential for eventual success.

8. **Utilizing Affirmations**: Positive affirmations contain surprising power to reinforce mental imagery. Repeating phrases that align with your desired future helps ingrain the vision deeper into your subconscious mind.

9. **Engaging Emotions**: Connecting this visualization process with the emotions that achieving the goal will invoke makes it more vivid and compelling. It's not just about seeing the future but feeling what it will be like.

10. **Monitoring Progress**: Keeping track of progress and celebrating small victories along the way helps you to reinforce your own belief in the vision. Recognizing growth and learning experiences adds to that motivation.

11. **Seeking Professional Guidance if Needed**: Sometimes, professional coaches or therapists trained in visualization techniques can provide the missing ingredient to guide you in using these methods most effectively. I have personally seen a hypnotherapist at times, which has deepened my visualization practice.

ESTABLISH YOUR CORE VALUES

Q: **How did you identify and define your core values, and how have they influenced your journey to success?**

A: During college, I spent a transformative semester abroad in Vienna. While there, I found myself at a crossroads that would eventually define my core values and the path to my success.

A family friend introduced me to the League of Innovators, a pioneering program in Canada that offered mentorship to the "Top 10 Young Entrepreneurs" under the age of 23. The program provided invaluable support, including $10,000 in cash and free office space at the newly built Hootsuite HQ2. Around the same time, I received an offer to play professional basketball in Vienna—a high school dream come true.

The choice between these two opportunities was both thrilling and revealing. My decision to join the League of Innovators was driven by an intense vision I had cultivated and a hunger to learn from the best.

Through this program, I had the privilege of engaging in confidential, closed-door conversations with accomplished entrepreneurs. They shared their deepest regrets, hardest lessons, and their intimate experiences with success and failure. During those conversations, a recurring theme emerged: the importance of aligning personal values with one's career choices and lifestyle.

During this time, I observed a stark contrast. The entrepreneurs who used their values as a decision-making filter were fulfilled, while those who strayed from their values felt burnout and dissatisfaction. One entrepreneur's poignant regret about not reflecting his values in his business resonated deeply with me.

Inspired by these insights, my partner and I undertook a reflective exercise to identify our own values. We started with a long list of words, circling those that resonated with us individually. Then we sorted these words into categories— eliminating, retaining, and merging them until we had a distilled list. We carefully defined each value, eliminating any ambiguity, and creating a clear guidepost for our lives.

A decade later, these values continue to ring true for me. They serve as a permanent GPS, directing my choices and influencing my journey to success. This experience not only shaped my understanding of entrepreneurship but also instilled a deep conviction in living a life that aligns with my core values—a lesson that I carry with me to this day.

Q: **Can you share an example of a time when aligning your actions and decisions with your values led to a more fulfilling and purpose-driven life?**

A: Every dollar you spend is a signal of what you value, even as it casts a vote for the type of world you want to live in. The same is true when it comes to investing. My favorite investments are the ones that have the strongest fit with my values. Take Othership as an example.

Othership is a Breathwork app and hot-cold therapy physical space, unlike anything you could imagine. At the time its founders were starting Othership, COVID lockdowns were at their peak. Opening a 60-person sauna and ice baths in downtown Toronto sounded like a terrible idea. But the vision behind Othership turned out to be so much more than a spa. It was a movement to make mental health accessible and to combat loneliness. It was an idea I've personally been passionate about for years. So when a friend decided to do it, I put my money where my mouth was. This is an investment that I likely would have passed on had it not been for using my values as a filter for my investment decisions. And now I'm so grateful that I have been included in their journey. *(Maybe we gift readers of my book with a year free to the Othership app!)*

Q: **What advice would you give to readers who are struggling to identify their core values?**

A: *Print out a list of common values,* circle all the ones that you resonate with, refine the list, pick your top 3-5 and then create a one sentence manifesto for each world. *Memorize them…or put them somewhere easy to reflect on.*

UNLOCK YOUR INNER GENIUS
THROUGH SELF-BELIEF

Q: **How important is self-belief in unlocking one's true potential? Can you share an experience where cultivating self-confidence led to breakthrough results?**

A: During my time in China for the G20 YEA, I was in the process of selling my first technology business, ShareShed™. An organized meeting with Sanfo, China's largest sports equipment company, unexpectedly led to an invitation to participate in a 10 KM trail race. Despite not being a runner, I was confident I could complete it.

However, a last-minute switch turned the 10 (Kilometer) KM race into a grueling 100 KM ultra-marathon across the Great Wall and over five mountains. On a dark and early Saturday morning, I found myself standing with thousands of Chinese racers—the only foreigner, facing a challenge far beyond what I had anticipated.

The race was not just physically demanding but mentally harrowing. At the 28.4 km mark, I felt like I was suffering from heatstroke, my ankles swollen and brain feeling like it was cooking. But my newly-found racing team (who had adopted me at the last minute) fortified me with just the needed encouragement and support. Mary, an English-speaking member, told me, "If you're going to quit then quit, but as long as you're with us, then it's one foot in front of the other."

Mary's words ignited something within me. I remember a quote about endurance being 30% physical and 70% mental, and I realized that this was my test. I decided to keep going, one foot in front of the other, for 27 hours non-stop.

Navigating treacherous mountain trails in torrential rain—dealing with unexpected obstacles like palm-sized spiders and fueling myself with the limited vegan options available. As I faced these and so many other challenges, the journey was an awakening for me, because it became an exercise in sheer willpower and determination. At times, it felt like I was going to collapse, but my body stayed upright.

When I finally crossed the finish line, I was overwhelmed by exhaustion. And yet the sense of accomplishment I felt upon completion was an even greater emotion. I raced back to the hotel and made my flight, reflecting on how the weekend had completely reshaped my understanding of what I was capable of doing...and the newfound awareness that with a Positive Mental Attitude *all things are possible.*

I had faced a challenge that I thought would defeat me at 28.4 KM. Yet, with determination, resilience, and the support of strangers who became friends, I completed 100 KM without training, over five mountains, non-stop. This experience was a powerful reminder that you may undertake anything successfully once you set your mind to do so. It's not just about physical strength; it's about the belief in oneself and the mental fortitude to push beyond perceived limitations.

Since that race, the mindset that I cultivated while negotiating those Chinese mountains has proven true countless times in other areas of my life. It taught me that the real barriers we face are often the ones we place on ourselves, and with self-belief and determination, we can overcome them.

Visit this link to see photos from this race; they truly are something everyone should see: https://docs.google.com/presentation/d/1dVKvNI6DHBG1shtGjID6_ceA4t09gqzYCazK8T2dKuU/edit?usp=sharing

Q: What strategies or exercises do you recommend for readers to overcome self-doubt and tap into their inner genius?

A: Do very hard things. Make a mental note of the hard thing you did, and call upon those extremely difficult challenges that you've overcome in the past as fuel to know that you can do anything.

Q: Have you ever faced moments of self-doubt during your journey, and if so, how did you overcome them?

A: Yes, many times. I've found the best way to eliminate self-doubt is by talking through it—either with yourself or someone who's judgment you trust. I had lunch recently with my long-time mentor and friend, Ryan Holmes. During lunch, I told him that I was going to stay with my company until it became a wild success or I went down with the ship. He pointed out that my mindset was a limiting belief. He said it's great to be persistent but it's better to be intentional and to know when to take a step back and/or make yourself replaceable. (Whenever you choose to do that, you free yourself as well.) My family, friends and mentors have always proven to be a source of energy when I doubt myself.

SELECTING YOUR MENTORS

Q: How have mentors played a role in your personal and professional growth? Can you share a specific mentorship experience that had a significant impact on your journey?

A: Mentors have played a massive role in my life. My first mentor, outside of family and friends that I looked up to, was when I was 13 years old. Travis Hayes was only 5 years older than I, and yet he took me under his wing as a basketball and essentially life coach. I grew up in a community where multiple generations would spend time together, and bonded together through a love for basketball. In high school, former Harlem

Globetrotter Mel Davis became my mentor, which as I mentioned earlier was focused a lot less on basketball and a lot more on life. See the Tweet thread regarding our relationship — https://twitter.com/danielmdubois/status/1482417642220802048?s=20

I entered college without any business mentorship. My first mentors and intellectual network mostly included my professors. I would visit them during office hours and ask them for advice on how to start a business, and everyone to the man (and woman) advised me to write a Business Plan. I made a 30-page plan without testing a single assumption. My business school provided me with so much information. And yet business school teaches you more about how to become a good manager than becoming an entrepreneur. I was so desperate to connect with someone who could truly help me go from zero to one and launch a company that I Googled "Web development Vancouver" and started to call dozens of companies. I didn't have any money to pay them.

So I said: "I'm making a documentary on starting a sharing economy company. And *you* can sponsor the documentary with services instead of cash." I was rejected by everyone. With one company I went pretty far into the sales cycle, only to have the founder tell me that he hoped to have his kid grow up to be doing what I was doing at 20 years old. I then drove from Vancouver to San Francisco to create a documentary series on *The Sharing Economy* where I interviewed top thought leaders such as the business partner of Rachel Botsman who gave the original TEDx Talk that inspired me to commit to the concept of "the sharing economy" in the first place.

I interviewed employees at companies such as Google and Facebook to hear their thoughts on this emerging trend. I met with the first ever co-housing company, the first co-working space in SF, and at the time, I interviewed a small but promising company called *Airbnb*. These became my first mentors that had domain expertise.

Even then, I still didn't know how to build a tech company from scratch, and then one day I received a call back from a designer who had previously missed my call. To my surprise and delight, he offered to meet me for a beer and (at least) listen to my story. After hearing what I had to say, he loved both my vision and my passion and offered to provide a logo for free, as well as make intros to other people in his network who could mentor me. The CMO of Capilano University started to resonate with the many ideas I had and agreed to meet me to help me brainstorm some of my strategies for marketing.

As a follow up, the CMO also had my story featured as their first blog post when they launched the university's series of blogs online. That story was soon picked up by a local newspaper and then later by national news. Before long, the President of my university would meet with me anytime to support what I was doing. It felt like the entire school was pushing me up a mountain. I was selected to emcee the university's biggest Networking Event of the year—my first and only public speaking appearance with 200 people there.

A couple weeks later, the University President, the CMO and other members of the C-suite invited me to a meeting. They asked me at the end of the meeting if I would be comfortable giving the welcome talk to 2,000 new students at the opening ceremony. I told them that I had learned to be "comfortable with discomfort," and that I would welcome the challenge even though it was 10 times the audience I'd originally had from my only other speaking appearance.

They all paused as if to deliberate something not on the agenda: Then the CMO said, "I'm going to up the ante. How would you feel about speaking in front of 20,000 people?" I don't quite remember what happened after that other than the C-suite saying there might be an opportunity in October, even though nothing had yet been confirmed.

I went home and told my brother about the meeting, and he immediately responded: "You know what they're referring to, right?" He did. I didn't. In fact, I had no idea.

My brother said, "WE Day.[6] You can't buy a ticket. You have to earn one through service. It's a stadium filled with youth who worked all year to earn a ticket." It was the first I'd ever heard of WE Day. I ran upstairs and watched an introductory video. The video started, "Born out of a dream…" And it showed a stadium of youth, screaming at the top of their lungs, all motivated by a dream for making an impact.

---

6   WE Day. The world's largest youth charity.

The video highlighted its past speakers: Malala Yousafzai, Nobel Prize laureate and advocate for girls' education; Selena Gomez, Singer, actress, and UNICEF ambassador; Prince Harry, British royal and advocate for veterans and mental health; Al Gore, Former Vice President of the United States and environmental activist; Magic Johnson, Basketball legend and philanthropist.

Seeing all this, I started to ball my eyes out. What began with pure hustle but no direction, or even mentorship on how to start a business, had now led up to an entire university being in my corner. On October 17, 2013, I spoke on the importance of holding onto the passion we all share for impact when we're young and not letting that go as we age. Not letting your idealistic dreams fade as we enter the system.

A group of amazing college friends and I raised $30 K for children's cancer, leading up to me speaking at *WE Day*, nearly all of which were small donations from other college students at school. At *WE Day*, I made a promise to myself that I have kept to this day: that I would only spend my time and energy on projects that move society forward in a meaningful way.

After I gave my talk at WE Day, I was invited to a one-on-one meeting with Kofi Annan, Secretary-General of the United Nations. He shook my hand and put his other hand over the top of mine. He didn't let go as he stared deeply into my eyes and told me the importance of following your heart and purpose with relentless discipline. Kofi Annan wouldn't remember our interaction but his words will always provide a special kind of mentorship for me.

It wasn't until I was accepted into *The League of Innovators* that I found a proper mentor-mentee fit for what I value and the impact I want to have in the world. Ryan Holmes and Meredith Powell gave me my start with that program. We read three books a month on top of countless mentorship office hours and fireside chats. In the first month, we read *The Lean Start Up, Team of Rivals*, and *The Psychology of Achievement*. *The Lean Start Up* became my philosophy for how to rapidly experiment. *Team of Rivals* taught me about team-building. And *The Psychology of Achievement*, a book I've probably read 30 times, became my all-time favorite book. I view those books and those authors as my mentors despite never having met them. (What Peter often refers to as, "Mentors/Virtual or Real.")

Q: **What qualities do you look for in mentors, and how do you establish meaningful connections with them?**

A: My first network came from League of Innovators and going through EO's GSEA. At first, I was excited to meet anyone who was a professional but quickly bonded with people who shared a thirst for putting a dent in the universe. I look for value alignment, especially when it comes to a passion for impact. I established a relationship by going to them for advice. To me, it's very strange to ask someone to be a mentor. So I never asked anyone to mentor me. Instead, I would reach out by asking to meet to discuss a specific challenge I was facing. You can learn from anyone. And it's always best to have a specific ask since important people don't want to waste their time. It's also important to try to be as human and helpful as possible to everyone in your life, including your mentors since all relationships are best grounded in authenticity.

Mentors aren't a means to an end. During League of Innovators, I would always follow up with speakers who gave us fireside chats. Out of the 10 young entrepreneurs that went through the program, I was the only one who kept in contact with *all the speakers.* Often one of the other young entrepreneurs would come to me and ask if they could gain access to one of the past speakers, even though we had the same opportunity to connect with those prospective mentors. Many of my mentors became my first investors.

There's a classic saying that becomes a paradox: "If you want advice, ask for money. If you want money, ask for advice." Mindful of that, I was able to raise $1M in my early 20s because of the amount of people that I consistently went to for advice. Not because I wanted to raise money but because I had a beginner's mind and wanted to build my vision. I'd ask for feedback, then go out and either action the advice I received or tell the "mentors" why I didn't do what they had recommended.

They saw my traction and my grit. Before I knew it, Praveen Varshney who was a judge at the GSEA in Vancouver said it might make sense for me to take on outside capital. I went to Ryan Holmes, founder of the billion-dollar tech company, Hootsuite, and he agreed and then followed up by telling me a valuation that he thought would be fair. Then I went to Manny Padda, past President of *EO Vancouver* who agreed.

After that, they became my first three investors…followed by the Mayor of Vancouver, the first investor in Uber and Salesforce, and a total of 17 dream mentors. The top entrepreneurs in Canada and one of the top Silicon Valley tech investors were, all of a sudden, my bosses. If I was to have a job I'd be reporting to someone else early in their career with only a dream to have the level and depth of mentorship from the people who then had a vested interest in my success.

Ten years later, I still keep in contact with these mentors/investors. As I'm writing this, my last meeting was with Lance Tracy who invested in my first company a decade ago and sold one of his own companies for over half a billion dollars ($500 M), cash. There's something truly special about building relationships in your early 20s, primarily due to the *Law Of Compounding Returns*. The Law Of Compounding Returns is something that applies—not just to investments but also to relationships as well.

One day when I was early into building my first company, I received a LinkedIn connection request from someone I didn't know. I was told by one professor to accept anyone who sends a request since everyone is a professional. That same day, someone said to only accept people you know so that your connections on LinkedIn are a clean database of your real contacts. This person was almost the first person that I rejected. As I hovered over the reject button, I decided that if I reject them then there will be no learning about whether or not that was a good or bad decision. I decided to accept to see if anything came from it and, if not then, I'll reject people I didn't know moving forward.

He immediately sent me a message asking me to judge a pitch competition downtown. My default answer when I was in my early 20s was always "yes." At the end of the pitch competition, I worked the room until I was one of the last people there along with the organizer. He then said, "You know what? You'd be a great panelist for our sharing economy panel at our largest event of the year in Banff next month."

One month later I was in Banff, Alberta, Canada and was able to meet with Steve Wozniak, Co-Founder of Apple. He was the speaker after my panel, so the room was packed, mostly with those waiting for us to finish so they could hear from the legendary "Woz."

I also shared the panel with Aaron Rifkin, Airbnb Country Manager for Canada who went on to lead the Americas. Airbnb was my all-time favorite company and one that I went on to give talks about when I started doing my speaking circuit on the sharing economy. Aaron Zifkin invited my girlfriend (now wife) and me to meet him that evening in the Banff Springs Hotel outdoor hot tub. We then ended up going for dinner and bonded over our shared values. Aaron ended up joining my advisory board, and years later I joined Airbnb full-time on Aaron's team—something that brought me on the journey of a lifetime. This all started with that LinkedIn request—the one I nearly rejected yet ended up completely changing my life...all in a way that is unimaginable had I not accepted that initial connection request.

During that event in Banff, I also met Josh Crumb, a top entrepreneur who raised $100 M for his company shortly after we met. He heard my story on stage and said he wants to support in any way he can. When he found out that I live in Vancouver, Josh told me that he did the Grouse Grind with Chip Wilson, Founder of Lululemon and I'd be welcome to join them one morning. After a few follow-ups, Josh invited me to do the Grouse Grind with him and Chip, meeting them at 5:55 a.m. at the base of Grouse. I woke early the following morning to a text from Josh, saying that he needed to cancel, since his software engineers were awake in Europe and he needed to put out some fires.

Since I was already up I figured I might as well go do the Grind on my own. I borrowed my dad's old carpet-cleaning van and during that dark early morning while I was driving up toward the base of Grouse Mountain, a Rolls Royce started to tailgate me. Who else in the world could that be other than the legendary Chip Wilson. When we parked, I went up to Chip who was with another friend and introduced myself. I told him that I was a friend of Josh Crumb, who had to cancel but who was also someone I hadn't wanted to interrupt, even as I informed him that I'd decided to do the Grind on my own. At that point, Chip absolutely insisted that I join them.

Chip Wilson is one of the most impressive entrepreneurs of our generation. He expressed so much interest and curiosity in me and what I was doing. He was generous with his advice. At the end of our hike together he asked for my contact details and said he'd reach out when he next went for a hike.

Before I knew it, Chip and I were taking weekly hikes together with a small group of people in his life. He'd send out an email with the time to meet at the base of Grouse or the UBC stairs. Chip was even kind enough to pick me up and drop me off along the way. I learned a ton from Chip, including the impact that *Good to Great* had on him and the fact that Lululemon wouldn't have existed had it not been for the personal awareness that he developed from Landmark. Years later when I joined EO (Entrepreneurs' Organization), I hosted Chip Wilson for a private fireside chat on our network.

FAST FORWARD: I'm now in YPO (Young Presidents Organization). And in a few months, I'm day-chairing the YPO "Legends of Vancouver" event with 30 members starting with the 94-year-old, Jim Pattison in his boardroom, immediately followed by none other than Chip Wilson. Once again, if it hadn't been for accepting a LinkedIn connection request, none of this would have happened.

MAKING YOUR DREAMS ATTAINABLE: SETTING SMART GOALS

Q: What is the importance of setting SMART goals that are aligned with one's vision? Can you provide an example from your own experience?

A: The Importance of Setting SMART Goals Aligned with One's Vision through the Lens of the OODA Loop.

At its core, the OODA Loop (*Observe, Orient, Decide, Act*) is a systematic and iterative process that helps organizations and individuals respond rapidly and effectively to change. Coupled with the SMART goal framework (*Specific, Measurable, Achievable, Relevant, Time-bound*), the OODA loop can drive efficient decision-making and fast-paced actions toward the realization of a well-defined vision.

- **Observe — The Rationale for Specificity**: To navigate through challenges, one must be acutely aware of their environment. In terms of goal-setting, this translates to having a clear, **specific** understanding of what you aim to achieve. Without specificity, your observation may lack direction, making it challenging to ascertain whether you›re on the right track.

- **Orient — Grounding in Relevance**: As you gauge the effectiveness of your plans, the orientation phase helps realign and pivot actions as needed. Your goals must be **relevant** to the bigger picture—your overarching vision. Only by setting relevant goals can you ensure that every twist, turn, and reorientation moves you closer to that vision.

- **Decide — The Power of Measurability**: Decisions must be data-informed. With *measurable* goals, you can quantify your progress, thus restructuring *decision-making* to become more objective and less reliant on guesswork. Metrics provide clarity on whether you're moving closer to or further from your targets.

- **Act — Time-bound and Achievable Actions**: It's not just about acting, but acting decisively and promptly. When goals are *time-bound,* there's an inherent sense of urgency, ensuring that actions are taken without unnecessary delay. Additionally, for any action to be impactful, it must be based on *achievable* objectives. Overly ambitious goals can lead to inaction due to perceived difficulty, whereas goals that stretch yet remain within reach can propel forward momentum.

The cyclic nature of the OODA Loop ensures continuous learning and adaptation. By embedding SMART criteria within this cycle, there's a structured pathway for that adaptation, anchored by clear, realistic, and actionable goals.

Finally, consider the competitive advantage. In today's dynamic environment, organizations or individuals that can navigate the OODA Loop more swiftly than their competitors can disrupt, innovate and lead. Setting SMART goals within this framework ensures not only that you're moving faster but also in the right direction, making every decision and action count toward achieving your vision.

Q: **How do you break down big dreams into actionable steps? What strategies or techniques do you recommend for tracking progress?**

A: As a company, we use the Entrepreneurs Operating System. As an individual, I've used the Painted Picture exercise that I described earlier.

Breaking down big dreams into actionable steps and tracking progress is crucial for any entrepreneur or business, and the Entrepreneurial Operating System (EOS) offers a structured approach to do just that. Here's a breakdown using EOS principles:

VISION/TRACTION ORGANIZER (V/TO)™

- **10-Year Target ™**: Start by identifying your big dream or vision, which EOS refers to as your 10-Year Target™. This is where you see your company in 10 years.

- **3-Year Picture™**: Break this 10-year goal down further. How does your company look in three years, and what are the major milestones you need to achieve to be on track for your 10-Year Target?

- **1-Year Plan**: Now, refine it and hone it down to just the year ahead. What are the most important things to accomplish this next year to stay on track for your 3-Year Picture and 10-Year Target?

ROCKS

- EOS emphasizes the concept of "Rocks" — these are your 90-day priorities. By focusing on 90-day cycles, you ensure that your team maintains momentum and alignment. Each Rock should be clear, actionable, and have a defined owner.

- Rocks can be established for the company as a whole, as well as for individual team members.

SCORECARD

- To track progress, EOS recommends using a weekly Scorecard. This scorecard contains 5 to 15 high-priority, actionable numbers that give you a pulse on your business.

- These numbers can include metrics like revenue, profit margin, customer satisfaction, etc. They help ensure the company is on track and alert the team to potential issues before they become major problems.

LEVEL 10 MEETING™

- Hold regular (weekly) Level 10 Meetings to check in on progress. These meetings have a set agenda that includes reviewing the scorecard, checking the status of Rocks, discussing any issues, and resolving them.

- This consistent check-in helps hold everyone accountable and ensures that progress is being made toward the bigger vision.

ISSUES LIST

- Maintain an ongoing Issues List for your organization. Whenever a challenge arises that can't be immediately resolved, add it to this list.

- During Level 10 Meetings, the team works together to IDS *(Identify, Discuss, and Solve)* these issues.

VISIONARY AND INTEGRATOR ROLES:

- EOS identifies two key roles: the Visionary (the big dreamer) and the Integrator (the person who makes things happen).

- By having both these roles (sometimes filled by one person, but often two different individuals), there's a balance between keeping an eye on the big dream and breaking it down into more bite-sized actionable steps.

RECOMMENDATIONS FOR TRACKING PROGRESS:

1. **Stay Consistent**: Keep the rhythm of your *Level 10 Meetings* and regularly review your Scorecard.

2. **Use Digital Tools**: There are various tools available that are EOS-friendly and can help in tracking Rocks, To-Dos, and the Issues List. Traction® Tools and Ninety.io are a couple of examples.

3. **Be Transparent**: Share progress, challenges and wins with the whole team. When everyone is informed, they're more likely to stay aligned and motivated.

Remember, breaking down big dreams into actionable steps requires clarity, commitment, and consistent review. By using the EOS model as your guide, you can ensure that you're not only dreaming big but also making those dreams a reality.

Q. **Have you ever faced challenges in achieving your goals, and if so, how did you overcome them?**

A. Absolutely, when I face challenges, I go back to self-reflection, journaling, and finding clarity. This goes back yet again to the OODA Loop.

CULTIVATING A SUCCESS MINDSET

Q: **How does belief play a role in shaping one's reality and achieving success? Can you share a mindset shift that had a significant impact on your journey?**

A: It starts with a dream. Next comes a strong belief in that dream. Believe works on a subconscious level which drives 95% of our existence. My mom started a company called *Women Arise International,* which had a mission to empower women to dream big, believe in their aspirations and achieve their goals. Their slogan was "Dream, Believe, and Achieve." Our lives are a self-fulfilling prophecy. Everything is invented in our minds. What we believe to become true often does with honesty and conviction.

Q: **What techniques or practices do you recommend for overcoming limiting beliefs and developing empowering thoughts and attitudes?**

A: That comes in a sequence of steps:
1. *Self-awareness and shrinking the "Unknown, unknowns" in your Johari Window.* This can take place through self-reflection, a mindset of curiosity and constructive feedback from others.

2. *Move your energy.* This can be done by working out, yoga, acupuncture, massage, breathwork such as my favorite breathwork app that I referenced earlier, Othership.

3. *Find a method for transformation that fits your present needs:* I'm currently going through the *Dalian Method (DM),* an advanced self-heal-

ing system developed by Mada Eliza Dalian. It's a modern-day method designed for personal transformation and healing by addressing the root causes of physical, mental, and emotional challenges. This method combines the elements of healing, meditation and psychotherapy.

HERE'S A BREAKDOWN OF ITS KEY PRINCIPLES:

- **The Holistic Approach**: DM looks at a person as a whole — mind, body, and spirit. It believes that every physical ailment has a root in the suppressed subconscious thoughts and emotions, and by addressing them, healing can occur.

- **Self-Inquiry and Awareness**: The method places a strong emphasis on self-awareness and self-inquiry. It encourages individuals to look within, find suppressed emotions and release them.

- **Transforming the Ego-Mind**: One of the main objectives of the Dalian Method is to transform the ego-mind and help individuals transform their limiting beliefs and unconscious thought patterns.

- **Using the Body as a Guide**: DM believes that the body stores memories of every experience, emotion, and thought. By reading these memories, the method can pinpoint root causes of ailments and challenges.

- **Erasing Energetic Blocks**: The method aims to identify and erase energetic blocks in the body's meridian system. By doing this, it allows suppressed emotions to surface and be released.

- **Self-Healing**: While Mada Dalian and trained facilitators can guide individuals through the process, the ultimate goal is to equip people with tools to heal themselves. It's a method that empowers individuals to take charge of their own healing journey.

The Dalian Method involves a combination of verbal expression, breath, and bodywork. It's not just about talking through problems but actively working to release them from the body and mind.

As with any healing or therapeutic method, it's essential to approach it with an open mind and consult with professionals or practitioners to understand if it's the right fit for one's personal journey.

Q: **How do you maintain a success-oriented mindset during challenging times or when faced with obstacles?**

A: I've worked the muscle of positivity for years and a superpower of mine is keeping my cool when sh*t hits the fan. I stay focused on the mission at hand and find a way to overcome the obstacle. Always ask the question: *"How could this be made possible?"* There are no such things as problems, only solutions.

Here's a story of overcoming an everyday obstacle: I was running late for a flight back to Canada. That evening we were hosting a team Canada Airbnb holiday party with the entire team and their partners. My flight was scheduled to land with just enough time to make it to dinner. When I arrived at the airport, it was horrifically busy in a way that no one had ever seen before. There were no other flights back to Toronto that day. And yet here I was: attempting to make my flight with nearly blind optimism that I had any chance of making it. I was in the security line when my scheduled departure took place.

When I made it through security, I flat out sprinted to my gate which was closed with the doors shut. I saw a check-in agent. I politely smiled and said, "I know I'm coming across as overly optimistic, but is there any way that I can still catch this flight."

She laughed and said, "Boarding already closed a while ago. There's not a chance."

Instead of dwelling on the importance of me making it back or being overly stressed, I smiled and said, "Is there ever a world where boarding closes and you can still make a flight?"

She thought about it and then said, "The jet bridge has already been disconnected and the door for the flight is closed. So at this point, no."

I then smiled and said, "That makes sense. Have you ever seen someone make a flight once the door to the plane is shut? There has to be a way."

She then thought about it and ran to the computer. She typed quickly and said, "This computer system is already shut down," which prompted her to run over the second computer.

Now my co-conspirator in this unique challenge, she yelled, "There's 20 seconds of hope!" She then paged the airplane to open the door and reconnect the flight bridge. She said due to a late check-in they had to honor the minimum amount of a check-in window.

Before I knew it, I was sitting in the first row of the plane and the first person that the individual next to me said was, "Who are you?!" with a giant grin. *Punchline:* I was able to make it back to the Christmas party with a healthy dose of both domain and gratification…and just a little bit smarter for the experience.

TURNING CHALLENGES INTO OPPORTUNITIES

Q: How do you approach challenges or obstacles on your journey to success? Can you share a specific example of how you turned a challenge into an opportunity?

A: I've found that some of the best founder stories are often when you turn a challenge you're experiencing first hand into an opportunity. Take Airbnb for example, Brian and Joe didn't have money to pay rent and at the same time there was a design conference with all the hotels sold out. They created something called AirBedAndBreakfast.com and hosted three strangers in their living room on air mattresses. They made three new friends, helped people who were attending the design conference and came up with the money to make their rent payment. When I moved from Vancouver to Toronto to join Airbnb full-time, I hired a Realtor to help me find a place to buy. An executive from Airbnb found out I was buying a place and told me that there was a good chance I'd move from Toronto to San Francisco within the next year: provided I bought a place and sold it a year later. At that point I wasn't getting any further ahead financially and had to face the reality of time, costs and hassles associated with home ownership.

Consequently, I ended up renting, thinking that I'd be in Toronto for a year at most…and ended up spending 5 years there. Inside that period of time, the real estate market doubled in value.

During my time at Airbnb, I experienced how binary renting or owning can be. I knew there had to be a better way for people like me who wanted the benefits of owning with the freedom of renting. Turns out there are millions of North Americans who feel underserved in this same way. KEY is now the market leader for attainable homeownership where you own a home while maintaining the freedoms and flexibility of renting. A lived experience and challenge turned into a quest towards creating the type of world I want to live in.

Q: **What strategies or mindset shifts do you recommend for reframing obstacles and embracing the growth and learning that come from facing challenges? And how do you maintain resilience and stay motivated during difficult times?**

A: The constant reminder that there's always a solution and that if it was easy, it would already be done. Resilience goes down drastically when you don't tend to your fundamentals—such as sleep, nutrition and exercise. Resilience is a muscle that gets better with use. I work on hard things, remember all the obstacles I've overcome, and draw on that as motivation when times get challenging. I embrace change and welcome the challenge of being comfortable in discomfort.

THE KEY TO PROGRESS

Q: **What is the importance of taking consistent action toward goals? Can you share a personal experience where consistent action led to significant progress?**

A: Consistent discipline drives compounding results when focused on the right area. When I was at Airbnb, one of my main KPIs was booking value for specific markets. I had a large GEO that I was managing, including most of Canada and multiple states in Eastern USA.

This is a huge geo to move the needle. So I divided my time *1) By a work strategy,* including how to operate within regulations and spent time working with legal, comms and policy to open up markets where there was uncertainty, and *2) By rolling up my sleeves and taking daily actions that would quantifiably move the market forward.* Since my GEO was so large, I decided to focus on the biggest opportunity. It also felt like Airbnb, as a business model, was working so well that monkeys could run a market and it would still prosper since the company had consistent 100% YOY (Year Over Year) growth.

After doing an analysis, I found that North Carolina had about 10% of the amount of supply as other online booking sites. Every day I spent time unpacking why North Carolina was one of Airbnb's smallest markets despite being the 5th most domestically visited state in the US. I realized it was due to trust accounting laws and some gray area that prohibited property managers from utilizing Airbnb. At the time, Airbnb was focused on urban markets and there were very few property managers on the platform. In fact, someone said I would potentially be shown the door if I vocalized support for property managers since Airbnb's brand was very much focused on supporting residents to make their rent or mortgage payments instead of supporting entrepreneurs like property managers.

Property managers controlled nearly the entire vacation rental market and there were multiple property managers with 1,000+ homes under management in the Outer Banks alone (most homes were 16+ bedrooms). Once I worked through the gray area, none of the property managers wanted to use Airbnb because they felt threatened. (Did they, or Airbnb, have a lock on the customer? That was the quandary that haunted them but one that could be dealt with.)

Instead of sitting behind my computer and discussing tactics in meeting rooms, I decided that consistent action toward relationship-building which would eventually earn the trust of a few property managers to give this a go. So I rolled up my sleeves, and every day I would start in the basement of the Canadian head office at MaRS in Toronto in a meeting room I had to myself—one that happened to be an old morgue turned into a storage room.

I would start every day with 20 calls, which would take three hours. I would cold-call property owners and start building relationships with them. Similar to Peter Thomas, I knew for every 20 calls, half would pick up, 5 would be open to a meeting and one would sign up within 3 months. I found that it was much easier to open a dialogue when I mentioned that I was planning to visit their town and would inquire from there whether or not they'd be open to meeting in person.

After that, I started to visit North Carolina once a month. The three weeks I wasn't in North Carolina were spent planning the next trip using an offline Google Map with pins for all the property managers. We organized one *"market blitz"* where managers from other states came to North

Carolina for one week, and where we *"painted the state Rouche!"* (The signature coral color of the Airbnb logo.)

At Airbnb, like many companies, you have a goal and a stretch goal. If you hit 70%, it's considered you hitting your goal. If you hit 100% then you've hit your stretch goal. The idea in principle is that you should always hit 70% but if you hit 100% then the goal was wrong since it was too easy a milestone to achieve. If you were to work your butt off and do everything right then end the quarter in the high 90 percentile, then that would be perfect. It wasn't long into the quarter that North Carolina became the first market in North America to hit the stretch goal. I kept the daily habit of a minimum of 20 calls. I would always start with this. Everything else for strategic planning or responding to anything internal or external would come after. By the end of the quarter, I hit over 700% of the stretch goal. Automation always follows human action. Both my story and the founding scenario of Airbnb come down to doing things that don't scale. *Consistent discipline leads to consistent results.* Once you find out what works, you can find out how to replicate those results.

Q: What strategies do you recommend for cultivating a positive attitude, staying motivated, and remaining committed to one's dreams?

A: I go back to the hard things I've overcome in the past and how I've built a track record of mastering difficult times: *One foot in front of the other* is my mantra. What you focus on matters. I focus on the positive.

Breathwork, self-reflection, meditation, and all the good things that go with them. Understand that there is no better way to predict the future than reflecting on what you do today. There are no secrets and it's all there for you when you put in the work. I'd say it's also much easier to be disciplined than to not be. The person who isn't disciplined spends way more time with less results.

A Prime Example: In high school, I barely ever did my homework. I cared much more about my clothing line and basketball. I would cram for an exam and do just well enough to pass. Finally, someone at the end of grade 12 said to me that if I did my homework then I wouldn't need to cram so hard for an exam, since the exam is based on the semester of homework that everyone else did. Not only did I have to outperform because I had zeros for not doing homework but I was also at a disadvantage because I didn't have that previous knowledge.

It rocked my world when I heard this and made me feel as if I'd be much better off had I embraced consistent discipline during my high school years. I graduated high school with 186 unexcused absences in my grade 12 years and, after walking across the stage, I peeked with uncertainty into my folder to see if a graduation certificate was even in there… or if I'd even passed.

Lesson learned: in college, I committed to having consistent discipline and doing my homework on-time, and as a result quickly rose to the very top of my class. I received multiple academic scholarships and even made money off traveling Europe for 7 months on exchange.

Q: How do you overcome procrastination and stay focused on your priorities? What time management techniques or strategies do you employ?

A. I've recently started to track my time and realized that I've been spread thin on a number of different initiatives without being able to go as deep as I'd like on any of them. Many of my projects have their results tied to the forced function of my energy.

I started to play around with how I've been investing my time and quickly realized that *Intentional Consistent Discipline = Results.*

This made me more of an *Essentialist.* I've started saying "no" to a lot more. I've been aware of what gives me energy and what takes away my energy. I've committed that 90% of what I'm working on will give me energy. While 10% are items I have to do but don't give or take away my energy. Now, close to 0% of what I work on takes away my energy. In the last year, those numbers were very different before I started to think this way. It is a kind of *Zero-Sum Game* that actually pays dividends, because I've actually been able to narrow down what is absolutely valid and what is absolutely not.

These days, I live off my calendar in a way that I time-block (such as writing-in my book right now) or going to the gym. I limit having to make decisions by following a simple meal routine and regular workout plan. I found that I was making a ton of decisions…and that my brain was way more maxed-out than the average person.

So I decided that I would eliminate the notice and embrace the philosophy of the *Essentialist* I just mentioned. This approach is best described with the German phrase: *Weniger aber besser,* "Less but better." Originated by minimalism Designer Dieter Rams, it is architectural in origin but applies to so many aspects of life as well. Your brain is a hard drive. So it's best to not use up your RAM drive (No relation to Dieter) unconsciously and focus energy on deliberate areas in line with your values and the world you want to create without distraction.

Q: What advice would you give to readers who struggle with taking action and making progress toward their dreams?

A: What if you just do it? Done is better than perfect. Write out that one thing you need to do to move your dream forward today and do that one thing.

THE MEANING OF ATTITUDE, MOTIVATION, AND COMMITMENT

Q: How important is resilience in bouncing back from failure and setbacks? Can you share a time when a positive attitude helped you overcome challenges?

A: In October of 2016, on a mild sunny fall day, I was biking back from giving a guest lecture at UBC. It was an exciting transitional time in my life where I was in the midst of selling my business, ShareShed™, involving multiple companies that I was in due-diligence with. My phone rang, and it was my life-partner Lucy.

Right away she said, "Have you talked with your mom?" I said "no." And she said "Call her," in a seriously concerned tone.

I called my mom who is filled with the same amount of energy and love for life as my good friend Peter Thomas.

When she picked up I could tell that she wasn't herself. She told me that she was at the hospital and that the doctors had presented her with the prognosis that she had Stage 4 Pancreatic Cancer—with only a month to live. I dropped everything and embarked on a healing journey with my mom and Lucy which took us to Mexico. The chances of beating Stage Four *pancreatic cancer* was less than 1% but that didn't faze us. If anyone was to be included in that other 1%, it was my mom. We met this challenge head-on and had fun every step of the way.

The journey was extremely healing in many ways…and yet also very revealing. My mom had been a victim of sexual abuse from the age of four to finally being raped at gunpoint when she was fourteen. We learned that pancreatic cancer is a dis-ease that is often related to unresolved trauma. My mom went on a personal journey to come to total forgiveness for the person who abused her and those who didn't believe her. Many of her memories were repressed.

She came to such an amazing place with her total forgiveness and love that she truly felt emotionally healed despite her health rapidly declining by the day. Two days before she passed, she asked me to take her picture as she was lifted up on a stretcher to be taken by an ambulance to palliative care.

When I asked her why, she smiled and said, "for my book" with the belief that she was still going to make it and that this was just another scene of how resilient we can be with faith. For me, I felt total ownership over the journey with my mom. We weren't victims but took accountability for my mom's health, the toll subconscious trauma had taken on her life, and the outcome that we were committed to doing our best to accomplish. When she passed, I felt a sense of overwhelming gratitude for the two months we had together on her journey with cancer and the amazing people who rallied together to help support her. To this day, it still doesn't feel quite real, and it is the greatest loss I can fathom.

Having said that, I look back with gratitude for our 25 years together: my parents coming to visit us in Vienna and touring a dozen countries together in three weeks; or my parents coming to Thailand together to attend the Global Student Entrepreneurship Awards in which I was participating. She was the most positive person I had ever known. And I've been blessed to have inherited that positivity.

Despite her not being here, her resilience and loving, supportive energy have gone on to impact so many lives that I know it will continue to have a ripple effect for eternity. We all have a much larger impact on others than we can imagine. The people we impact go on to impact others. They have children and those children are raised to be more resilient and positive based on their parent's muscle of positivity and resiliency.

Q: Impossible to top a story like that. And It helps to summarize who you are and where you are in your life. And yet we need to ask for A Summary. Is there anything you'd like to add to this phenomenal list of insights?

A: I think there are two things that are the most pivotal decisions you can make during this journey we spend on Planet Earth. One is the choice of your life-partner—your wife, your mate. And Nathaniel Branden (in *The Psychology of Romantic Love)* was right: In a relationship 1+1 never equals 2. It is either more than 2 or less than 2. In my case, with my life-partner Lucy it is so much more than 2 and as such the very definition of synergy.

Lucy is very supportive of me and yet manages to be so while fully engaged in her own practice as a licensed psychotherapist.

She has her own group of coaches and psychotherapists that she has banded together in a company called Inward. And as it seems that Peter Thomas has sprinkled some of his entrepreneurial DNA on this, it is now self-sustaining and running perfectly on autopilot. This in turn frees up so much of Lucy's time to be a good mother and also pursue those other things she enjoys.

As for me, at 32 I'm doing exactly what I love—and that is setting up Angel capital with the most enterprising and sophisticated team of financial experts I have ever known—20 people that have mastered the fine art of venture capital and investment banking. At this point, I spend my time running a very large Angel Network—investor communities that include the top 10% of the best Venture Capitalists in the world. That's a pretty heady group to hang out with. And though our track record isn't perfect, we have enjoyed some phenomenal successes and expect to stay on course for that for some time to come.

In this case, the trope holds true: "If you love what you're doing, you never have to work another day again as long as you live." At this stage of my life, that's a pretty prospect. So, I'll just keep on keeping on—learning and growing and trying to be a bit better every day...and celebrating some milestones along the way.

~DD

CHAPTER 27

Conclusion

On the Pacific Ocean 9.14.23

I'm happy to say that today's my birthday: Number 85 (and it's just a number)! Nevertheless, it's a milestone in so many more ways than one. And I've just been presented with the most wondrous gift of all—this book, *The Dream Factory,* with the help of my brilliant powerful, overachieving, Genius contributors. So here we are!

This may be the most difficult chapter I've ever written in any book. And yet in some ways it comes as the easiest, if for no other reason than I have so many phenomenal people to thank for putting this "High Achiever's Anthology" together as something unique. And that's just the starting point. Because it is a major milestone, and yet so much more than that...

First, let me congratulate you, dear readers, on reaching the exhilarating conclusion of *The Dream Factory!* Throughout this transformative journey, we have explored the depths of your potential, armed you with invaluable tools, and ignited the fire within to chase your dreams relentlessly and achieve them—every one! As we wrap up our adventure together, let us reflect on the profound transformation that has taken place within you.

Remember, milestones are not just destinations but reflections of the progress made on your unique path. Revel in the fact that you've found your own Genius, and all that this implies. Embrace the significance of celebrating milestones and let them fuel your continued pursuit of excellence. Each milestone celebration brings you closer to the realization of all that you desire, instilling in you a greater Belief in Self—that plus the awareness that you are capable of achieving your own level of greatness on this very private path to

The Dream Factory. By recognizing achievements, setting meaningful goals, acknowledging progress, expressing gratitude, creating rituals, reflecting and learning and inspiring others, you have infused your journey toward self-discovery with joy, motivation, and a sense of fulfillment.

Genius inventor, chemist and creator of "The Scientific Method" Sir Francis Bacon once observed: "If I begin with certainties, I will end with doubts. But if I begin with doubts, I will end with certainties." Bacon was right in that regard, but left out one key ingredient: *the determination to achieve a desired result.*

When I embarked on the journey to write *The Dream Factory* I had no idea where it would lead me. But it turned out to be a rocket ride to the stars, exceeding my expectations in so many ways. Yet, in a sense, it has also unfolded exactly as I had envisioned. Because it has become the story of another dream realized in so very many ways. And, as we all know by now: *Dreams are never entirely achieved in a void.*

I want to start this letter of appreciation with thanks to my life partner and the love of my life, Rita, who inspires me daily with her kindness and beautiful spirit. It is her constant support for the last 37 years makes it so special just to wake up each morning.

Before I start to thank everyone, I would also like to give a special mention to my writing mentor Robert Joseph Ahola. Without his guidance, skills, perception, and the uncanny ability to read my mind, this book would never have seen the light of day. Robert, you are an indispensable part of this journey, and I'm deeply grateful for your unwavering support.

Finally, I'd like to extend my heartfelt gratitude to some longtime extraordinary friends: Renie Cavallari, Mikhail Naumov, Marcia Meyer, Daniel Dubois, Yarden Zilber, Joe Polish, David Hodgson and Bronwyn Bridges. More than contributors, these Renaissance human beings are also geniuses and role models in every sense of the word. And the wisdom that they have collectively infused into the core of this work has filled it with a heart, soul and mental clarity that will inspire entrepreneurs (both young and mature) for many years to come. What's more, their canny, brilliant insights have helped to craft a game plan that—if followed—can help anyone discover their own personal brilliance and reshape the course of their lives.

I have met so many of these wonderful people such as Mikhail, Daniel, David and Bronwyn through our joint participation in the Entrepreneur's Organization (EO). The Entrepreneurs Organization (EO) has as its top gifting entity a program called the Global Students Entrepreneurs Awards (or GSEA) as we call it. In it, the applicants must be students at a recognized university, own and run their own companies, and apply to compete in a "Shark Tank" type competition. All four of these young entrepreneurs were winners in various competitions over the years. David specifically was the international winner for 2023. And Bronwyn Bridges won the Canadian competition for that same year.

Currently, the EO enjoys a membership numbering over 18,000 CEOs, and has created a new level of mentorship and networking for high-achievers in more than 80 different countries in the "free world." At present, I serve as Chairman Emeritus of this extraordinary organization. And I am honored to do so as a way of paying back this group for the many times I was blessed to find mentors to guide me on my path. So much so, that it has been my life goal to pass this gift on to coming generations…and in every possible way to "pay it forward."

The philosopher/poet Ralph Waldo Emerson once wrote: "The purpose of life is not to be happy. It is to be useful, to be honorable, to be compassionate, to have it make some difference that you have lived and lived well."

A goal I have is to change the world in a positive way. And the way I have chosen to change it for the better is to encourage young people to recognize their own Genius. Throughout my eight and a half decades on this planet, starting as a fully-fledged entrepreneur at the age of 27, I've been fortunate to cross paths with hundreds of geniuses who have guided me on my journey. To each of you (and you know who you are) I carry your wisdom and inspiration always in my heart.

As we bring *The Dream Factory* to its conclusion, I want to express my deeply felt indebtedness to everyone who has been a part of this remarkable adventure. Together, we've created something extraordinary: a testament to *the power of dreams* and a celebration of the human spirit.

With profound appreciation and endless gratitude,
Peter H. Thomas, Author
Aboard *Happiness II*

Acknowledgment

A special acknowledgment to the EO Global Student Entrepreneur Awards (GSEA), as a personal inspiration to me in the writing of this book. The EO Global Student Entrepreneur Awards (GSEA) is the premier global competition for students who own and operate a business. Nominees compete against their peers from around the world in a series of local and national competitions in hopes to qualify for the GSEA Global Finals. GSEA supports student entrepreneurs who require much-needed mentorship, recognition and connections to take their businesses to the next level of success. Support for this magnificent association has been a passion of mine for several years as I continue on my journey to try to help inspire and mentor others. It has been oxygen for the spirit for me to be able to continue to do so.

Glossary of Terms

(Entrepreneurs' Acronyms and more...)

ACV	Annual Contract Value
AI	Artificial Intelligence
Airbnb	Air Bed and Breakfast (even though virtually none provide "breakfast")
AMC	Attitude Motivation Commitment
ARR	Annual Recurring Revenue
ASAP	As Soon As Possible
BHAG	Big Hairy Audacious Goals
B2B	Business to Business
B2C	Business to Consumer
CEMENT	Contribute. Empower. Mentor. Educate. Network. Train.
CFE	Clarity. Focus. Execution.
CHAT GPT	CHAT Generative Pre-Trained Transformer
CPU	Cost Per Unit
CTA	Call to Action
CTR	Click Through Rate
DAU	Daily Active Users
DM	Dalian Method
DTC	Direct to Consumer
EBITDA	Earnings Before Interest, Taxes, Depreciation and Amortization.

EOS	Entrepreneurial Operating System
EPS	Earnings Per Share
EQ	Emotional Quotient
FOLO	Fear Of Losing Out
FOMO	Fear Of Missing Out
FUD	Fear, Uncertainty and Doubt
GMV	Gross Merchandise Value
GPS	Global Positioning System
GQ	Genius Quotient
HLA	High Leverage Activities
ICP	Ideal Customer Profile
IDS	Identify. Discuss. Solve.
IP	Intellectual Property
IPO	Initial Public Offering
IT	Information Technology
KPI	Key Performance Indicator
LOI	Letter of Interest (also Letter of Intent)
MCAT®	Medical College Admissions Test
MIT	Most Important Things
MOLO	More Of Less Of
NDA	Non-Disclosure Agreement
OCD	Obsessive Compulsive Disorder
OODA	Observe. Orient. Decide. Act.
OOO	Out Of Office - not on vacation just out of office
OPP	Other People's Problems
P2P	Peer To Peer (also Person To Person)
PPC	Pay Per Click
$P + S \times R = A$	*Passion plus Skill times Repetition equals Achievement.*
QA	Quality Assurance
QC	Quality Control
R&D	Research and Development

RFP	Request For Proposal
SEO	Search Engine Optimization
SLA	Service Level Agreement
SMART	Specific, Measurable, Attainable, Realistic, Time-Bound
SOP	Standard Operating Procedure
SWOT	Strengths, Weakness, Opportunities and Threats
TBD	To Be Determined
UI	User Interface
UX	User Experience
VC	Venture Capital
VM	Virtual Machine
WIFM	What's In It For Me
WIFT	What's In It For Them
YOY	Year Over Year

"The secret of genius is to carry the spirit of the child into old age, which means never losing your enthusiasm"

—Aldous Huxley

About the Author

Peter H. Thomas is an internationally renowned mega-entrepreneur and motivational speaker who has influenced audiences and mentored young business people all over the world. Chairman Emeritus of the Entrepreneurs Organization (EO), Peter has authored four other groundbreaking books, including *Be Great, Never Fight With a Pig, Life Manual,* and *Business Ground Rules. The Dream Factory* is the summation of his success philosophy, as well as a melding of the best of the best of his other works up to now. A citizen of the world, Peter lives with his wife Rita in Phoenix Arizona, USA, Kelowna, British Columbia, Canada Puerto Vallarta, Mexico and aboard his yacht, *Happiness II.*

Printed in the USA
CPSIA information can be obtained
at www.ICGtesting.com
LVHW050854040324
773188LV00001BA/4